Microsoft® Windows® PowerShell™ Programming for the Absolute Beginner

Jerry Lee Ford, Jr.

THOMSON

COURSE TECHNOLOGY

Professional ■ Technical ■ Reference

The Thomson Course Technology PTR logo and related trade dress are trademarks of Thomson Course Technology, a division of Thomson Learning Inc., and may not be used without written permission.

Microsoft, Windows, and PowerShell are either registered trademarks or trademarks of Microsoft Corporation in the United States and/or other countries. Seinfeld is a copyright of Sony Pictures Entertainment.

All other trademarks are the property of their respective owners.

Important: Thomson Course Technology PTR cannot provide software support. Please contact the appropriate software manufacturer's technical support line or Web site for assistance.

Thomson Course Technology PTR and the author have attempted throughout this book to distinguish proprietary trademarks from descriptive terms by following the capitalization style used by the manufacturer.

Information contained in this book has been obtained by Thomson Course Technology PTR from sources believed to be reliable. However, because of the possibility of human or mechanical error by our sources, Thomson Course Technology PTR, or others, the Publisher does not guarantee the accuracy, adequacy, or completeness of any information and is not responsible for any errors or omissions or the results obtained from use of such information. Readers should be particularly aware of the fact that the Internet is an ever-changing entity. Some facts may have changed since this book went to press.

Educational facilities, companies, and organizations interested in multiple copies or licensing of this book should contact the Publisher for quantity discount information. Training manuals, CD-ROMs, and portions of this book are also available individually or can be tailored for specific needs.

ISBN-10: 1-59863-354-6

ISBN-13: 978-1-59863-354-2

Library of Congress Catalog Card Number: 2006907921

Printed in the United States of America

07 08 09 10 11 PH 10 9 8 7 6 5 4 3 2 1

THOMSON

COURSE TECHNOLOGY

Professional ■ Technical ■ Reference

Thomson Course Technology PTR,
a division of Thomson Course Technology
25 Thomson Place
Boston, MA 02210
http://www.courseptr.com

Publisher and General Manager, Thomson Course Technology PTR:
Stacy L. Hiquet

Associate Director of Marketing:
Sarah O'Donnell

Manager of Editorial Services:
Heather Talbot

Marketing Manager:
Mark Hughes

Acquisitions Editor:
Mitzi Koontz

Marketing Coordinator:
Adena Flitt

Project Editor:
Jenny Davidson

Technical Reviewer:
Keith Davenport

PTR Editorial Services Coordinator:
Erin Johnson

Interior Layout:
Shawn Morningstar

Cover Designer:
Mike Tanamachi

Indexer:
Sharon Shock

Proofreader:
Kate Welsh

To my wonderful children, Alexander, William, and Molly,
and my beautiful wife, Mary.

ACKNOWLEDGMENTS

This book represents the culmination of hard work from a number of individuals to whom I owe many thanks. For starters, there is Mitzi Koontz, for helping me get this book started and for her support as acquisitions editor. I also owe a special debt of gratitude to Jenny Davidson, who served as the book's project/copy editor and worked hard to help keep me straight and ensured that everything came together like it was supposed to. Thanks also go out to Keith Davenport, who as the book's technical editor provided me with invaluable insight, guidance, and advice. Finally, I'd like to thank everyone else at Thomson Course Technology PTR for all their contributions and hard work.

ABOUT THE AUTHOR

Jerry Lee Ford, Jr. is an author, educator, and an IT professional with over 18 years of experience in information technology, including roles as an automation analyst, technical manager, technical support analyst, automation engineer, and security analyst. Jerry has a master's degree in Business Administration from Virginia Commonwealth University in Richmond, Virginia. He is the author of 19 other books and co-author of two additional books. His published works include *Microsoft Windows Shell Scripting for the Absolute Beginner*, *Microsoft Windows Shell Scripting and WSH Administrator's Guide*, *Perl Programming for the Absolute Beginner*, *VBScript Professional Projects*, *Microsoft Visual Basic 2005 Express Edition Programming for the Absolute Beginner*, *Beginning REALbasic*, *Learn VBScript in a Weekend*, *Learn JavaScript in a Weekend*, and *Microsoft Windows XP Professional Administrator's Guide*. He has over five years' experience as an adjunct instructor teaching networking courses in Information Technology. Jerry lives in Richmond, Virginia, with his wife, Mary, and their children, William, Alexander, and Molly.

Contents

INTRODUCTION

Welcome to *Microsoft Windows PowerShell Programming for the Absolute Beginner*. *Windows PowerShell* is a next-generation command shell for Microsoft operating systems. A *command shell* or *shell* is a text-based interface that sits between the user and the operating system, which most people loosely refer to as the command prompt. In the case of the Windows PowerShell, the shell is both a user interface and a new scripting language, both of which have been redesigned from the ground up to facilitate the secure administration of Windows operating systems.

The goal of this book is to teach you everything you need to know in order to begin developing your own Windows PowerShell scripts. This will, of course, include learning how to interact with the Windows PowerShell command line. It will also involve learning a little about Microsoft's .NET Framework. At the same time, you learn how to work with other Windows technologies, such as the Windows registry, as you learn how to become a PowerShell programmer.

WHY WINDOWS POWERSHELL SCRIPTING?

Windows PowerShell is a next-generation command shell developed by Microsoft to run on its latest generation of Windows operating systems. As a shell, you interact with Windows PowerShell from the command line. One of the things that makes the PowerShell different from cmd.exe, the previous Windows command shell, is that PowerShell has been redesigned as an object-based environment that is tightly integrated with Microsoft's .NET Framework. As such, the PowerShell is far more powerful and advanced than its predecessor. At the same time, Microsoft worked hard to make Windows PowerShell backward compatible. The Windows shell will accept and process the same commands as the previous Windows shell, thus preserving any knowledge and experience you may already bring with you while also introducing you to a whole new set of capabilities.

Microsoft provides the Windows PowerShell as a free add-on to Windows operating systems. Its new scripting language has been designed from the ground up to support object-based programming, thus providing systems administrators and computer hobbyists with a tool for automating just about any Windows activity.

Windows PowerShell makes for a great starter language for first-time programmers and hobbyists. Professional programmers will also benefit from this new scripting technology, which provides more robust and powerful scripting capabilities than that provided by any other Windows scripting language. You will find that more often than not, you can develop scripts to automate a given task much more quickly and efficiently using the Windows PowerShell than can be done using other scripting languages, thus saving valuable time and freeing you up to move on to tackle other tasks.

In short, whether you are interested in learning your first programming language or are looking for an introduction to PowerShell scripting that teaches you how to develop PowerShell scripts with which you can leverage your existing knowledge of .NET programming, this book should serve you well. If Windows is your operating system of choice, Windows PowerShell scripting provides you with access to a scripting environment that is unmatched by other scripting languages. In addition, learning Windows PowerShell scripting will provide you with a programming background from which you can then make the jump to other .NET programming languages.

This book will teach you Windows PowerShell scripting. To help make learning fun and interesting, you will learn how to program through the development of computer games. By the time you have finished this book, not only will you have access to a collection of working sample scripts, but you also will have laid a foundation upon which you can move on and begin to tackle real-world challenges.

WHO SHOULD READ THIS BOOK?

My goals in writing this book are to show you how to interact with the Windows PowerShell, to teach you the fundamentals of how to develop and execute PowerShell scripts, and to help you become an effective programmer. I do not make any assumptions regarding your previous programming experience, although prior programming experience is obviously helpful. I do, however, expect you to have a working familiarity with Windows.

I think that you will find this book's unique approach of teaching through the development of computer games both entertaining and highly productive. Learning through the creation of computer games not only helps keep things fun but it also provides a unique opportunity to experiment with a programming language.

If you are a first-time programmer or a computer hobbyist, you should find this book's systematic building block approach to programming very helpful, allowing you to master basic fundamentals before moving on to more advanced topics. By investing your time and energy in learning how to program using Windows PowerShell scripting, you will develop a programming foundation that translates well to other scripting languages such as VBScript,

JavaScript, Python, and Perl, as well as .NET programming languages such as C#, C++, and Visual Basic. Professional programmers will also benefit from this book by using it as a quick start guide to PowerShell scripting.

WHAT YOU NEED TO BEGIN

In order to work with Windows PowerShell, your computer must run one of the following operating systems.

- Windows XP
- Windows Server 2003
- Windows Vista

When writing this book, I worked on a computer running Windows XP. Therefore, all of the figures and examples that you will see were generated on that particular operating system. However, everything you see should apply to Windows Server 2003 and Windows Vista as well.

In addition to running a supported operating system, your computer must also have Microsoft .NET Framework version 2.0 or higher installed. As of the writing of this book, Windows PowerShell was a free download provided by Microsoft and could be downloaded and installed from the Microsoft PowerShell website located at

www.microsoft.com/windowsserver2003/technologies/management/powershell/default.mspx.

If necessary, you can get the latest version of .NET by going to msdn.microsoft.com/netframework/.

Beyond a supported version of Windows, .NET 2.0, and a copy of Windows PowerShell, you do not need anything else to get started or to perform all the exercises outlined in this book. Of course, you will need a text editor of some type with which you will create and save PowerShell script files. For starters, you can user the Windows Notepad application. However, you may find it beneficial to download and install a code editor that is specifically designed to support PowerShell script development. If you skip ahead to Appendix B, "What Next?," you will find information about two such applications, both of which were free as of the time of this writing.

HOW THIS BOOK IS ORGANIZED

As I sat down and designed the overall structure of this book, I did so with the intention that it be read from cover to cover. However, if you have prior programming experience, you may instead choose to read this book by going through the first two chapters in order to learn a few specifics about working with Windows PowerShell. You might then jump around a bit to different chapters based on your specific needs and experience. However, Windows PowerShell comes equipped with an entirely new programming language. As such, it is probably a good idea that you spend some time reading Chapters 4 through 7, which cover the basics of the Windows PowerShell scripting language.

Windows PowerShell Programming for the Absolute Beginner is organized into four parts. Part I is made up of three chapters that focus on providing you with an introduction to the Power-Shell and its capabilities. These chapters outline the basic steps involved in interacting with the PowerShell command prompt and in creating and executing PowerShell scripts, and they provide an overview of object-based scripting and the PowerShell's relationship with the .NET Framework.

The second part consists of four chapters, which together provide you with a review of the PowerShell scripting language. Each chapter focuses on a different collection of topics. You will learn how to store and retrieve data. You will also learn how to implement conditional logic and to set up loops in order to automate repetitive tasks and process large collections of data. Lastly, you will learn how to improve the overall organization of your PowerShell scripts using functions.

The third part is made up of three chapters, each of which covers an advanced topic. These topics include learning how to work with files and folders, developing PowerShell scripts to automate system administration tasks, and learning how to track down and debug errors.

Finally, The fourth part consists of two appendices and a glossary. The appendices address the material that you will find on this book's companion website as well as provide you with suggestions on where you can go online to learn more about Windows PowerShell. Lastly, the glossary provides access to a comprehensive list of terms used throughout the book.

A detailed review of the information provided by each chapter of this book is provided here.

- **Chapter 1, "Introducing Windows PowerShell."** This chapter provides you with an introductory overview of the Windows PowerShell. You will learn about the different technologies that make up and support Windows PowerShell, including object-oriented programming and the .NET Framework. You will also learn how to start the PowerShell and to interact with it using commands and cmdlets. In addition, you will learn how to configure the PowerShell to run scripts and to develop and execute your first PowerShell script.

- **Chapter 2, "Interacting with the Windows PowerShell Command Line."** This chapter provides a thorough review of how to interact with the Windows PowerShell command line and how to work with its built-in cmdlets. You will also learn to access help information and to formulate command input.

- **Chapter 3, "Object-Based Scripting with .NET."** Windows PowerShell requires .NET in order to execute. This chapter provides an overview of .NET and its relationship to Windows PowerShell. You will learn about the .NET class library and how to work with structured objects.

- **Chapter 4, "Working with Variables, Arrays, and Hashes."** This chapter's primary focus is to show you different ways that you can store and retrieve data. This will include learning how to define and access variables, arrays, and hashes. You will also learn how to work with PowerShell's special variables.

- **Chapter 5, "Implementing Conditional Logic."** In this chapter you will learn how to apply conditional logic in order to analyze data and selectively choose between different logical execution paths. You will learn how to evaluate strings, numbers, and Boolean data.

- **Chapter 6, "Using Loops to Process Data."** This chapter shows you how to create loops in order to efficiently execute commands over and over again, thus facilitating the processing of large amounts of data. You will also learn how to conditionally break out of loops when predetermined conditions occur.

- **Chapter 7, "Organizing Scripts Using Functions."** This chapter introduces you to functions and explains how to use them to improve the overall organization and readability of your PowerShell script files. This includes learning how to call on functions for execution as well as how to pass arguments to functions for processing and to set up functions to return data back to calling statements.

- **Chapter 8, "Working with Files and Folders."** This chapter will teach you how to interact with and control files, folders, and disks. You will learn how to open and close files and to read and write information to and from them.

- **Chapter 9, "Basic System Administration."** The primary focus of this chapter is to demonstrate how to develop PowerShell scripts that automate various system administration tasks, such as how to access system information and network resources. In addition, you will learn how to interact with the Windows registry.

- **Chapter 10, "Debugging PowerShell Scripts."** This chapter focuses on teaching you how to track down and fix any error that may occur as you work on your PowerShell scripts. The topics covered include how to trap and recover from errors, how to pause script execution by establishing breakpoints, and how to trace script execution using debug mode.

- **Appendix A, "What's on the Companion Website?"** This appendix provides a review of the materials that can be found on this book's companion website (www.courseptr.com/downloads). This material includes copies of all the PowerShell game scripts covered in this book.

- **Appendix B, "What Next?"** This appendix is designed to provide you with suggestions and tips for furthering your Windows PowerShell scripting education. It includes suggestions for additional reading and points you to various PowerShell resources available on the Internet, including PowerShell IDEs, user groups, and blogs.
- **Glossary.** This unit provides a glossary of terms used throughout the book.

CONVENTIONS USED IN THIS BOOK

In order to help you get the most out of this book and to help organize the material in an efficient and comprehensive manner, I have implemented a number of conventions that will help with the overall organization and presentation of this book's material. These conventions are outlined below.

 HINT. Suggestions and ideas for different ways things can be done in order to help you become a better and more efficient Windows PowerShell programmer.

 TRAP. Situations where mistakes and errors often are made and advice on how to deal with these situations.

 TRICK. Tips, tricks, and programming shortcuts that you can use to work faster and more efficiently.

IN THE REAL WORLD

Explanations and demonstrations of how certain programming techniques are applied to solve specific real-world problems.

CHALLENGES

At the end of each chapter, you will learn how to create a new computer game. I will then present you with a series of suggestions to follow up on in order to further enhance and improve both the chapter game project and your programming skills.

Part

I

Windows PowerShell Basics

C H A P T E R

INTRODUCING
WINDOWS POWERSHELL

indows PowerShell is a next-generation command shell that runs on Windows XP, Windows 2003, and Windows Vista. As a command shell, PowerShell provides a command-line interface that administrators and computer hobbyists can use to directly interact with and control the Windows operating system. PowerShell also includes its own scripting language that has been custom designed to interact with Microsoft's .NET Framework and to take advantage of the resources that .NET provides. In this chapter, I will introduce you to PowerShell and PowerShell scripting. This will include learning how to install and configure the shell as well as how to use it to execute commands and run your first PowerShell script. By the end of this chapter, you will have created your first PowerShell script game and have a good understanding of the steps involved in working with PowerShell and creating and executing PowerShell scripts.

Specifically, you will learn:

- A little bit about PowerShell's history
- How to install PowerShell and configure it to run scripts
- About the basic components that make up PowerShell
- About cmdlets and how to use them to formulate commands and script statements
- How to get help regarding different PowerShell commands

PROJECT PREVIEW: THE KNOCK KNOCK JOKE GAME

In this chapter and in each chapter that follows, you will learn how to create a computer game using Windows PowerShell scripting. In this first game, you will create a script that tells several knock knock jokes. The script is designed to interact with the user by prompting the user to enter input at appropriate moments.

The game begins by clearing the screen and then displaying a prompt that says Knock Knock!, as shown in Figure 1.1.

FIGURE 1.1

The Knock Knock Joke game begins by prompting the user to guess who is there.

As a response, the user is expected to enter the string **Who is there?**, exactly as shown in Figure 1.2.

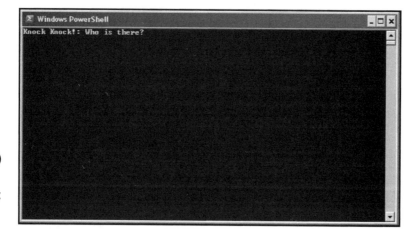

FIGURE 1.2

The user must respond by typing the string **Who is there?**.

If the user types anything other than **Who is there?**, the script will continue to prompt the user until he responds correctly, as demonstrated in Figure 1.3.

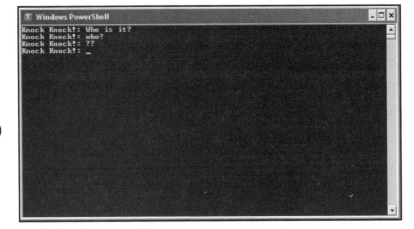

FIGURE 1.3

If necessary, the game will continue to prompt the user to respond correctly.

Once the user provides the correct response, the game responds with an answer of "Orange." In response, the player is required to enter the string **Orange who?**, as demonstrated in Figure 1.4.

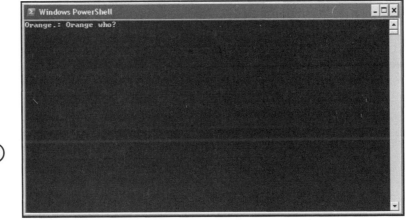

FIGURE 1.4

The player is required to respond **Orange who?**.

Next, the script displays the joke's punch line, as shown in Figure 1.5.

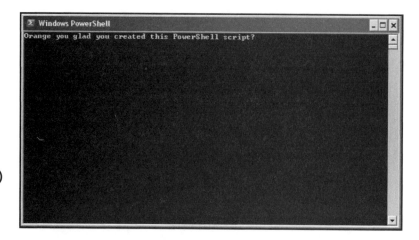

FIGURE 1.5

Finally, the joke's
punch line is
displayed.

The game displays the punch line for five seconds before clearing the screen and starting the process of telling another joke. In total, the game tells three jokes, pausing for five seconds at the end of each joke to display a punch line. Finally, once the last joke has been told, the information shown in Figure 1.6 is displayed for three seconds, after which the screen is cleared and the PowerShell command is redisplayed.

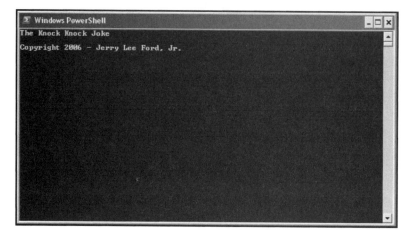

FIGURE 1.6

The script ends
by displaying
information about
itself and its
author.

Now that you have had a quick preview of the operation of the Knock Knock Joke game, let's spend a little time learning more about PowerShell and PowerShell scripting. After this, we'll turn our attention back to the development of the game script at the end of the chapter.

GETTING TO KNOW WINDOWS POWERSHELL

Most operating systems' command shells consist of a small number of internal commands, which the shell runs internally when executed. Because the number of commands provided by traditional shells is limited, large numbers of utility programs (or external commands) are later developed to supplement built-in shell commands in order to provide missing functionality. These utility programs run outside of the shell, generating their own processes. These utility programs may or may not support a command syntax that is similar to that of its associated command shell. The end result is a command line and shell scripting environment that is inconsistent and difficult to learn due to syntax inconsistencies.

 Throughout this book, the terms Windows PowerShell and PowerShell are used interchangeably.

Enter the Windows PowerShell, which provides access to well over one hundred commands in the form of cmdlets, each of which shares a common syntax, making the command line and scripting environment far more predictable and easy to learn. When developing Windows PowerShell, one of Microsoft's goals was to make the learning curve for PowerShell as easy as possible. Therefore, it incorporated as many cmd.exe and UNIX shell features as it could into Windows PowerShell.

Windows PowerShell has many other features that further differentiate it from traditional command shells. These features include:

- A C#-styled syntax
- Access to over one hundred cmdlets providing access to .NET Framework classes
- Support for regular expressions
- A provider model that provides Windows PowerShell with access to hierarchical repositories including the Windows file system and the Windows registry
- The ability to shorten commands and script statements by supplying abbreviated forms of keywords

A Little History Lesson

Going all the way back to the first version of Windows, every version of Windows has included a command shell. The original command-line shell was named Command.com. When Windows NT was released, Microsoft added cmd.exe as the operating system's new command shell. cmd.exe remained the Windows command shell when both Windows

2000 and Windows XP were released. As much of an improvement as cmd.exe was over Command.com, it never provided the kind of comprehensive access to the Windows operating systems that, for example, UNIX and Linux users and administrators are accustomed to.

Windows has successfully made the leap from the Windows desktop to become a major player in corporate data centers all around the world. However, its lack of a world-class shell has plagued Windows administrators. When Microsoft released the Windows Script Host, or WSH, in 1998, things improved significantly. Using the WSH, Windows administrators could develop automation scripts using either VBScript or JScript. Later, third-party developers released WSH-compatible scripting languages that included Perl, Rexx, and Python. Still, when compared to UNIX, command-line access has continued to remain a major deficiency for Windows.

By creating Windows PowerShell and providing it with an entirely new scripting language, capable of accessing resources provided by the .NET Framework, Microsoft has provided Windows users and administrators with access to a command shell that now has access to resources formerly only available to GUI-based programming languages like Visual Basic .NET.

Integration with .NET

Unlike traditional command shells, which manipulate text, Windows PowerShell treats everything as objects. An *object* is a self-contained resource that stores information about itself in properties and provides program code, in the form of methods, that can be used to interact with it. For example, a file is an object. So is a disk drive and a folder.

All objects are derived from a class that defines the object and its properties and methods. An object's *properties* describe particular features of the object. For example, a file has a name, a file extension, and a file size, among many other properties. Objects also have built-in collections of code, referred to as *methods*, which can be programmatically called upon to access and interact with objects. For example, files can be opened, read from, written to, closed, and deleted.

The .NET Framework provides the Windows PowerShell with access to a huge library of classes. The .NET Framework *class library* is a hierarchical collection of classes that defines the data type of objects that can be instantiated using the classes as templates. Within the framework, classes are often based on other classes, creating parent and child relationships. A child class (or subclass) inherits base object definitions from its parent class and includes its own modifications. These classes and subclasses are made available to the PowerShell in the form of *cmdlets*, which are built-in commands that provide access to specific system resources.

TRICK Classes, objects, properties, and methods can be difficult for new programmers to understand. To help make them easier to understand, consider the following analogy: A car manufacturer might have a library of blueprints (class library) which are used in the making of new cars. An individual blueprint (class) defines everything required to create a new type of car (object).

Individual cars are created or instantiated based on the blueprint. For example, a car company might have a master set of blueprints for building a particular model of a car. Using this one blueprint (class), the car company can create (instantiate) as many new cars (objects) as it wishes. By default, each car produced using the same class has the same set of properties and methods. Each car that is created from the same blueprint inherits a predefined set of attributes (properties). For example, every car has a color. By modifying the value of its color property, each car or object can be given a different color.

If the car company wants, it can pay an engineer to create a new set of blueprints for a new car, using the other set of blueprints as a starting point. As a result, the new set of blueprints would represent a subclass of the parent class and any new cars created from the new set of blueprints, though similar to cars created by the parent class, would have their own unique subset of shared properties and methods.

A basic understanding of objects is essential for any Windows PowerShell programmer because the PowerShell interacts with objects in just about everything it does. As such, Windows PowerShell scripting is often referred to as an object-based scripting language. It is called an *object-based* scripting language because, unlike object-oriented programming languages, PowerShell programmers typically work with objects that have already been created as opposed to defining and creating entirely new objects themselves. That is not to say that a PowerShell programmer cannot create new objects; it is just not something that is commonly needed.

PowerShell Versus cmd.exe

On the surface there are many similarities between cmd.exe and the PowerShell. As far as everyday tasks go, you should be able to use the PowerShell in place of cmd.exe. However, under the covers, PowerShell is many times more advanced than its predecessor. As has already been stated, PowerShell has direct access to resources provided by the .NET Framework and a brand new scripting language specifically designed to support interaction with .NET resources via cmdlets.

Another difference between the manner in which cmd.exe and PowerShell execute is the manner in which data is passed between commands. Both shells support the use of pipes to move data between commands. However, the type of data moved is completely different.

A *pipe* is a logical connection between two commands that supports the passage of one command's output to another command where it is received as input.

With cmd.exe, data is passed as text. Unfortunately, the output of one command often does not come back in a format required by the second command. As such, shell script programmers typically have to add additional programming logic to their scripts to reformat one command's output into a format the other command can accept. Window PowerShell uses an object pipeline that allows the receiving cmdlets to access properties and methods of objects generated by other cmdlets. With object piping, the programmer is relieved of the responsibility of formatting object data, significantly simplifying the scripting process.

Table 1.1 lists a number of additional key differences between cmd.exe and PowerShell. As you can see, Windows PowerShell boasts many key improvements, which you will learn more about as you work your way through this book.

TABLE 1.1   KEY WINDOWS SHELL DIFFERENCES

Feature	cmd.exe	PowerShell
Regular Expressions	No	Yes
Exception Handling	No	Yes
Array Support	No	Yes
Functions	No	Yes
Script Signing	No	Yes
Tab Completion	Limited	Yes

INSTALLING AND CONFIGURING WINDOWS POWERSHELL

In order to install Windows PowerShell, your computer must meet the following requirements.

- Your computer must be running Windows XP, Windows 2003, or Windows Vista
- Microsoft .NET Framework must be installed

As of the writing of this book, Windows PowerShell was a free download provided by Microsoft and could be downloaded and installed from the Microsoft PowerShell website, located at http://www.microsoft.com/windowsserver2003/technologies/management/powershell/default.mspx

Windows PowerShell downloads as a self-extracting executable that you can install by double-clicking on it. If your computer is not already running version 2.0 or higher of the .NET Framework, you must download and install it before you can install and run Windows PowerShell. If you attempt to install Windows PowerShell without .NET installed, you will see a popup dialog message instructing you to install it and the Windows PowerShell installation process will stop.

If necessary, you can get .NET by going to http://msdn.microsoft.com/netframework and downloading it. Once .NET has been installed, you can install Windows PowerShell. The install of PowerShell does not take long and ends with the addition of the Windows Power-Shell group on the All Programs menu, as demonstrated in Figure 1.7.

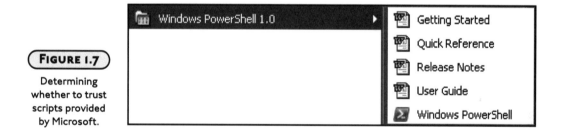

FIGURE 1.7

Determining whether to trust scripts provided by Microsoft.

Although Microsoft markets the Windows PowerShell as a secure environment for both command-line execution and scripting, the addition of a new shell and scripting language opens up the potential for exploitation by hackers. As such, Microsoft forces you to explicitly decide whether you trust Microsoft as a publisher of PowerShell scripts. Your choices are

- [D] Do not run
- [R] Run once
- [A] Always run
- [?] Help

Responding by entering A and pressing the Enter key allows you to run PowerShell scripts developed by Microsoft. Another security feature implemented by Microsoft is the inability to run scripts by double-clicking on them from the Windows desktop. Microsoft also forces you to make one more decision before you can start running PowerShell script files on your computer by establishing an execution policy that permits PowerShell scripts to run at one of three security levels, as outlined below.

- **Allsigned.** Only permits scripts that have a trusted signature to execute on your computer.
- **Remotesigned.** Permits PowerShell scripts downloaded from the web to run only if they are from a trusted source.
- **Unrestricted.** Allows any PowerShell script to run on your computer.

Before PowerShell will allow you to run your first PowerShell script, you will need to set one of Windows PowerShell's execution policy settings. For example, to allow any PowerShell script to run on your computer, you would enter the following command at the PowerShell command prompt.

```
Set-Executionpolicy Unrestricted
```

 Your choice of what execution policy to set should be based on your scripting needs and security requirements. If you decide later that you want to change your Windows PowerShell execution policy, you may do so at any time by re-executing the `Set-Executionpolicy` command and passing it one of the options listed above.

INTERACTING WITH THE POWERSHELL COMMAND PROMPT

The Windows PowerShell provides programmers with access to well over 100 cmdlets (pronounced command-lets), each of which is a .NET class that provides access to specific system resources. Like traditional command shells, the Windows PowerShell uses pipelines to pass data between cmdlets; however, instead of passing data as text, data is passed as objects. The inherent advantages of this approach include:

- When accessed from the command line, data is returned and displayed as text
- When data is passed from cmdlet to cmdlet, it is passed as objects or structured data
- Data passed between cmdlets is automatically converted into any format that is appropriate based on the current situation

Cmdlets also share access to a universal set of options. These options provide you with the ability to specify how errors are handled as well as to run cmdlets using a `-WHATIF` option that lets you see the effect that a command would have without actually making any changes. Cmdlets also support a `-CONFIRM` option that allows you to prompt the user for approval before execution within scripts.

Windows PowerShell cmdlets use a naming syntax that consists of verb-noun pairs. The verb is always on the left-hand side and is separated from the noun by a hyphen. The verb describes the action that is to take place and the noun identifies the target to be acted upon. Nouns are specified in a singular form. For example, the Get-* verb is a universal verb used to retrieve resources such as objects and properties. Using the Get-* verb and the Property noun, you could, for example, retrieve information about a given object's properties (e.g., Get-Property).

By combining the Get-* verb with the Help noun, you can execute the Get-Help cmdlet to get help on any cmdlet. For example, Figure 1.8 demonstrates how to use the Get-Help cmdlet, which retrieves information about other cmdlets, to get information about the Read-Host cmdlet.

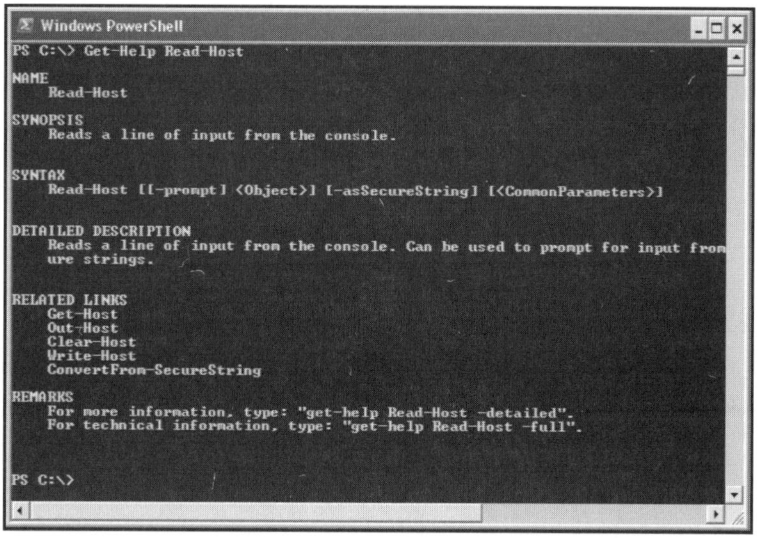

FIGURE 1.8

Examining help information about the Read-Host cmdlet.

Starting a New PowerShell Session

To start a new Windows PowerShell session, select on Start > All Programs > Windows PowerShell. A new Windows command console is opened and the Windows PowerShell command prompt is displayed, as demonstrated in Figure 1.9.

Executing PowerShell Cmdlets

You interact with the PowerShell by submitting commands at the command prompt, which typically looks something like PS C:\>, as demonstrated in Figure 1.10. PS is simply an abbreviation for PowerShell. C:\ represents the current working directory, and the > character indicates that PowerShell is ready to receive input. You enter commands for PowerShell to process by typing them in and pressing Enter. What happens next depends on the command you entered. By default, any command you type is processed and any output is returned as text, as demonstrated in Figure 1.10.

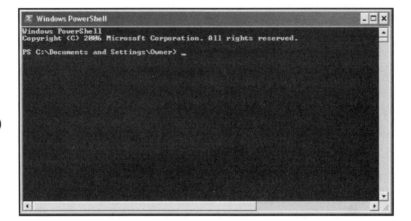

FIGURE 1.9

Access to the PowerShell is provided via the Windows command console.

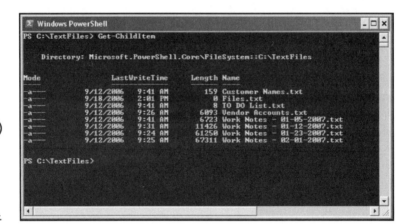

FIGURE 1.10

The Get-Childitem cmdlet displays the contents of the current working directory.

The command executed in Figure 1.10 is the Get-Childitem cmdlet, which retrieves the contents of a folder. Since a path was not specified, the current working directory was used. In order to help users and administrators make the transition to working with Windows PowerShell as easy as possible, Microsoft has developed a collection of cmdlet aliases that can be used in place of actual cmdlet names. Within the Windows PowerShell, an *alias* is a link to a particular cmdlet. In many cases, Microsoft has created multiple aliases for a given cmdlet. For example, since a user or administrator may find it difficult at first to remember to use `Get-Childitem` in order to display the contents of a folder, Microsoft has created an alias of `dir` for this cmdlet. You can therefore type `dir` in place of `Get-Childitem` and you receive the same exact results, as demonstrated in Figure 1.11.

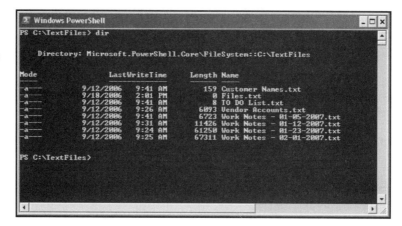

FIGURE 1.11

`dir` is an alias for the `Get-Childitem` cmdlet provided to help Windows users and administrators make the switch from cmd.exe to the Windows PowerShell.

Recognizing that not everybody is an experienced Windows user or administrator, Microsoft has also created an alias of `ls` for the `Get-Childitem` cmdlet in order to help smooth the transition to Windows PowerShell for users and administrators with a Linux or UNIX background. As Figure 1.12 shows, entering `ls` at the PowerShell command prompt results in the exact same results as the previous two examples.

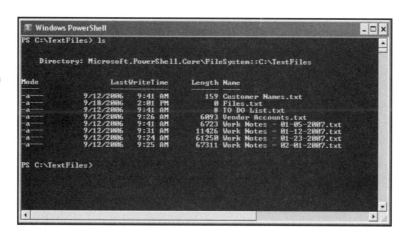

FIGURE 1.12

`ls` is an alias for the `Get-Childitem` cmdlet provided to help Linux and UNIX users and administrators make the switch to the Windows PowerShell.

HINT

Window PowerShell provides access to over 100 cmdlets, most of which have at least one alias. You will find a complete list of Windows PowerShell cmdlets in Chapter 3, "Object-Based Scripting with .NET".

Other Types of Commands

It is important that I do not leave you with the impression that the only types of commands that you can run from the Windows PowerShell command prompt are cmdlets. In fact, you can run any executable file. One way to locate executable files is by using the Get-Command cmdlet as demonstrated below.

```
Get-Command *.exe
```

In response, PowerShell will display a listing of all the executable files it can find. If you examine this list you will probably see a number of executable files that you are already familiar with. For example, you could start the Notepad application by typing **notepad** and pressing Enter at the PowerShell command prompt.

A Short PowerShell Workout

The best way to become familiar with Windows PowerShell is to begin working with it. In this section, you will get the chance to do just that. Specifically, I will provide you with a series of command-line examples that will give you a feel for the types of cmdlets supported by Windows PowerShell as well as the overall syntax involved in executing them.

For starters, let's execute a command that provides a list of all active processes currently running on the computer. This can be accomplished using the Get-Process cmdlet as demonstrated by the following.

```
PS C:\Get-Process
```

Handles	NPM(K)	PM(K)	WS(K)	VM(M)	CPU(s)	Id	ProcessName
17	2	540	1396	25	0.03	27784	AcroTray
78	3	1948	2024	33	0.20	27212	ALCXMNTR
103	5	1132	2464	32	0.05	2020	alg
305	8	2992	1228	60	2.08	27840	BackWeb-137903
987	4	2128	396	34	225.42	28156	CFD
529	6	1636	3468	26	40.89	536	csrss
527	14	15732	24388	103	147.00	27920	explorer
91	3	1076	3244	35	0.56	1160	FINDFAST
94	3	872	2348	35	0.11	28436	hpgs2wnd
91	3	868	2228	35	0.09	28356	hpgs2wnf
78	3	1140	2540	35	0.69	27332	hpotdd01
61	2	912	2316	31	0.17	28184	HpqCmon

```
13        1      380      1120     17     0.03     28100 hpsysdrv
17        2      496      1448     24     0.03     27312 hpwuSchd
43        2      504      1208     15     0.08      1324 HPZipm12
0         0      0        16       0                   0 Idle
6613      2      904      1324     17     0.16      1880 OPXPApp
357      11    28860    28288     151     3.97     30076 powershell
104       3      896      136      34     0.09     29704 realsched
300       7     2004     3700      36     7.75       608 services
21        1      164      340       4     0.06       472 smss
154       6     6256     5228      53     3.94      1068 spoolsv
209       5     3092     3564      62     0.20       788 svchost
335      13     1872     3048      37     1.55       836 svchost

PS C:\>
```

In response to the Get-Process cmdlet, Windows PowerShell displays a structured table complete with headings that lists each active process on the computer as well as a bunch of other information related to each process. Most cmdlets accept parameters that you can alter to further specify how to want them to execute. As you have already seen, by itself the Get-Process cmdlet retrieves a list of all the processes running on your computer. This cmdlet also support an optional -ProcessName parameter that lets you specify a process that it should look for as demonstrated here.

```
PS C:\Get-Process -ProcessName Winword

Handles   NPM(K)   PM(K)   WS(K)   VM(M)   CPU(s)      Id ProcessName
-------   ------   -----   -----   -----   ------      -- -----------
216       9        7312    18192   93      1,103.81 30516 WINWORD

PS C:\>
```

In this example, the Get-Process command has been instructed to display information about the Winword process (if it is running). As you can see, cmdlet parameters begin with a hyphen followed by the name of the parameter being specified and then the actual parameter. Cmdlet syntax is very straightforward but also very strict. However, the extra discipline also makes Windows PowerShell syntax easier to learn and remember.

The Windows PowerShell is flexible in many circumstances; often you only need to type in as much as is required to uniquely identify a parameter from other parameters. As a result, you could retype the previous example as shown next and Windows PowerShell will recognize that the argument being passed is the Process-Name parameter.

```
PS C:\> Get-Process -p winword

Handles     NPM(K)     PM(K)     WS(K)     VM(M)     CPU(s)     Id ProcessName
-----       ----       ----      ----      ----      ----       -- -----------
225         10         7496      18456     99        2,004.70   30516 WINWORD

PS C:\>
```

Many cmdlets, including the Get-Process cmdlet, define positional parameters, allowing you to pass arguments to the cmdlet without explicitly specifying the parameter they are supposed to match up against. For example, since the first parameter expected by the Get-Process cmdlet is the -ProcessName parameter, you can omit the -ProcessName or -p and supply just the name of a process. The cmdlet will automatically assume that the first argument you pass to it is the name of a process, as demonstrated below.

```
PS C:\> Get-Process winword

Handles     NPM(K)     PM(K)     WS(K)     VM(M)     CPU(s)     Id ProcessName
-----       ----       ----      ----      ----      ----       -- -----------
225         10         7476      18476     99        2,031.17   30516 WINWORD


PS C:\>
```

Also, you can cast a somewhat wider net and view all of the processes whose names begin with the letter w, as demonstrated here.

```
PS C:\> Get-Process w*

Handles     NPM(K)     PM(K)     WS(K)     VM(M)     CPU(s)     Id ProcessName
-----       ----       ----      ----      ----      ----       -- -----------
67          2          1492      1172      14        0.03       1452 wdfmgr
428         46         6948      3408      51        6.08       564 winlogon
214         9          7300      18204     92        1,206.08   30516 WINWORD
32          1          328       684       15        0.03       1580 WLService
27          2          464       1568      25        0.05       27752 wscntfy
142         8          5820      8136      56        0.53       1600 WUSB54Gv4

PS C:\>
```

HINT Most cmdlets allow you to refine their execution by passing them additional information for processing as arguments. In the case of the preceding `Get-Process w*` example, the * wildcard character was passed along with the w character.

In this example, the `Get-Process` cmdlet processes retrieve a list of all active processes whose names begin with the letter w, as specified by the w* argument that was passed to the cmdlet for processing.

TRICK The * character is a wild card character that is used in pattern matching. Its purpose is to set up a match with any number of characters. For example, T*p would match any of the following strings

- Tp
- Top
- Tooooooop

The ? character is another wildcard matching character, used to set up a pattern match with a single character. For example, T*p would match Tip or Top but not Tooooooop.

If you have previous command-line experience, then the examples you have just seen should look reasonably familiar. If you don't have a lot of command-line experience, don't worry; you will by the end of this book, and examples such as these will eventually become second nature to you. Before moving on, let's look at one more command-line example.

In this example, the `Get-Process` cmdlet is used to retrieve a list of all active processes whose names begins with the letters wi. Next, using a technique known as *object piping*, the results of this command are passed to the `Format-Table` cmdlet. The `Format-Table` cmdlet displays command output in a table format, allowing you to specify a number of optional parameters. In this example, the `-groupby` property is used to instruct the cmdlet to organize output by process name, as demonstrated below.

```
PS C:\> Get-Process wi* | Format-Table -groupby ProcessName

    ProcessName: winlogon

Handles    NPM(K)    PM(K)    WS(K)    VM(M)    CPU(s)    Id ProcessName
-------    ------    -----    -----    -----    ------    -- -----------
428        46        6948     3408     51       6.08      564 winlogon
```

```
ProcessName: WINWORD

Handles     NPM(K)      PM(K)       WS(K)       VM(M)       CPU(s)      Id ProcessName
-----       -----       ----        ----        ----        -----       -- -----------
224         10          7500        18484       99          2,120.91    30516 WINWORD

PS C:\>
```

WINDOWS POWERSHELL SCRIPTING

Windows PowerShell scripts are plain text files with a .ps1 file extension. These script files are made up of one or more PowerShell script statements. Once created, PowerShell scripts are executed like any PowerShell command or cmdlet; you just type in its name at the PowerShell command line and optionally pass any arguments required by the script.

Windows PowerShell comes complete with its own brand-new scripting language, which supports a full range of programming language features, including support for the following:

- variables, arrays, and hashes
- conditional logic statements
- looping statements
- functions
- error handling

 You will learn about the Windows PowerShell programming language in Chapters 3–7.

SIMPLIFYING POWERSHELL SCRIPT EXECUTION

To run a PowerShell script, all that you have to do is type in the name of the script at the PowerShell command prompt. In response, the PowerShell will search every folder in your default search path looking for the specified PowerShell script.

 I suggest that you create a new folder named something like MyScripts and use it as the storage location for all your PowerShell script files; this will make your script files easy to find.

To see the contents of your default path, start PowerShell and type **$env:path**, as demonstrated here.

```
PS C:\> $env:path
```

In response you should see output similar to this.

```
C:\Perl\bin\;C:\WINDOWS\system32;C:\WINDOWS;C:\WINDOWS\System32\Wbem;c:\Python2
2;C:\Program Files\Windows PowerShell\v1.0\
PS C:\Documents and Settings\Owner>
```

This output shows that on my computer, the PowerShell will search each of the following folders looking for the specified PowerShell script file.

```
C:\Perl\bin\
C:\WINDOWS\system32
C:\WINDOWS
C:\WINDOWS\System32\Wbem
c:\Python22
C:\Program Files\Windows PowerShell\v1.0\
```

There are a number of different options open to you for making your Windows PowerShell scripts easy to execute. For starters, you can store your PowerShell scripts in one of the folders that is already listed in your default path. However, this is probably not a good idea. It is a much better idea to store them someplace that works better for you and to run your PowerShell scripts from there. One way to do this is to switch over to the folder where your PowerShell scripts are stored and then precede the name of your PowerShell script with a ./ when running them.

```
PS C:\> cd c:\ShellScripts
PS C:\> ./knockknock.ps1
```

By appending ./ in front of your PowerShell script filename, you temporarily add the current folder to your search path, thus letting PowerShell find it. A more permanent way of dealing with things is to permanently add your script folder to your default search path, which you can do by right-clicking on My Computer, selecting Properties, and then selecting the Advanced property sheet on the System properties dialog. Next, click on the Environment Variables button, locate the path variable in the System variables list located at the bottom of the window, and then click on the Edit button and append a semicolon followed by the full path name of your script folder to the end of the path string. Once you have finished making this modification, you will need to reboot your computer for the change to take effect.

BACK TO THE KNOCK KNOCK JOKE GAME

Okay, it is time to turn your attention back to the development of this chapter game's project, the Knock Knock Joke game. The creation of this script will demonstrate the mechanics involved in creating and running PowerShell scripts. In addition, this game will demonstrate how to develop a PowerShell script that can interact with the user by retrieving command-line input and displaying text output.

At this point in the book, it is not expected that you will understand what each script statement does or how it works. You will learn the basics of the PowerShell scripting language later in Chapters 4–6. For now, your primary focus should be on learning the steps involved in script creation and execution.

Designing the Game

It is always a good idea to spend a little time planning out the design and organization of your PowerShell scripts before you begin writing them. This will help reduce errors and decrease the amount of time it takes to get the job done. As you saw earlier in this chapter, the script begins by clearing the screen and then prompting the player to answer two questions correctly before displaying the punch line for the first joke. Two additional jokes are then told in succession. The game ends after displaying a little information about itself and its author.

As you can see, the series of steps required to tell a joke is not terribly complicated. To develop the PowerShell script file, you will assemble it in eight steps, as outlined here:

1. Create a new script file and add an initial statement that clears the screen.
2. Display the first line of the first joke and wait for the player to respond.
3. Display the second line of the first joke and wait for the player to respond again.
4. Displays the first joke's punch line.
5. Pause script execution to give the player a chance to enjoy the joke.
6. Tell the script's second joke
7. Tell the script's third joke
8. Display closing script and author information.

Creating a New PowerShell Script

Begin by opening your preferred text or script editor and saving a new script file named KnockKnock.ps1. Next, add the following statement as the first line in the script file.

```
Clear-Host
```

HINT .ps1 is PowerShell's standard file extension. You will be using it for all the PowerShell game scripts you create in this book.

Clear-Host is a Windows PowerShell cmdlet. When executed, it clears out any text currently displayed in the Windows command console, preparing it for the display of new text.

HINT If you prefer, you can also clear the Windows command console by substituting the clear or cls command for the Clear-Host command. clear and cls are both aliases for Clear-Host. Window PowerShell supports well over 100 cmdlets, most of which have at least one alias. You will find a complete list of Windows PowerShell cmdlets in Chapter 3.

Prompting the Player to Begin the Game

Now it is time for the game to display the first joke's opening "Knock Knock!" string and wait for the player to respond by typing in the string **Who is there?**. To complete this portion of the script, add the following statements to the end of the script file.

HINT A *string* is a series of zero or more characters surrounded by double quotation marks.

```
$userReply = ""

while ($userReply -ne "Who is there?"){
    $userReply = read-host "Knock Knock!"
}
```

The first statement declares a variable named $userReply, assigning it an empty string. This variable will be used by the while loop block that follows to store and analyze the input keyed in by the user. The while loop has been set up to execute until the player enters the expected response. Note that it is the single statement located inside the while loop that displays the opening "Knock Knock!" string prompt, which it does using the Read-Host cmdlet to read a line of input from the Windows command console.

HINT A *variable* is a pointer to a location in memory where a value is stored. You will learn more about variables in Chapter 4, "Working with Variables, Arrays, and Hashes." A *loop* is collection of one or more statements that is repeatedly executed as a unit. You will learn more about loops in Chapter 6, "Using Loops to Process Data."

Collecting Additional Player Input

Once the player has provided the correct response to the opening "Knock Knock!" prompt, the game needs to display the joke's setup line, which is accomplished by adding the following statements to the end of the script file.

```
Clear-Host

while ($userReply -ne "Orange who?"){
    $userReply = read-host "Orange."
}
```

As you can see, the first statement shown here clears the Windows command console screen. Next, a while loop executes using the Read-Host cmdlet to display a prompt of "Orange.". The player must then respond by entering "Orange who?" in order for the game to continue.

Displaying the Punch Line

Once the player has provided the correct response, the script displays the first joke's punch line. This is accomplished by adding the following statements to the end of the script file.

```
Clear-Host
Write-Output "Orange you glad you created this PowerShell script?"
```

The first statement clears the Windows command console screen. The second statement displays a text string containing the first joke's punch line using the Write-Output cmdlet.

 HINT By default, the Write-Output cmdlet writes a line of text to the Windows command console screen.

Pausing Between Jokes

After each joke is told, the game is supposed to pause for five seconds to give the player an opportunity to read the joke's punch line. This is accomplished by adding the following statement to the end of the script file.

```
Start-Sleep -Seconds 5
```

This statement executes the Start-Sleep cmdlet, telling it to pause script execution for five seconds.

Telling the Second Joke

At this point, the script's first joke has been presented to the user. Now it is time to write the code statements required to tell the game's second joke. The code statements required to complete this task are almost identical to the statements that presented the first joke, except for some slightly different content in the text strings that make up the text of the joke. This code, shown below, must be added to the end of the script file.

```
Clear-Host

while ($userReply -ne "Who is there?"){
    $userReply = read-host "Knock Knock!"
}

Clear-Host
while ($userReply -ne "Orange who?"){
    $userReply = read-host "Orange."
}

Clear-Host
Write-Output "Oranges are oranges but this is PowerShell scripting!"

Start-Sleep -Seconds 5
```

Telling the Third Joke

The code statements responsible for telling the game's third joke are shown next. These statements need to be added to the end of your PowerShell script file.

```
Clear-Host

while ($userReply -ne "Who is there?"){
    $userReply = read-host "Knock Knock!"
}

Clear-Host
while ($userReply -ne "Banana who?"){
    $userReply = read-host "Banana."
}
```

```
Clear-Host
Write-Output "Orange you glad I didn't say orange?"

Start-Sleep -Seconds 5
```

As you can see, these code statements are almost identical to the statements that presented the first and second jokes, except for some slightly different text string content.

Displaying Game and Author Information

The Knock Knock Joke game ends by clearing the Windows command console screen, displaying a little information about the game and the game's author, and, after a three-second pause, clearing the screen and ending. The code statements that make this happen are shown next and should be added to the end of your script file.

```
Clear-Host

Write-Output "The Knock Knock Joke"
Write-Output ""
Write-Output "Copyright 2006 - Jerry Lee Ford, Jr."

Start-Sleep -Seconds 3

Clear-Host
```

The Final Result

At this point, your new Windows PowerShell script should be complete. Since this is your first PowerShell script and since you built it in a series of different steps, I've gone ahead and laid out a full copy of the entire script here so that you can make sure that you did not miss anything when keying your copy of the script.

```
Clear-Host

$userReply = ""

while ($userReply -ne "Who is there?"){
    $userReply = read-host "Knock Knock!"
}
```

```
Clear-Host
while ($userReply -ne "Orange who?"){
    $userReply = read-host "Orange."
}

Clear-Host
Write-Output "Orange you glad you created this PowerShell script?"

Start-Sleep -Seconds 5

Clear-Host

while ($userReply -ne "Who is there?"){
    $userReply = read-host "Knock Knock!"
}

Clear-Host
while ($userReply -ne "Orange who?"){
    $userReply = read-host "Orange."
}

Clear-Host
Write-Output "Oranges are oranges but this is PowerShell scripting!"

Start-Sleep -Seconds 5

Clear-Host

while ($userReply -ne "Who is there?"){
    $userReply = read-host "Knock Knock!"
}

Clear-Host
while ($userReply -ne "Banana who?"){
    $userReply = read-host "Banana."
}
```

```
Clear-Host
Write-Output "Orange you glad I didn't say orange?"

Start-Sleep -Seconds 5

Clear-Host

Write-Output "The Knock Knock Joke"
Write-Output ""
Write-Output "Copyright 2006 - Jerry Lee Ford, Jr."

Start-Sleep -Seconds 3

Clear-Host
```

Assuming that you have not made any typos, your Knock Knock Joke script should be ready to run. If you run into any errors, then you have made a typo somewhere. If this is the case, you will need to go back and review your work and find where you made a mistake.

SUMMARY

This chapter has taught you a lot about Windows PowerShell and Windows PowerShell scripting. You learned what makes Windows PowerShell different from its predecessor and examined its major features and components. You learned how to install and configure its execution. You learned how to execute cmdlets and to create and run Windows PowerShell scripts. You learned how to get help on different PowerShell commands. On top of all this, you created your first Windows PowerShell game, the Knock Knock Joke game.

The Knock Knock Joke game is admittedly not the most advanced PowerShell script. Still, if you are new to programming, you may not yet understand everything that you see. Don't worry about that for now. The important thing for you to take away from the development of this script is a basic understanding of the mechanics involved in creating and executing a Windows PowerShell script.

When it comes to computer games, there is always room for improvement. Before you move on to the next chapter, I recommend that you spend a little more time working on the Knock Knock Joke game by trying to implement the following list of challenges.

CHALLENGES

1. As currently written, the Knock Knock Joke game presents players with three somewhat bland jokes. I suggest that you replace these jokes with knock knock jokes of your own.

2. With only three jokes, the Knock Knock Joke game does not take very long to complete. Give the player a better experience by expanding the number of jokes that are told.

3. Once you have added your own jokes to the Knock Knock Joke game, take credit for your work by modifying the developer information that is displayed at the end of the script.

INTERACTING WITH THE
WINDOWS POWERSHELL
COMMAND LINE

I n order to work effectively with the Windows PowerShell and to develop PowerShell scripts, you must have a solid understanding of how to interact with Windows from the PowerShell command line. This chapter will provide you with instruction on how to configure the Windows command console in order to create a better working environment with which to interact with Windows PowerShell. This will include learning how to configure the command console layout and to specify your default working directory. This chapter will also explain how to take advantage of Windows PowerShell's built-in tab completion feature in order to save time and reduce errors when keying in commands. You will also learn how to use Windows PowerShell to navigate and access different types of system resources, including the Windows registry, environment variables, and disk drives. On top of all this, you will learn how to create your second PowerShell game, The Story of the Three Amigos.

Specifically, you will learn how to:

- Set a default working directory for your PowerShell sessions
- Customize the Windows command console
- Reduce the time required to complete commands by taking advantage of tab completion
- Use Windows PowerShell to access different hierarchical data stores

PROJECT PREVIEW: THE STORY OF THE THREE AMIGOS

In this chapter you will learn how to create a new computer game that tells The Story of the Three Amigos. Key pieces of this mad-lib styled story are collected from the user in the form of responses to seemingly unrelated questions. The end result is a story that is never told the same way twice. The Story of the Three Amigos begins by displaying its title page, as shown in Figure 2.1.

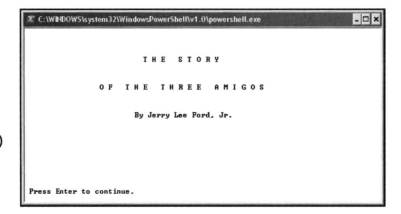

FIGURE 2.1

The Story of the Three Amigos is told a page at a time.

The Story of the Three Amigos is a mad-lib styled game in which player input is collected and plugged into key places in the story to allow the user to participate in the story-telling experience. Before asking any questions, the game informs the users of what is expected from them, as shown in Figure 2.2.

FIGURE 2.2

The Story of the Three Amigos is an interactive story that depends on user input.

In total, the user is asked four questions without knowing in advance the context in which the answers will be used. Figure 2.3 provides an example of one of the questions asked by the game.

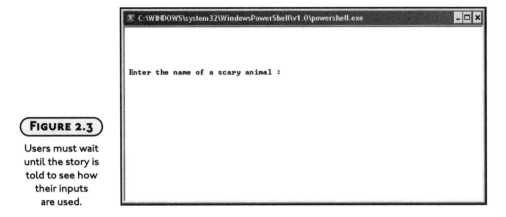

FIGURE 2.3

Users must wait until the story is told to see how their inputs are used.

Once the game has collected all of the information that it requires, it begins telling The Story of the Three Amigos a page at a time. The first page of the story is shown in Figure 2.4.

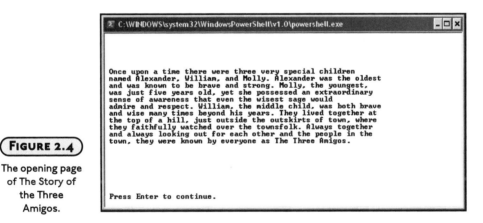

FIGURE 2.4

The opening page of The Story of the Three Amigos.

As users read through each page of the story, they will notice how the answers they provided have affected the manner in which the story is told, as demonstrated in Figure 2.5.

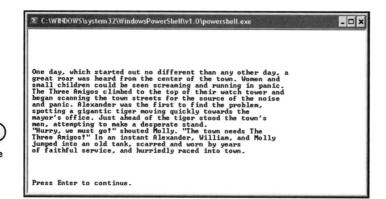

FIGURE 2.5

The second page of The Story of the Three Amigos.

Figure 2.6 shows the next page of the story, which explains how the story's heroes defeat their enemy and save the townsfolk.

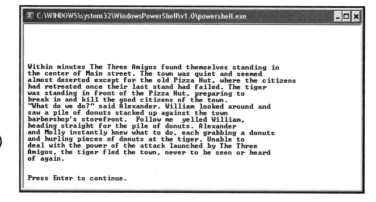

FIGURE 2.6

The third page of The Story of the Three Amigos.

The Story of the Three Amigos ends, like so many stories, with a happy ending, as shown in Figure 2.7.

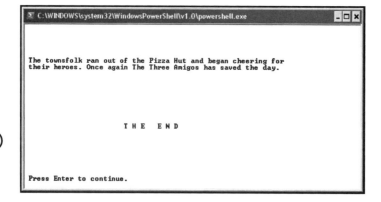

FIGURE 2.7

The last page of The Story of the Three Amigos.

By the time you have finished the Windows PowerShell script that makes up The Story of the Three Amigos, you should have a good understanding of the mechanics involved in creating and executing Windows PowerShell scripts.

ACCESSING WINDOWS POWERSHELL

As you have already seen, you can start a new Windows PowerShell session by clicking on Start > All Programs > Windows PowerShell. When first started, the Windows command console appears and, after a moment, displays the following information.

```
Windows(R) PowerShell
Copyright (C) 2006 Microsoft Corporation. All rights reserved.


PS C:\>
```

By default, Windows PowerShell displays its name and copyright information each time it is started. The name and copyright information is followed by a blank line and the Windows PowerShell command prompt. The command prompt displays, by default, the Windows PowerShell's current working directory.

There are plenty of other ways to start new Windows PowerShell sessions. For example, you could also click on Start > Run and then type **PowerShell** in the Run window that appears, as shown in Figure 2.8.

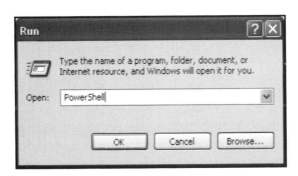

FIGURE 2.8

Starting Windows PowerShell from the Run window.

When started from the Run window, Windows gives you the opportunity to pass arguments to the Windows PowerShell at startup. For example, if you wanted to prevent the display of the Windows PowerShell name and copyright information, you should type **PowerShell –nologo** into the Run window and click on OK. The end result would be a new Windows PowerShell session that starts up by displaying the PowerShell command prompt only.

You can also start a new PowerShell session from within a cmd.exe shell console session by typing **PowerShell** at the command prompt and pressing Enter. In response, a new PowerShell session is started within the current command window. When done working with the PowerShell session, you can close it and return to the cmd.exe session by typing **Exit** at the PowerShell command line and pressing Enter.

Another way to start up a new Windows PowerShell session is to create a desktop shortcut for it, which you can do by clicking on Start > All Programs, right-clicking on the Windows PowerShell icon, then selecting Create Shortcut. This adds a PowerShell shortcut to the Windows PowerShell group, which you can then drag and drop onto your Windows desktop.

Another way of creating a shortcut for Windows PowerShell is to right-click on an open area of the Windows desktop and, when prompted, select New > Shortcut. This will start a Create Shortcut wizard, whose job is to walk you through the process of setting up new shortcuts. Type **PowerShell** in the Type the Location of the Item field and click on Next. Next type **Windows PowerShell** in the Type a Name for This Shortcut field and click on Finish.

CUSTOMIZING THE WINDOWS POWERSHELL WORKING ENVIRONMENT

Regardless of how you start a Windows PowerShell session, you will find yourself working with it from within the Windows command console application. The good news is that the Windows command console provides you with access to a rich set of commands and features that help give you greater control over the manner in which you interact with the PowerShell and that can also be used to help you work faster and more efficiently.

Customizing Windows PowerShell Shortcuts

Placing a shortcut to the Windows PowerShell on your desktop provides convenient access. One way to make the shortcut an even more convenient tool is by modifying its Start in field to point to the folder where you have decided to store all your Windows PowerShell script files. This way, all you have to do is double-click on your Windows PowerShell icon and a new session will start up, using the specified folder as your current working directory.

The steps required to modify your Windows PowerShell shortcut as described above are outlined in the following procedure.

1. Right-click on your Windows PowerShell shortcut and select Properties. The Windows PowerShell Properties dialog box will appear.

2. Type the full path name for your PowerShell script folder in the Start in field, as demonstrated in Figure 2.9.

3. Click on OK.

The next time you start up a new Windows PowerShell session using this shortcut, the Windows command console will appear and a new PowerShell session will be started with the specified folder set as your current working directory, as demonstrated in Figure 2.10.

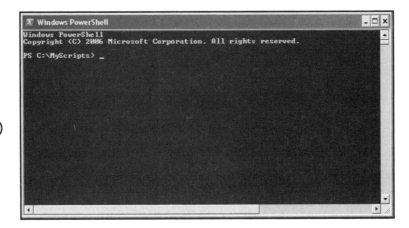

Configuring the Windows Command Console

Windows PowerShell is accessed through the Windows command console. By default, the Windows command console displays text in a window that is 45 lines long and 120 characters wide. All text is displayed as white text on a blue background. As a Windows PowerShell programmer, it is important that you know how to work with the Windows command console and that it is configured to suit your personal preferences.

As the sections that follow will demonstrate, the Windows command console is highly configurable, allowing you to modify its appearances and behavior in a number of ways. In addition, it provides you with a number of handy editing commands for interacting with the Windows PowerShell.

 To help improve the presentation of figures in this book, I have modified my version of the Windows command console to be 25 characters long and 80 characters wide. Also, I have set up text to display as black characters on a white background.

Windows Command Console Customization Options

In order to customize the Windows command console, you must first open it up, which you can do by starting a new Windows PowerShell session. Once opened, right-click on the Command Prompt icon located in the upper-left corner of the command console's title bar and then select Properties from the context menu that appears. This will open the Windows PowerShell Properties dialog window. This dialog is organized into four property sheets. Each of these sheets controls a different aspect of the Windows command console. You configure the Windows command console's behavior and appearance by modifying the attribute information shown on these property sheets.

 Even though this section highlights the configuration of the Windows command console using Windows XP, the information provided here should also broadly apply to both Windows 2003 and Windows Vista.

Modifying Command Console Options

The first property sheet on the Properties window is the Options tab, as shown in Figure 2.11. From here you can modify the following Windows command console attributes:

- **Cursor Size**. Determines whether the command console cursor appears in a small, medium, or large size.

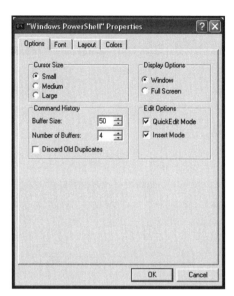

FIGURE 2.11

The Options property sheet provides access to console attributes that control cursor size and command history as well as display and edit settings.

- **Command History**. Determines the size of the command console's buffers, which affects the number of commands the command console stores and retrieves, as well as the number of buffers in use and whether or not duplicate commands are saved as part of the command console's command history.

- **Display Options**. Determines whether the command console opens in its default window view or in full-screen mode.

- **Edit Options**. Determines whether QuickEdit mode and Insert mode are enabled. QuickEdit is a command console feature that supports the copying of text from the command window and the pasting of text to the command prompt. Insert mode controls whether text is inserted or overwritten when editing text keyed in at the command prompt.

Modifying Command Console Font Attributes

The second property sheet on the Properties window is the Font tab, as shown in Figure 2.12. From here you can modify the font size and font type used by the Windows command console.

Changes to font size also affect the size of the Windows command console. The Windows Preview area provides you with visual feedback regarding the effects of making a font size change.

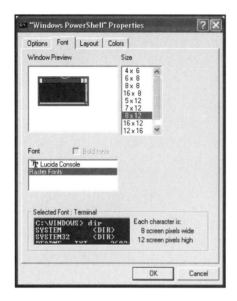

FIGURE 2.12

Configuring font
attributes for
the Windows
command
console.

The Font property sheet also allows you to change the font type used by the Windows command console. The effects of a font type selection are made immediately apparent in the Selected Font: Terminal section of the Font property sheet. Depending on the font that you select, the Bold fonts attribute, located just above the list of available fonts, is enabled. When enabled, console text appears bold, which, depending on your preferences, may make console text easier to read.

Changing the Layout of the Windows Command Console

The third property sheet on the Properties window is the Layout tab, as shown in Figure 2.13. From here you can set the Windows command console's initial size and display location.

Changes made to Layout attributes are immediately reflected in the Window Preview portion of the Layout property sheet. Configuration changes are made by modifying any of the following settings:

- **Screen Buffer Size**. The Width setting specifies the number of characters that are displayed on a single line. The Height setting specifies the number of lines of text that can be stored in memory, thus controlling the number of lines that you can scroll back and view.

- **Window Size**. The Width setting specifies the number of characters that are displayed on a single line. The Height setting specifies the number of lines of text the command console displays by default. Regardless of these settings, you can always manually resize the Windows command console like any other Windows application by right-clicking on its edges and dragging them to a new location. It should be noted, however, that the Windows command console cannot be resized any larger than the height and width values set in the Screen Buffer Size section.

• **Window Position.** You can set the starting location of the Windows command console by modifying these settings to specify the exact location where the Windows command console should be displayed when started. Position is set by specifying the pixel count of the left and right corner of the Windows command console's upper-left corner. A *pixel* (picture element) represents the smallest area that can be displayed or printed. Optionally, you can allow Windows to determine the proper location for the Windows command console by leaving the default Let System Position Window attribute selected.

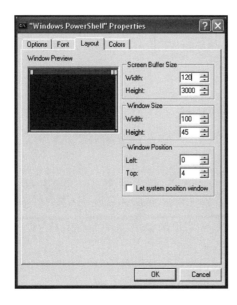

FIGURE 2.13

Modifying
Windows
command
console default
screen size and
Windows
position.

TRICK I recommend that you set the Screen Buffer Size Height setting to three times the height of the Window Size setting. This will allow you to scroll back through several pages of previously executed commands and command output.

Changing Command Console Color Attributes

The fourth property sheet on the Properties window is the Colors tab, as shown in Figure 2.14. From here you can change the Windows command console's foreground and background colors.

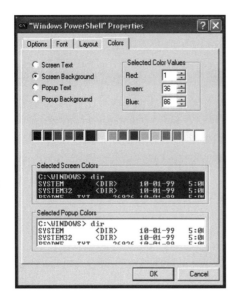

FIGURE 2.14

Modifying the
Windows
command
console
foreground and
background color
attributes.

The left side of the top portion of the Colors property sheet provides access to four different options. To configure these options, select them one at a time and then select a color from the color strip located in the middle of the property sheet. The four options include:

- **Screen Text**. Specifies the color used to display text.
- **Screen Background**. Specifies the color used to display the command console's background color.
- **Popup Text**. Specifies the color used to display the text color of the Windows command console's Command History dialog box.
- **Popup Background**. Specifies the color used to display the background color of the Windows command console's Command History dialog box.

If you prefer, you can specify a custom color instead of a selecting a color from the color strip by selecting one of these four configuration options and then specifying various levels of red, green, and blue using the scrollbar controls located in the Selected Color values section in the top-right corner of the Colors property sheet.

The bottom half of the Colors tab provides a visual preview of the effect of any changes made to the Windows command console and its Command History dialog box.

Going forward, I have set the screen background color of the Windows command console to white and the screen text color to black. This will **generate** screen figures that are more legible and easier to read for the rest of the book's game scripts.

Windows Command Console Editing Features

Because you access and interact with the Windows PowerShell within the Windows command console, you have access to a host of helpful editing features that are built into the console. For example, you can edit any command already typed in at the command prompt by using the left and right arrow keys to move back and forth to locations within the command and then use the Backspace or Delete keys to remove characters from the command.

In addition to this basic command-editing capability, you can use any of the edit features shown in Table 2.1 to take control of the command line and edit and execute commands.

TABLE 2.1   WINDOWS COMMAND CONSOLE EDIT COMMANDS

Edit Feature	Result
Up Arrow	Moves back one position in the command-line history buffer.
Down Arrow	Moves forward one position in the command-line history buffer.
Page Up	Moves to the first command stored in the command-line history buffer.
Page Down	Moves to the last command stored in the command-line history buffer.
Home	Jumps the cursor to the beginning of the command line.
End	Jumps the cursor to the end of the command line.
Control+Left	Moves the cursor to the left a word at a time.
Control+Right	Moves the cursor to the right a word at a time.

 HINT The Windows command console maintains a list of commands that are executed during the current working session. This list is referred to as the *history buffer*.

 TRICK You can also view a listing of the commands stored in the Windows command console's history buffer by pressing the F7 key. In response, the Windows command console displays a window like the one shown in Figure 2.15.

FIGURE 2.15

Viewing and executing commands stored in the Windows command console history buffer.

```
0:  Get-Process
1:  Get-Help
2:  Get-alias
3:  Get-Process  winword
```

Note that to the left of each command in the history buffer is a number. You can execute any command in the list by typing its associated number and pressing the Enter key. If the buffer contains more commands than can be displayed at one time, you can use the up and down arrows to move up and down in the history buffer in order to locate the command you are looking for.

WINDOWS POWERSHELL EDIT ENHANCEMENTS

In addition to inheriting access to all the edit features provided by the Windows command console, Windows PowerShell also provides you with access to a couple of PowerShell-specific editing capabilities that you can use to work smarter and faster from the Windows PowerShell command prompt.

Tab Completion

One powerful Windows PowerShell feature that merits explicit recognition is tab completion. Tab completion allows you to type a part of a command and then hit the Tab key to get assistance in filling out the rest of the command. For example, if you type **get-** at the PowerShell prompt and then press the Tab key, PowerShell responds by displaying the following:

```
Get-Acl
```

If this is the command you want, press Enter to accept this selection. Otherwise, press Tab again to see the next available suggestion. If you continue to press Tab, PowerShell will continue to show you additional suggestions until it exhausts the available list, after which it starts over again, letting you loop back through the list of suggestions. For example, if you were to continue to press Tab in the current example, you would eventually see each of the following suggestions.

```
Get-Alias
Get-AuthenticodeSignature
Get-ChildItem
Get-Command
Get-Content
Get-Credential
Get-Culture
Get-Date
Get-Eventlog
Get-ExecutionPolicy
Get-Help
```

```
Get-History
Get-Host
Get-Item
Get-ItemProperty
Get-Location
Get-Member
Get-PfxCertificate
Get-Process
Get-PSDrive
Get-PSProvider
Get-PSSnapin
Get-Service
Get-TraceSource
Get-UICulture
Get-Unique
Get-Variable
Get-WmiObject
```

The obvious advantage of tab completion is that you do not have to remember all of a command to be able to key it in. You only have to remember enough to help PowerShell identify the broad category and then start pressing Tab. Tab completion applies to more than just helping you key in cmdlets; it can also assist you in filling in filenames based on the contents of the current working directory, variable names, and property names. For example, enter the following statements at the PowerShell command prompt and press Enter.

```
$x = "Once upon a time..."
```

This statement creates a variable named $x and assigns it a value consisting of a text string. Next, type **$x.** and then press the Tab key. In response, PowerShell will display the first of a series of possible matches based on the contents of the command being formulated. In this example, PowerShell will display methods appropriate for working with a variable that contains a text string. When a method is selected, it is appended to the end of your current command along with an opening left parenthesis, leaving it up to you to supply any additional arguments and then the obligatory closing right parenthesis. For example, if you were to keep pressing the Tab key until the ToLower(suggestion was displayed and then you pressed the Enter key, you would end up with the following results.

```
$x.ToLower(
```

TRICK

The ToLower() method is used to convert all of the characters that make up a string to all lowercase characters. To finish off the previous example, all you would need to do is add the closing right parenthesis and then press Enter, as demonstrated here:

```
PS C:\> $x = "Once upon a time..."
PS C:\> $x.ToLower()
once upon a time...
PS C:\>
```

Alternatively, you could press the Enter key to select the ToLower(suggestion and then type the closing right parenthesis and press the Enter key twice as shown here.

```
PS C:\> $x = "Once upon a time..."
PS C:\> $x.ToLower(
>> )
>>
once upon a time...
PS C:\>
```

In this example, PowerShell did not execute the specified command when you first pressed the Enter key because it knew the command was not complete. Instead, it left you in Edit mode as indicated by the absence of the command prompt and the presence of the >> characters on the left side of the screen. When you supplied the required closing right parenthesis and then pressed the Enter key, PowerShell remained in Edit mode, allowing you to add to the command if necessary. Pressing Enter a second time without entering any text closed Edit mode and instructed PowerShell to execute your command.

The Get-History Cmdlet

You can also get your hands on entries stored in the history buffer using the Get-History cmdlet. This cmdlet accesses history buffer commands and inserts them into the Windows PowerShell pipeline, allowing to you programmatically access and manipulate them. For example, using the Get-History cmdlet, you could display a list of commands stored in the history buffer, as demonstrated here.

```
PS C:\MyScripts> Get-History

  Id CommandLine
  -- -----------
```

```
1 Get-Process
2 Get-Alias
3 Get-Help
```

With this information now in your possession, you can execute any of the commands in the history buffer using the `Invoke-History` cmdlet, which takes as an argument a number representing the position of a command in the history buffer. For example, to execute the second command listed in the previous example, you would enter the following command at the PowerShell command prompt and press Enter.

```
Invoke-History 2
```

While this may seem like a lot of work just to find and re-execute a simple two-word cmdlet, the real value of the `Get-History` and `Invoke-History` cmdlets comes into play when you find yourself repeatedly executing a series of complex and lengthy commands. Not only will you be able to work faster, but also, once you have your commands entered correctly, you can re-execute them over and over again without making any typos.

NAVIGATING HIERARCHICAL DATA STORES

Traditional command shells are designed to interact with and navigate the computer's file system. The file system is a hierarchical data store made up of drives, folders, and files. In the cmd.exe shell, the `dir` command is used to display the contents of the current working directory and the `cd` command is used to navigate the file system's hierarchical structure. Similar commands are available in Windows PowerShell (the `Get-ChildItem` and `Set-Location` cmdlets).

However, unlike traditional shells, Windows PowerShell does not limit itself to just the computer's file system. Instead, Windows PowerShell has the ability to access and navigate many different hierarchical data stores, including:

- Alias commands
- Environment variables
- Windows PowerShell functions
- The Windows registry
- Variables
- Certificates

In order to facilitate the access of different hierarchical data stores, Windows PowerShell implements a provider model that exposes different hierarchical data stores in a manner that simulates a file system. As such, not only can you access these different data stores, but you can do so using familiar commands (e.g., `cd` or `Set-Location` and `dir` or `Get-ChildItem`).

You can view a listing of all the providers supported by Windows PowerShell by executing the Get-PSProvider cmdlet, as demonstrated here.

```
PS C:\MyScripts> Get-PSProvider
```

Name	Capabilities	Drives
Alias	ShouldProcess	{Alias}
Environment	ShouldProcess	{Env}
FileSystem	Filter, ShouldProcess	{C, D, A, E...}
Function	ShouldProcess	{Function}
Registry	ShouldProcess	{HKLM, HKCU}
Variable	ShouldProcess	{Variable}
Certificate	ShouldProcess	{cert}

As this cmdlet shows, each provider is represented as a drive. Alternatively, you can use the Get-PSDrive cmdlet to display a listing of available drives and the provider with which they are associated, as demonstrated here.

```
PS C:\> Get-PSDrive
```

Name	Provider	Root	CurrentLocation
A	FileSystem	A:\	
Alias	Alias		
C	FileSystem	C:\	
cert	Certificate	\	
D	FileSystem	D:\	
E	FileSystem	E:\	
Env	Environment		
F	FileSystem	F:\	
Function	Function		
G	FileSystem	G:\	
H	FileSystem	H:\	
HKCU	Registry	HKEY_CURRENT_USER	
HKLM	Registry	HKEY_LOCAL_MACHINE	
I	FileSystem	I:\	
J	FileSystem	J:\	
Variable	Variable		

You can access any of the drives exposed by Windows PowerShell providers using the Set-Location cmdlet. For example, to switch from the default C: drive to the logical Env drive, you would type

```
PS C:\> cd Env:
PS Env:\>
```

 The Env drive provides access to system environmental variables maintained by the Windows operating system.

Once you have targeted a given drive, you can display its contents using the Get-ChildItem cmdlet, just as if it were a physical disk drive, as demonstrated here.

```
PS C:\> cd Env:
PS Env:\> Get-ChildItem
```

Name	Value
Path	C:\Perl\bin\;C:\WINDOWS\system32;C:\WINDOWS;C...
TEMP	C:\DOCUME~1\Owner\LOCALS~1\Temp
SESSIONNAME	Console
PATHEXT	.COM;.EXE;.BAT;.CMD;.VBS;.VBE;.JS;.JSE;.WSF;....
USERDOMAIN	HP
PROCESSOR_ARCHITECTURE	x86
SystemDrive	C:
APPDATA	C:\Documents and Settings\Owner\Application Data
windir	C:\WINDOWS
PCToolsDir	C:\Documents and Settings\All Users\Start Men...
TMP	C:\DOCUME~1\Owner\LOCALS~1\Temp
USERPROFILE	C:\Documents and Settings\Owner
ProgramFiles	C:\Program Files
FP_NO_HOST_CHECK	NO
HOMEPATH	\Documents and Settings\Owner
COMPUTERNAME	HP
USERNAME	Owner
NUMBER_OF_PROCESSORS	2
PROCESSOR_IDENTIFIER	x86 Family 15 Model 2 Stepping 9, GenuineIntel
SystemRoot	C:\WINDOWS
ComSpec	C:\WINDOWS\system32\cmd.exe

```
APPDATA                  C:\Documents and Settings\Owner\Application Data
windir                   C:\WINDOWS
PCToolsDir               C:\Documents and Settings\All Users\Start Men...
TMP                      C:\DOCUME~1\Owner\LOCALS~1\Temp
USERPROFILE              C:\Documents and Settings\Owner
ProgramFiles             C:\Program Files
FP_NO_HOST_CHECK         NO
HOMEPATH                 \Documents and Settings\Owner
COMPUTERNAME             HP
USERNAME                 Owner
NUMBER_OF_PROCESSORS     2
PROCESSOR_IDENTIFIER     x86 Family 15 Model 2 Stepping 9, GenuineIntel
SystemRoot               C:\WINDOWS
ComSpec                  C:\WINDOWS\system32\cmd.exe
LOGONSERVER              \\HP
CommonProgramFiles       C:\Program Files\Common Files
PROCESSOR_LEVEL          15
PROCESSOR_REVISION       0209
ALLUSERSPROFILE          C:\Documents and Settings\All Users
OS                       Windows_NT
HOMEDRIVE                C:

PS Env:\>
```

Because of the manner in which Windows PowerShell abstracts different hierarchical data structures, you can access parts of the Windows registry just as easily as a physical disk drive or the local Env drive. The Windows registry is organized into a series of high-level keys. Windows PowerShell provides access to two of these keys, as outlined in Table 2.2.

TABLE 2.2 REGISTRY KEYS ACCESSIBLE BY WINDOWS POWERSHELL		
Registry Key	**Abbreviation**	**Description**
HKEY_LOCAL_MACHINE	HKLM	Stores information about system-configuration settings that affect all users of the computer.
HKEY_CURRENT_USER	HKCU	Stores information about the currently logged on user's configuration settings.

To access either of the two registry keys listed in Table 2.2, you must reference its abbreviated name, as demonstrated here.

```
PS C:\> cd HKCU:
PS HKCU:\> Get-ChildItem


    Hive: Microsoft.PowerShell.Core\Registry::HKEY_CURRENT_USER


SKC  VC Name                          Property
---  -- ---                          ----
  2   0 AppEvents                     {}
  0   1 bfgt                          {status}
  1   1 Console                       {LoadConIme}
 11   1 Control Panel                 {Opened}
  0   2 Environment                   {TEMP, TMP}
  1   6 Identities                    {Identity Ordinal, Migrated5, Last Us...
  0   0 Network                       {}
  4   1 Printers                      {DeviceOld}
  0   0 RemoteAccess                  {}
  0   7 S                             {AutodiscoveryFlags, DetectedInterfac...
 60   0 Software                      {}
  0   0 UNICODE Program Groups        {}
  1   0 VBGames                       {}
  0   1 vivfile                       {(default)}
  2   0 Windows 3.1 Migration Status  {}
  0   1 SessionInformation            {ProgramCount}
  0   7 Volatile Environment          {LOGONSERVER, CLIENTNAME, SESSIONNAME...


PS HKCU:\>
```

In this example the HKEY_CURRENT_USER key has been accessed and displayed.

 HINT You will learn how to programmatically interact with the Windows registry including how to store and retrieve data, in Chapter 9, "Basic System Administration."

BACK TO THE STORY OF THE THREE AMIGOS

Okay, it is time to turn your attention back to the chapter's main game project, The Story of the Three Amigos. The development of this is game will demonstrate how to create a script that can interact with the player by displaying messages, retrieving command-line input, and applying simple programming logic to control the operation of the script.

TRICK

Going forward, I plan to develop a script template file that will be used as the basis for all new Windows PowerShell scripts. You will find a copy of this script template, named PSTemplate.ps1, on the book's companion website (www.courseptr.com/downloads). The purpose of this script template is to provide additional documentation for each new script file. For now, this template, shown below, will provide a place to document the script's name, version, author, date, and description. Later, I'll modify the template again when covering functions in Chapter 7, "Organizing Scripts Using Functions."

```
# ********************************************************************
#
# Script Name:
# Version:
# Author:
# Date:
#
# Description:
#
#
# ********************************************************************
```

Note that this template consists of a series of comment lines. *Comments* are text embedded within script files that helps to document the scripts, but which is otherwise ignored when the script is executed. In Windows PowerShell, the # character serves as a comment indicator. Anything that follows a # character in a script is considered a comment. Comments can be placed on their own line or placed at the end of a script statement.

Before writing the first line of code, it is important to spend a little time planning out the script's overall design. The Story of the Three Amigos will begin by displaying a title page. Next, the user is informed that her participation is required to tell the story, after which four questions are presented. Each answer that is provided must be saved. The text that makes up the story must then be laid out. In addition, the variables containing the user's answers must be strategically placed at specific locations within the story text. Lastly, closing credits and copyright information should be displayed.

As you can see, the overall logical flow of The Story of the Three Amigos is fairly simple. To set it up, you will complete its development in eight steps.

1. Create a new script file using the PowerShell template and add opening statements.
2. Declare variables used throughout the script file.
3. Display the introduction screen.
4. Display game instructions.
5. Collect first player input.
6. Collect additional player input.
7. Display the opening portion of the story.
8. Display the rest of the story.

Creating a New Script

The first step in creating The Story of the Three Amigos is to open the PowerShell template file and save it as a new file named ThreeAmigos.ps1. Next, modify the comment statements at the top of the script file, as shown here.

```
# ********************************************************************
#
# Script Name: ThreeAmigos.ps1 (The Story of the Three Amigos)
# Version:     1.0
# Author:      Jerry Lee Ford, Jr.
# Date:        January 1, 2007
#
# Description: This PowerShell script is a mad-lib styled game that tells
#              a humorous story using input provided by the player.
#
# ********************************************************************
```

Next, let's add the script's first statement.

```
#Clear the Windows command console screen
Clear-Host
```

As you can see, the script begins by executing the Clear-Host cmdlet to clear the display area of the Windows command console. To make things perfectly clear, I have added a comment just above the Clear-Host command, explaining what the command will do when executed.

Declaring Script Variables

The next step in the development of The Story of the Three Amigos is to declare all of the variables that will be used to store the input provided by the user when responding to each of the game's four questions. This is accomplished by appending the following statements to the end of your PowerShell script file.

```
#Define the variables used in this script to collect player input
$animal = ""    #Stores the name of an animal supplied by the player
$vehicle = ""  #Stores the name of a vehicle supplied by the player
$store = ""     #Stores the name of a store supplied by the player
$dessert = ""  #Stores the name of a dessert supplied by the player
```

Note that I have assigned descriptive names to each variable that help to provide an indication of the type of data that they will store.

Displaying the Introduction

The next step in assembling your new Windows PowerShell script is to append the following statements to the end of the script file.

```
#Display the game's opening screen
Write-Host
Write-Host
Write-Host
Write-Host
Write-Host "                        T H E    S T O R Y"
Write-Host
Write-Host
Write-Host
Write-Host "              O F  T H E    T H R E E    A M I G O S"
Write-Host
Write-Host
Write-Host
Write-Host "                        By Jerry Lee Ford, Jr."
Write-Host
Write-Host
Write-Host
Write-Host
Write-Host
Write-Host
```

```
Write-Host
Write-Host
Write-Host
Write-Host
Write-Host " Press Enter to continue."

#Pause script execution and wait for the player to press the Enter key
Read-Host
```

As you can see, these statements consist of a number of Write-Host cmdlet statements that display the story's opening screen. Note the placement of the Read-Host cmdlet. When executed, it will pause the script and wait until the user presses the Enter key.

Providing Player Instructions

Now let's add the statements that provide the user with instructions for interacting with the story by appending the following statements to the end of the script file.

```
#Clear the Windows command console screen
Clear-Host

#Provide the player with instructions
Write-Host
Write-Host
Write-Host
Write-Host
Write-Host
Write-Host
Write-Host
Write-Host " This is an interactive mad-lib styled story. Before it can be"
Write-Host
Write-Host " told, you must answer a few questions."
Write-Host
Write-Host
Write-Host
Write-Host
Write-Host
Write-Host
Write-Host
Write-Host
```

```
Write-Host
Write-Host
Write-Host
Write-Host
Write-Host
Write-Host " Press Enter to continue."

#Pause script execution and wait for the player to press the Enter key
Read-Host
```

As you can see, these first statements will clear the Windows command console screen. Then a series of Write-Host cmdlets are executed in order to display the text containing the game's instruction. Lastly, the Read-Host cmdlet pauses the script to give the user a chance to read the instructions before continuing.

Prompting the Player for Input

Now it is time to start collecting user input. The code statements required to display the story's first question and store the user's answer is shown next and should be appended to the end of the script file.

```
#Ask the player the first question
while ($animal -eq ""){

    Clear-Host  #Clear the Windows command console screen

    Write-Host
    Write-Host
    Write-Host
    Write-Host
    Write-Host
    Write-Host

    $animal = read-host " Enter the name of a scary animal "

}
```

Here, a while loop has been set up to control interaction with the user. Its main purpose is to prevent the user from simply pressing the Enter key without first typing in something. The user's answer is assigned to a variable named $animal.

HINT   Don't worry just yet about the workings of variables and while loops. These are covered in detail in Chapter 4, "Working with Variables, Arrays, and Hashes," and Chapter 5, "Implementing Conditional Logic."

Collecting Additional Inputs

Next, add the following code statements to the end of the script file. The statements are responsible for collecting the rest of the input required to tell the story.

```
#Ask the player the second question
while ($vehicle -eq ""){

    Clear-Host  #Clear the Windows command console screen

    Write-Host
    Write-Host
    Write-Host
    Write-Host
    Write-Host
    Write-Host

    $vehicle = read-host " Enter the name of a transportation vehicle "

}

#Ask the player the third question
while ($store -eq ""){

    Clear-Host  #Clear the Windows command console screen

    Write-Host
    Write-Host
    Write-Host
    Write-Host
    Write-Host
    Write-Host

    $store = read-host " Enter the name of your favorite store "

}
```

```
#Ask the player the fourth question
while ($dessert -eq ""){

    Clear-Host  #Clear the Windows command console screen

    Write-Host
    Write-Host
    Write-Host
    Write-Host
    Write-Host
    Write-Host

    $dessert = read-host " Enter the name of your favorite dessert "

}
```

As you can see, these statements are organized into three `while` loops, each of which is little more than a simple variation of the code statements used to prompt the user to provide an answer to the story's first question.

Displaying the Story's Opening

Now that the input needed to tell the story has been collected, it is time to begin displaying the text that makes up the story. For starters, add the following statements to the end of the script file.

```
#Clear the Windows command console screen
Clear-Host

#Provide the player with instructions
Write-Host
Write-Host
Write-Host
Write-Host
Write-Host
Write-Host " Once upon a time there were three very special children"
Write-Host " named Alexander, William, and Molly. Alexander was the oldest"
Write-Host " and was known to be brave and strong. Molly, the youngest,"
Write-Host " was just five years old, yet she possessed an extraordinary"
Write-Host " sense of awareness that even the wisest sage would"
Write-Host " admire and respect. William, the middle child, was both brave"
```

```
Write-Host " and wise many times beyond his years. They lived together at"
Write-Host " the top of a hill, just outside the outskirts of town, where"
Write-Host " they faithfully watched over the townsfolk. Always together"
Write-Host " and always looking out for each other and the people in the"
Write-Host " town, they were known by everyone as The Three Amigos."
Write-Host
Write-Host
Write-Host
Write-Host
Write-Host
Write-Host
Write-Host
Write-Host " Press Enter to continue."

#Pause script execution and wait for the player to press the Enter key
Read-Host
```

These statements clear the screen, display some story text, and then pause script execution until the user presses the Enter key.

Displaying the Rest of the Story

The code statements that display the remainder of the story are shown next and should be appended to the end of the script file.

```
#Clear the Windows command console screen
Clear-Host

#Provide the player with instructions
Write-Host
Write-Host
Write-Host
Write-Host
Write-Host
Write-Host
Write-Host " One day, which started out no different than any other day, a"
Write-Host " great roar was heard from the center of the town. Women and"
Write-Host " small children could be seen screaming and running in panic."
Write-Host " The Three Amigos climbed to the top of their watch tower and"
Write-Host " began scanning the town streets for the source of the noise"
```

```
Write-Host " and panic. Alexander was the first to find the problem,"
Write-Host " spotting a gigantic $animal moving quickly towards the"
Write-Host " mayor's office. Just ahead of the $animal stood the town's"
Write-Host " men, attempting to make a desperate stand."
Write-Host " `"Hurry, we must go!`" shouted Molly. "The town needs The"
Write-Host " Three Amigos!" In an instant Alexander, William, and Molly"
Write-Host " jumped into an old $vehicle, scarred and worn by years"
Write-Host " of faithful service, and hurriedly raced into town."
Write-Host
Write-Host
Write-Host
Write-Host
Write-Host " Press Enter to continue."

#Pause script execution and wait for the player to press the Enter key
Read-Host

#Clear the Windows command console screen
Clear-Host

#Provide the player with instructions
Write-Host
Write-Host
Write-Host
Write-Host
Write-Host
Write-Host
Write-Host " Within minutes The Three Amigos found themselves standing in"
Write-Host " the center of Main street. The town was quiet and seemed"
Write-Host " almost deserted except for the old $store, where the citizens"
Write-Host " had retreated once their last stand had failed. The $animal"
Write-Host " was standing in front of the $store, preparing to"
Write-Host " break in and kill the good citizens of the town."
Write-Host " `"What do we do?`" said Alexander. William looked around and"
Write-Host " saw a pile of $dessert stacked up against the town"
Write-host " barbershop's storefront. "Follow me," yelled William,"
Write-host " heading straight for the pile of $dessert. Alexander"
Write-host " and Molly instantly knew what to do, each grabbing a $dessert"
Write-Host " and hurling pieces of $dessert at the $animal. Unable to"
```

```
Write-Host " deal with the power of the attack launched by The Three"
Write-Host " Amigos, the $animal fled the town, never to be seen or heard"
Write-host " of again."
Write-Host
Write-Host
Write-Host " Press Enter to continue."

#Pause script execution and wait for the player to press the Enter key
Read-Host

#Clear the Windows command console screen
Clear-Host

#Provide the player with instructions
Write-Host
Write-Host
Write-Host
Write-Host
Write-Host
Write-Host
Write-Host " The townsfolk ran out of the $store and began cheering for"
Write-Host " their heroes. Once again The Three Amigos has saved the day."
Write-Host
Write-Host
Write-Host
Write-Host
Write-Host
Write-Host
Write-Host
Write-Host
Write-Host  "                         T H E   E N D"
Write-Host
Write-Host
Write-Host
Write-Host
Write-Host
Write-Host
Write-Host
Write-Host " Press Enter to continue."
```

```
#Pause script execution and wait for the player to press the Enter key
Read-Host

#Clear the Windows command console screen
Clear-Host
```

Take note of the variable names that are embedded inside the `Write-Host` statements that displayed the story text. When executed, each of these variables will automatically be replaced with the text string input provided by the user earlier in the script file. To help make the locations of these variables stand out, I have made them bold.

SUMMARY

This chapter has covered a number of different PowerShell topics designed to help you develop a solid understanding of how to interact with the PowerShell command line. You learned how to configure the Windows command console in order to customize your working environment. You learned how to configure the Window command shell to automatically use your Windows PowerShell script folder as your default working directory. You also learned how to work with tab completion and to use Windows PowerShell to navigate and access different types of system resources, including the Windows registry and environment variables.

Now, before you move on to Chapter 3, "Object-Based Scripting with .NET," I suggest you set aside a few extra minutes to work on and improve The Story of the Three Amigos by implementing the following challenges.

CHALLENGES

1. For starters, consider prompting the user to provide additional inputs and use her answers to further increase the unpredictability of the story.

2. Consider rewriting the story's ending to make it more exciting or to give it an unexpected and humorous twist.

3. Lastly, don't forget to modify the author credits by using your own name. In addition, you might want to add some additional information such as your website's URL or your e-mail address.

OBJECT-BASED SCRIPTING WITH .NET

indows PowerShell is tightly integrated with Microsoft's .NET Framework, which provides much of the supporting environment required to develop Windows applications and scripts. In this chapter you will learn how Windows PowerShell leverages .NET resources. You learn about the .NET class library and common language runtime. You will learn how to execute cmdlets and to use cmdlets to access object properties and methods. You will also review cmdlet aliases and learn how to create your own custom aliases. On top of all this, you will learn how to programmatically customize the Windows PowerShell and to develop the PowerShell Fortune Teller game.

Specifically, you will learn:

- How to create a profile.ps1 script file and use it to customize Windows PowerShell
- More background information regarding Windows PowerShell's integration with .NET
- How to use object pipelines to pass structured data between cmdlets
- How to create custom aliases

PROJECT PREVIEW: THE POWERSHELL FORTUNE TELLER GAME

This chapter's game project is the PowerShell Fortune Teller game. This game simulates a session with a virtual fortune teller who listens to player questions and then provides answers. The answers provided vary based on the fortune teller's mood, which changes based on the time of day that questions are asked. All questions are expected to be posed in such a way that Yes/No styled answers can be applied.

When first started, the game displays the welcome screen shown in Figure 3.1.

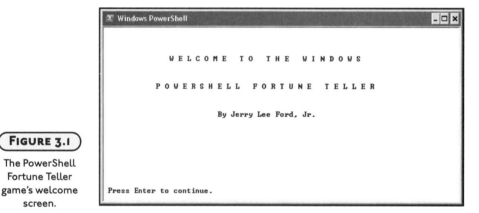

FIGURE 3.1

The PowerShell
Fortune Teller
game's welcome
screen.

Pressing Enter dismisses the welcome screen. Next, instructions are displayed that provide the player with guidance regarding the proper way to formulate questions, as shown in Figure 3.2.

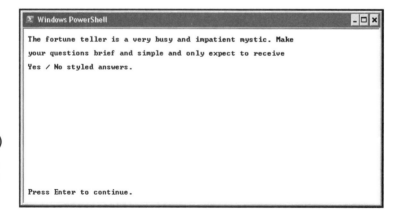

FIGURE 3.2

Players are given
guidance on how
to formulate
questions.

Next, the player is prompted to ask her question, as shown in Figure 3.3.

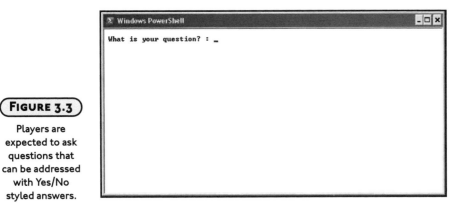

FIGURE 3.3

Players are expected to ask questions that can be addressed with Yes/No styled answers.

In response, the game randomly selects 1 of 8 possible answers and displays it, as demonstrated in Figure 3.4.

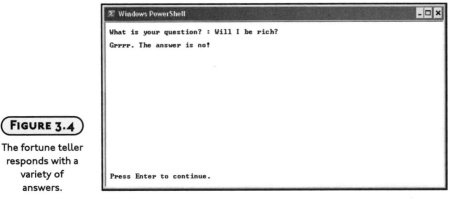

FIGURE 3.4

The fortune teller responds with a variety of answers.

The player is then prompted to either press Enter to ask the fortune teller another question or type **Q** to end the game, as shown in Figure 3.5.

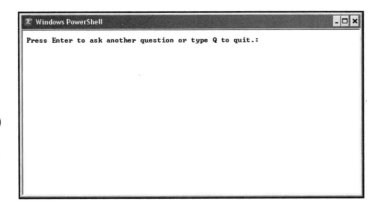

FIGURE 3.5

Players may ask the fortune teller as many questions as they wish.

The game ends by displaying a message suggesting that the player return and play again, as shown in Figure 3.6.

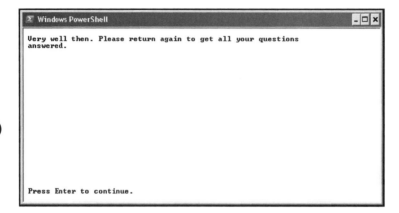

FIGURE 3.6

The game ends after inviting the player to return and ask more questions.

One Last PowerShell Customization Technique

Before we jump deep into a review of the .NET Framework and how Windows PowerShell uses cmdlets to access .NET resources, let's spend a few more minutes taking a look at one additional way in which you can customize Windows PowerShell. Only this time, instead of focusing on manual configuration, we'll look at how to programmatically script PowerShell configuration.

As you learned in Chapter 2, "Interacting with the Windows PowerShell Command Line," you can customize your Windows PowerShell working environment by making changes to a PowerShell shortcut in order to redirect it to a default working directory of your choice. Chapter 2 also showed you how to manually configure PowerShell attributes affecting cursor size, command history, font type and size, console size, as well as its color scheme.

In addition to manually configuring the Windows command console using the Windows PowerShell Properties window, you can also programmatically configure your PowerShell environment. To do so, you create a PowerShell script file named profile.ps1 and store it in one of the following folders.

- C:\Windows\System32\WindowsPowerShell\v1.0
- C:\Documents and Settings*UserName*\My Documents\WindowsPowerShell

If you create a profile.ps1 script and store it in the first folder listed above (C:\Windows\ system32\WindowsPowerShell\v1.0), it will automatically be run for every user of the computer each time a new Windows PowerShell session is started. If you create and store a profile.ps1 script in an individual user's My Documents\WindowsPowerShell folder, the PowerShell script will execute each time that user starts a new Windows PowerShell session but will not execute for other users.

By developing a profile.ps1 script, computer administrators can manage large numbers of computers by remotely deploying the script file to any number of computers, thus eliminating the need to visit and configure individual computers. For example, you might create a PowerShell script file similar to the following example and then distribute it to the C:\Windows\system32\WindowsPowerShell\v1.0 folder on all corporate computers to help ensure awareness of corporate computer policy.

```
# ***********************************************************************
#
# Script Name: Profile.ps1 (PowerShell Profile configuration Scripts)
# Version:     1.0
# Author:      Jerry Lee Ford, Jr.
# Date:        January 1, 2007
#
# Description: This PowerShell script contains commands that customize
#              the Windows PowerShell execution environment.
#
# ***********************************************************************


#Create a custom alias command
Set-Alias ds Write-Host

#Clear the Windows command console screen
Clear-Host

#Display custom greeting

ds
ds "This computer and network are private. By using this computer you agree"
ds "to all terms outlined in the company's security policy. Failure to comply"
ds "with these policies may result in criminal prosecution."
ds
```

When executed, this script creates a custom alias named ds, which creates a shortcut to the Write-Host cmdlet. You will learn more about aliases and how to create them later in this chapter. Next, the screen is cleared and then, using the newly created alias, a message is displayed regarding the company's security policy. Figure 3.7 demonstrates what the user will see each time a new Windows PowerShell session is started.

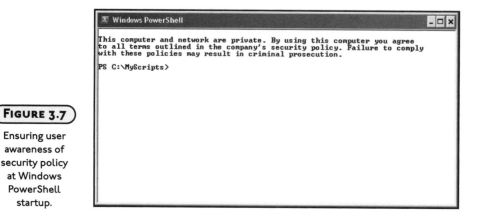

FIGURE 3.7

Ensuring user awareness of security policy at Windows PowerShell startup.

THE MICROSOFT .NET FRAMEWORK

The .NET Framework is a core component of modern Windows PowerShell scripting. Version 2 of the .NET Framework is a requirement for PowerShell script execution. It is therefore important that PowerShell programmers have a solid understanding of the .NET Framework's major components and the services it provides. For starters, .NET is a Microsoft framework designed to support desktop, network, and Internet-based applications and scripts. .NET also supports the development of mobile applications for devices such as PDAs.

 A *framework* is a collection of resources that facilitates the development of scripts and programs. The purpose of a framework is to alleviate much of the complexity involved in developing new programs and scripts by providing programmers access to a predefined collection of services and resources, allowing programmers to instead focus on the higher level logic required to solve a specific problem.

The .NET Framework is designed to support the development of applications and scripts in conjunction with any .NET-compliant application or script-development programming language. In fact, Microsoft has generated an entire suite of application-programming languages built around the .NET Framework. These languages include Visual Basic, C++, C#, and J#. Microsoft is promoting the .NET Framework as a key component in all its new programming languages. It should be no surprise, therefore that Microsoft decided to integrate support for .NET Framework into Windows PowerShell, giving it and its scripting language instant access to a enormous range of resources and commands.

Key .NET Framework Components

The .NET Framework acts as an interface between Windows PowerShell and the operating system. .NET is responsible for translating script code into a format that can be executed on your computer. Figure 3.8 shows the role the .NET Framework plays in supporting application and script development.

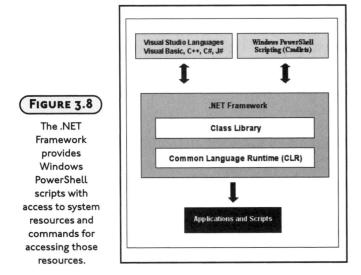

FIGURE 3.8

The .NET Framework provides Windows PowerShell scripts with access to system resources and commands for accessing those resources.

The .NET Framework consists of two key components, as outlined here.

- .NET Framework class library
- CLR (common language runtime)

Don't be too worried if there are elements in Figure 3.8 that you don't understand. I will cover each in detail in the sections that follow.

The .NET Class Library

Traditional command shells have a very limited recognition of data, typically recognizing only strings and numbers. However, Windows PowerShell enforces the use of tightly structured data. As a result, Windows PowerShell can work with many different types of data including, strings, dates, integers, floating-point numbers, Boolean data, and so on.

Structured data is also a key feature of the .NET Framework. With .NET, structured data is grouped into different collections to define complex structured classes. *Classes* are then used as a template for creating objects, which represent things that Windows PowerShell can access and manipulate. An *object* is a self-contained resource that contains information about itself as well as the code required to access and manipulate it. For example, a file, folder, and disk drive are all treated as objects by Windows PowerShell.

Objects have certain attributes or *properties* that define a particular characteristic of the object. For example, folders have names. Objects also provide access to predefined collections of code, referred to as *methods*, which can be executed in order to interact with and control the object. For example, a file object provides access to methods that can be used to perform all sorts of actions on the file, including opening, closing, and deleting it.

The Common Language Runtime

The *common language runtime* or *CLR* is responsible for converting Windows PowerShell scripts into an executable format that your computer can understand and run. The CLR also provides Windows PowerShell with other services, including:

- Compiling
- Security
- Memory Management
- Exception Handling

Accessing .NET Framework Resources

Windows PowerShell provides access to .NET Framework resources through cmdlets. Cmdlets provide access to .NET resources while at the same time hiding much of the complexity involved. As a PowerShell programmer, you do not have to worry about specific .NET classes or their properties and methods. All that you have to do is know which cmdlets to use in order to get at the type of resources required by your scripts. To see what I mean, consider the following series of examples.

In this first example, let's execute the Get-ChildItem cmdlet. The Get-ChildItem cmdlet retrieves a listing of objects representing each file and subfolder stored in the current working directory. The .NET Framework stores a lot of information, or properties, about file objects. However, by default, Windows PowerShell only displays a few of these properties, as demonstrated here.

```
PS C:\MyScripts> Get-ChildItem
```

```
    Directory: Microsoft.PowerShell.Core\FileSystem::C:\MyScripts


Mode            LastWriteTime            Length Name
----            -------------            ------ ----
-a---           9/24/2006   4:31 PM        3416 FortuneTeller.ps1
-a---           9/10/2006   1:42 PM        1077 KnockKnock.ps1
-a---           9/25/2006   1:28 PM         832 profile.ps1
-a---           9/23/2006   5:22 PM        7598 ThreeAmigos.ps1
-a---           9/9/2006    2:10 PM         130 UserInput.ps1

PS C:\MyScripts>
```

Here, the Mode, LastWriteTime, Length, and Name properties for each file object are displayed. Next, let's focus on a specific file, as shown here.

```
PS C:\MyScripts> Get-ChildItem profile.ps1


    Directory: Microsoft.PowerShell.Core\FileSystem::C:\MyScripts


Mode            LastWriteTime            Length Name
----            -------------            ------ ----
-a---           9/25/2006   1:28 PM         832 profile.ps1

PS C:\MyScripts>
```

In this example, profile.ps1 was passed as an argument to the Get-ChildItem cmdlet. As a result, only property information for that file object is played. Now that we are focused on the properties for a specific object, let's poke a little deeper and see what other types of property information .NET keeps for this object. The following example takes the output generated by the Get-ChildItem cmdlet and passes it to the Get-Member cmdlet. The Get-Member cmdlet is then passed an argument named -MemberType. This argument can take on different values. In this example, a value of Property is specified. The end result is the display of properties that the .NET Framework has for this particular file.

 Remember that Windows PowerShell views most everything as an object and objects have attributes that describe features of the object. The attributes are commonly referred to as *object properties*. As the preceding example demonstrated, most cmdlets allow you to pass data for processing in the form of arguments. In addition, most cmdlets return object data as command output. In the next example, the object data output generated by the Get-ChildItem cmdlet is passed as an argument to the Get-Member cmdlet for further processing.

```
PS C:\MyScripts> Get-ChildItem profile.ps1 | Get-Member -MemberType Property


    TypeName: System.IO.FileInfo

Name                MemberType   Definition
----                ----------   ----------
Attributes          Property     System.IO.FileAttributes Attributes {get;set;}
CreationTime        Property     System.DateTime CreationTime {get;set;}
CreationTimeUtc     Property     System.DateTime CreationTimeUtc {get;set;}
Directory           Property     System.IO.DirectoryInfo Directory {get;}
DirectoryName       Property     System.String DirectoryName {get;}
Exists              Property     System.Boolean Exists {get;}
Extension           Property     System.String Extension {get;}
FullName            Property     System.String FullName {get;}
IsReadOnly          Property     System.Boolean IsReadOnly {get;set;}
LastAccessTime      Property     System.DateTime LastAccessTime {get;set;}
LastAccessTimeUtc   Property     System.DateTime LastAccessTimeUtc {get;set;}
LastWriteTime       Property     System.DateTime LastWriteTime {get;set;}
LastWriteTimeUtc    Property     System.DateTime LastWriteTimeUtc {get;set;}
Length              Property     System.Int64 Length {get;}
Name                Property     System.String Name {get;}

PS C:\MyScripts>
```

As you can see, the .NET Framework stores a lot of properties that are not automatically displayed by the Get-Childitem cmdlet. However, this information is readily available to you, as the next example demonstrates.

```
PS C:\MyScripts> Get-ChildItem profile.ps1 | Select-Object name,extension,
directory


Name                     Extension      Directory
----                     ------—        ------—
profile.ps1              .ps1           C:\MyScripts

PS C:\MyScripts>
```

In this example, the Get-ChildItem cmdlet is once again used to retrieve information about the profile.pls file. However, this time the Select-Object cmdlet is used to retrieve and display different object properties, specifically the Name, Extension, and Directory properties.

Note that these names of the specific properties to be retrieved were passed as a comma-separated list of arguments.

 HINT The `Select-Object` cmdlet provides the ability to determine which objects being passed through the pipeline are kept or discarded. In the previous example, all objects returned by the `Get-ChildItem` cmdlet are discarded except for profile.ps1.

In short, unlike traditional command shells, which pass only a limited amount of data back in a simple text format, Windows PowerShell cmdlets provide you with direct access to all kinds of behind-the-scenes object information.

As previously stated, .NET Framework classes define all of the properties and methods associated with each object associated with a particular class. As such, you can also retrieve a listing of all the methods associated with a given object, as demonstrated next.

```
PS C:\MyScripts> Get-ChildItem profile.ps1 | Get-Member -MemberType Method
    TypeName: System.IO.FileInfo
```

Name	MemberType	Definition
AppendText	Method	System.IO.StreamWriter AppendText()
CopyTo	Method	System.IO.FileInfo CopyTo(String destFi...
Create	Method	System.IO.FileStream Create()
CreateObjRef	Method	System.Runtime.Remoting.ObjRef CreateOb...
CreateText	Method	System.IO.StreamWriter CreateText()
Decrypt	Method	System.Void Decrypt()
Delete	Method	System.Void Delete()
Encrypt	Method	System.Void Encrypt()
Equals	Method	System.Boolean Equals(Object obj)
get_Attributes	Method	System.IO.FileAttributes get_Attributes()
get_CreationTime	Method	System.DateTime get_CreationTime()
get_CreationTimeUtc	Method	System.DateTime get_CreationTimeUtc()
get_Directory	Method	System.IO.DirectoryInfo get_Directory()
get_DirectoryName	Method	System.String get_DirectoryName()
get_Exists	Method	System.Boolean get_Exists()
get_Extension	Method	System.String get_Extension()
get_FullName	Method	System.String get_FullName()
get_IsReadOnly	Method	System.Boolean get_IsReadOnly()
get_LastAccessTime	Method	System.DateTime get_LastAccessTime()

get_LastAccessTimeUtc	Method	System.DateTime get_LastAccessTimeUtc()
get_LastWriteTime	Method	System.DateTime get_LastWriteTime()
get_LastWriteTimeUtc	Method	System.DateTime get_LastWriteTimeUtc()
get_Length	Method	System.Int64 get_Length()
get_Name	Method	System.String get_Name()
GetAccessControl	Method	System.Security.AccessControl.FileSecur...
GetHashCode	Method	System.Int32 GetHashCode()
GetLifetimeService	Method	System.Object GetLifetimeService()
GetObjectData	Method	System.Void GetObjectData(Serialization...
GetType	Method	System.Type GetType()
InitializeLifetimeService	Method	System.Object InitializeLifetimeService()
MoveTo	Method	System.Void MoveTo(String destFileName)
Open	Method	System.IO.FileStream Open(FileMode mode...
OpenRead	Method	System.IO.FileStream OpenRead()
OpenText	Method	System.IO.StreamReader OpenText()
OpenWrite	Method	System.IO.FileStream OpenWrite()
Refresh	Method	System.Void Refresh()
Replace	Method	System.IO.FileInfo Replace(String desti...
set_Attributes	Method	System.Void set_Attributes(FileAttribut...
set_CreationTime	Method	System.Void set_CreationTime(DateTime v...
set_CreationTimeUtc	Method	System.Void set_CreationTimeUtc(DateTim...
set_IsReadOnly	Method	System.Void set_IsReadOnly(Boolean value)
set_LastAccessTime	Method	System.Void set_LastAccessTime(DateTime...
GetLifetimeService	Method	System.Object GetLifetimeService()
GetObjectData	Method	System.Void GetObjectData(Serialization...
GetType	Method	System.Type GetType()
InitializeLifetimeService	Method	System.Object InitializeLifetimeService()
MoveTo	Method	System.Void MoveTo(String destFileName)
Open	Method	System.IO.FileStream Open(FileMode mode...
OpenRead	Method	System.IO.FileStream OpenRead()
OpenText	Method	System.IO.StreamReader OpenText()
OpenWrite	Method	System.IO.FileStream OpenWrite()
Refresh	Method	System.Void Refresh()
Replace	Method	System.IO.FileInfo Replace(String desti...
set_Attributes	Method	System.Void set_Attributes(FileAttribut...
set_CreationTime	Method	System.Void set_CreationTime(DateTime v...
set_CreationTimeUtc	Method	System.Void set_CreationTimeUtc(DateTim...

```
set_IsReadOnly          Method      System.Void set_IsReadOnly(Boolean value)
set_LastAccessTime      Method      System.Void set_LastAccessTime(DateTime...
set_LastAccessTimeUtc   Method      System.Void set_LastAccessTimeUtc(DateT...
set_LastWriteTime       Method      System.Void set_LastWriteTime(DateTime ...
set_LastWriteTimeUtc    Method      System.Void set_LastWriteTimeUtc(DateTi...
SetAccessControl        Method      System.Void SetAccessControl(FileSecuri...
ToString                Method      System.String ToString()
```

```
PS C:\MyScripts>
```

As you can see, in this example the value passed as the -MemberType argument to the Select-Object cmdlet was changed from property to Method.

If all this talk about the .Net Framework, classes, objects, properties, and methods seems confusing or overwhelming, don't be alarmed. It takes times to fully understand and comprehend all this new technology. However, the good news is that as a Windows PowerShell programmer, you needn't be directly focused on .NET. Instead, all you have to do is become comfortable with working with cmdlets and let the .NET Framework worry about all the underlying complexities.

 HINT You can learn more about the .NET Framework by visiting www.microsoft.com/net.

EXECUTING CMDLETS

Cmdlets are key Windows PowerShell resources that provide access to .NET Framework resources. In total, there are over 100 cmdlets. Windows PowerShell cmdlets provide access to a host of commands, each of which is designed to perform a singular task. Individually, cmdlets provide access to specific resources and commands. However, the real power provided by cmdlets comes when they are used together as building blocks to formulate complex tasks.

You will learn more about how Windows PowerShell lets you combine cmdlets into complex statements in the next section. However, in order to work with the Windows PowerShell and to write PowerShell scripts, it helps to know a little something about each of the cmdlets that PowerShell makes available to you. To help you out, I have provided a complete list of PowerShell cmdlets in Table 3.1, along with a brief explanation of what each cmdlet does.

TABLE 3.1   WINDOWS POWERSHELL CMDLETS

Cmdlet	Description
Add-Content	Adds to the content(s) of the specified item(s).
Add-History	Adds entries to the session history.
Add-Member	Adds a user-defined custom member to an object.
Add-PSSnapIn	Adds one or more PSSnapIn(s) (containing additional collections of providers or cmdlets) to the current Ps console.
Clear-Content	Removes the content from an item or file while leaving the file intact.
Clear-Item	Sets the item(s) at the specified location to the "clear" value specified by the provider.
Clear-ItemProperty	Removes the property value from a property.
Clear-Variable	Removes the value from a variable.
Compare-Object	Compares the properties of objects.
ConvertFrom-SecureString	Exports a secure string to a safe, persistent format.
Convert-Path	Converts the path of the item given from a Ps path to a provider path.
ConvertTo-Html	Converts the input to an HTML table.
ConvertTo-SecureString	Creates a secure string from a normal string created by Export-SecureString.
Copy-Item	Calls a provider to copy an item from one location to another within a namespace.
Copy-ItemProperty	Copies a property between locations or namespaces.
Export-Alias	Exports an alias list to a file.
Export-Clixml	Produces a clixml representation of a Ps object or objects.
Export-Console	Exports the changes made to the current console. This action overwrites any existing console file.
Export-CSV	Exports CSV strings from input.
ForEach-Object	Applies script blocks to each object in the pipeline.
Format-Custom	Formats output display as defined in additions to the formatter file.
Format-List	Formats objects as a list of their properties displayed vertically.
Format-Table	Formats the output as a table.
Format-Wide	Formats objects as a table of their properties.
Get-ACL	Gets the access control list (ACL) associated with a file or object.
Get-Alias	Returns alias names for cmdlets.

TABLE 3.1   WINDOWS POWERSHELL CMDLETS (CONTINUED)

Cmdlet	Description
Get-AuthenticodeSignature	Gets the signature object associated with a file.
Get-ChildItem	Retrieves the child items of the specified location(s) in a drive.
Get-Command	Retrieves basic information about a command.
Get-Content	Gets the content from the item at the specified location.
Get-Credential	Gets a credential object based on a password.
Get-Culture	Gets the culture information.
Get-Date	Gets the current date and time.
Get-EventLog	Gets event log data for the machine.
Get-ExecutionPolicy	Gets the effective execution policy for the current shell.
Get-Help	Opens the help files.
Get-History	Gets a listing of the session history.
Get-Host	Gets host information.
Get-Item	Returns an object that represents an item in a namespace.
Get-ItemProperty	Retrieves the properties of an object.
Get-Location	Displays the current location.
Get-Member	Enumerates the properties, methods, typeinfo, and property sets of the objects given to it
Get-PfxCertificate	Gets the PFX certificate information.
Get-Process	Gets a list of processes on a machine.
Get-PSDrive	Gets the drive information (DriveInfo) for the specified Ps drive.
Get-PSProvider	Gets information for the specified provider.
Get-PSSnapIn	Lists registered PSSnapIns.
Get-Service	Gets a list of services.
Get-TraceSource	Lists properties for given trace sources.
Get-UICulture	Gets the UI culture information.
Get-Unique	Gets the unique items in a sorted list.
Get-Variable	Gets a Ps variable.
Get-WmiObject	Produces a WMI object or the list of WMI classes available on the system.

TABLE 3.1 WINDOWS POWERSHELL CMDLETS (CONTINUED)

Cmdlet	Description
Group-Object	Groups the objects that contain the same values for a common property.
Import-Alias	Imports an alias list from a file.
Import-Clixml	Imports a clixml file and rebuilds the Ps object.
Import-CSV	Takes values from a CSV list and sends objects down the pipeline.
Invoke-Expression	Executes a string as an expression.
Invoke-History	Invokes a previously executed command.
Invoke-Item	Invokes an executable or opens a file.
Join-Path	Combines path elements into a single path.
Measure-Command	Tracks the running time for script blocks and cmdlets.
Measure-Object	Measures various aspects of objects or their properties.
Move-Item	Moves an item from one location to another.
Move-ItemProperty	Moves a property from one location to another.
New-Alias	Creates a new cmdlet-alias pairing.
New-Item	Creates a new item in a namespace.
New-ItemProperty	Sets a new property of an item at a location.
New-Object	Creates a new .NET object.
New-PSDrive	Installs a new drive on the computer.
New-Service	Creates a new service.
New-TimeSpan	Creates a timespan object.
New-Variable	Creates a new variable.
Out-Default	Sends output to the default formatter.
Out-File	Sends command output to a file.
Out-Host	Sends the pipelined output to the host.
Out-Null	Sends output to a null.
Out-Printer	Sends the output to a printer.
Out-String	Sends output to the pipeline as strings.
Pop-Location	Changes the current working location to the location specified by the last entry pushed onto the stack.
Push-Location	Pushes a location to the stack.

TABLE 3.1   WINDOWS POWERSHELL CMDLETS (CONTINUED)

Cmdlet	Description
Read-Host	Reads a line of input from the host console.
Remove-Item	Calls a provider to remove an item.
Remove-ItemProperty	Removes a property and its value from the location.
Remove-PSDrive	Removes a drive from its location.
Remove-PSSnapIn	Removes PSSnapIn(s) from the current console process.
Remove-Variable	Removes a variable and its value.
Rename-Item	Changes the name of an existing item.
Rename-ItemProperty	Renames a property at its location.
Resolve-Path	Resolves the wildcard characters in a path.
Restart-Service	Restarts a stopped service.
Resume-Service	Resumes a suspended service.
Select-Object	Selects objects based on parameters set in the cmdlet command string.
Select-String	Lets you search through strings or files for patterns.
Set-ACL	Sets a resource's Access Control List properties.
Set-Alias	Maps an alias to a cmdlet.
Set-AuthenticodeSignature	Places an authenticode signature in a Ps script or other file.
Set-Content	Sets the content in the item at the specified location.
Set-Date	Sets the system date on the host system.
Set-ExecutionPolicy	Sets the execution policy for the current shell.
Set-Item	Sets the value of a pathname within a provider to the specified value.
Set-ItemProperty	Sets a property at the specified location to a specified value.
Set-Location	Sets the current working location to a specified location.
Set-PSDebug	Turns Ps script debugging features on and off, and sets trace level.
Set-Service	Makes and sets changes to the properties of a service.
Set-TraceSource	Sets or removes the specified options and trace listeners from the specified trace source instance(s).
Set-Variable	Sets data in a variable and creates a variable if one with the requested name does not exist.

TABLE 3.1 WINDOWS POWERSHELL CMDLETS (CONTINUED)

Cmdlet	Description
Sort-Object	Sorts the input objects by property values.
Split-Path	Given a Ps path(s), it streams a string with the qualifier, parent path, or leaf item.
Start-Service	Starts a stopped service.
Start-Sleep	Suspends shell, script, or runspace activity for the specified period of time.
Start-Transcript	Starts a transcript of a command shell session.
Stop-Process	Stops a running process.
Stop-Service	Stops a running service.
Stop-Transcript	Stops the transcription process.
Suspend-Service	Suspends a running service.
Tee-Object	Sends input objects to two places.
Test-Path	Returns true if the path exists; otherwise, it returns false.
Trace-Command	Enables tracing of the specified trace source instance(s) for the duration of the expression or command.
Update-FormatData	Updates and appends format data files.
Update-TypeData	Updates the types.ps1xml file in the Microsoft shell.
Where-Object	Filters the input from the pipeline, allowing operation on only certain objects.
Write-Debug	Writes a debug message to the host display.
Write-Error	Writes an error object and sends it to the pipeline.
Write-Host	Displays objects through the user feedback mechanism.
Write-Output	Writes an object to the pipeline.
Write-Progress	Sends a progress record to the host.
Write-Verbose	Writes a string to the host's verbose display.
Write-Warning	Writes a warning message.

Although all the cmdlets listed in Table 3.1 are shown using initial uppercase spelling, cmdlets are not case sensitive. Therefore, the case that you use when keying them in is entirely up to you. While you shouldn't try to memorize this entire list of cmdlets, it is probably a good idea to bookmark this table so that you can come back to it when you need to. Once you have found a cmdlet that looks like it will suit the needs of your particular task, you can use the PowerShell Get-Help cmdlet to learn more about it. For example, Figure 3.9 shows a portion of the output that you will see when using the Get-Help cmdlet to look up information about the Write-Host cmdlet.

The Get-Help cmdlet retrieves information about any cmdlet or PowerShell topic. When executed without any parameters, this cmdlet displays a list of help topics. When passed a cmdlet name or topic, it displays information specific to that cmdlet or topic.

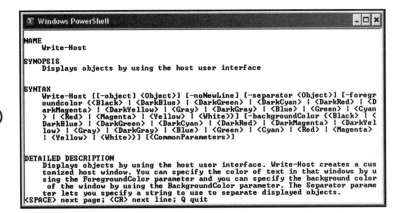

FIGURE 3.9

An example of how to use the Get-Help cmdlet to look up detailed cmdlet information.

If you do not have this book handy, you can use the Get-Command cmdlet to generate a complete list of available cmdlets. You can then use the Get-Help command to look up detailed information on any cmdlet that you see in the list.

WINDOWS POWERSHELL PLUMBING

Object pipelines are the conduit through which cmdlets pass object data to one another. Unlike traditional command shells, which only pass text data, Windows PowerShell passes different types of object data through its pipeline. You have already seen many examples of PowerShell object pipelines in use. The following examples are designed to further help you understand the versatility and power of PowerShell pipelines.

Let's begin by using the Get-ChildItem cmdlet to generate a list of files and folders located in the current working directory, as demonstrated here.

```
PS C:\> Get-ChildItem

    Directory: Microsoft.PowerShell.Core\FileSystem::C:\

Mode            LastWriteTime          Length Name
----            -------------          ------ ----
-a---      4/10/2003     1:19 AM       0 AUTOEXEC.BAT
-a---      4/10/2003     1:19 AM       0 CONFIG.SYS
-a---      10/11/2004    9:01 PM       1810432 ffastunT.ffl
-a---      2/20/2006     1:52 PM       1323 net_save.dna
-a---      6/24/2005     9:39 PM       584 Plugins
-a---      3/25/2005     3:29 PM       108 PS.PS
d----      4/10/2003     1:22 AM       Documents and Settings
d----      6/4/2003      8:58 PM       I386
d----      9/10/2006     3:19 PM       MyScripts
d-r--      9/9/2006      5:10 PM       Program Files
d----      4/21/2006     3:53 PM       temp
d----      9/15/2006     1:56 PM       WINDOWS

PS C:\>
```

Pipelines are created using the | character. Using pipelines, you can combine two or more cmdlets together to compose a logical statement that takes advantage of the combined capabilities of both cmdlets. For example, consider the following statement that takes the output generated by the Get-ChildItem cmdlet and passes it to the Sort-Object cmdlet.

```
PS C:\> Get-ChildItem | Sort-Object

    Directory: Microsoft.PowerShell.Core\FileSystem::C:\

Mode            LastWriteTime          Length Name
----            -------------          ------ ----
-a---      4/10/2003     1:19 AM       0 AUTOEXEC.BAT
-a---      4/10/2003     1:19 AM       0 CONFIG.SYS
d----      4/10/2003     1:22 AM       Documents and Settings
-a---      10/11/2004    9:01 PM       1810432 ffastunT.ffl
d----      6/4/2003      8:58 PM       I386
d----      9/10/2006     3:19 PM       MyScripts
```

```
-a---          2/20/2006   1:52 PM      1323 net_save.dna
-a---          6/24/2005   9:39 PM      584 Plugins
d-r--          9/9/2006    5:10 PM      Program Files
-a---          3/25/2005   3:29 PM      108 PS.PS
d----          4/21/2006   3:53 PM      temp
d----          9/15/2006   1:56 PM      WINDOWS

PS C:\>
```

HINT The Sort-Object cmdlet sorts a list of objects passed to it by other cmdlets, thus changing the order in which objects are passed down the pipeline. In the previous example, the sort operation was performed using the Name property. However, you can override this by specifying a different property. Likewise, you can change the default sort order from ascending to descending. To learn more about the Sort-Object cmdlet, type **Get-Help Sort-Object** at the Windows PowerShell command prompt.

As you can see, the output from the Get-ChildItem cmdlet has been removed from the pipeline, sorted, and then added back in ascending order by the Sort-Object cmdlet. Now that you have a sorted list of objects, let's process them even further. In this next example, the sorted list of objects in the pipeline is next processed by the Where-Object cmdlet.

```
PS C:\> Get-ChildItem | Sort | Where-Object { $_.Length -gt 200 }

    Directory: Microsoft.PowerShell.Core\FileSystem::C:\

Mode           LastWriteTime            Length Name
----           -------------            ------ ----
-a---          10/11/2004   9:01 PM     1810432 ffastunT.ffl
-a---          2/20/2006    1:52 PM     1323 net_save.dna
-a---          6/24/2005    9:39 PM     584 Plugins

PS C:\>
```

In this example, the Where-Object cmdlet, which removes objects failing to meet a specified criteria from the pipeline, is passed an expression enclosed within matching {} brackets. This expression takes each object passed through the pipelines, as represented by $_, and examines the value of its Length property to see if it is greater than 200. Note the use of the period (.) to connect the $_ to the keyword Length. This is an example of dot notation, which is simply a syntax used to identify an object property.

Again, don't get too hung up on the syntax used in the previous example to build the expression passed as an argument to the Where-Object cmdlet. You will learn everything you need to know about PowerShell statement syntax in Chapters 4–7. For now, the important thing to take away from this example is an understanding of pipelines and their use in passing structures between cmdlets in order to build complex logical statements.

The Where-Object cmdlet provides the ability to filter out unwanted objects from the pipelines based on input passed to it as an argument. In the previous example, the Where-Object cmdlet was instructed to remove any object whose Length property was less than 200 bytes.

$_ is a special variable created and maintained by Windows PowerShell. $_ is automatically assigned the name of the current object in the PowerShell pipeline and, in the case of the Where-Object cmdlet, to reference each object in a collection. In the previous example, the collection was composed of every file in the current working directory.

WORKING WITH ALIASES

As you have already seen with the Get-ChildItem cmdlet, the Windows PowerShell provides access to two different alias commands (dir and ls), each of which can be executed in place of this cmdlet in order to produce the same results. An *alias* is a shortcut to another cmdlet. Microsoft developed these aliases to help ease the transition from traditional command shells to Windows PowerShell. Table 3.2 provides you with a quick reference to all the aliases supported by the Windows PowerShell.

You can use the Get-Alias cmdlet to display a list of all the aliases supported by Windows PowerShell.

TABLE 3.2 WINDOWS POWERSHELL CMDLET ALIASES

Alias	Cmdlet	Alias	Cmdlet
ac	Add-Content	rp	Remove-ItemProperty
asnp	Add-PSSnapIn	rsnp	Remove-PSSnapIn
clc	Clear-Content	rv	Remove-Variable

TABLE 3.2 WINDOWS POWERSHELL CMDLET ALIASES (CONTINUED)

Alias	Cmdlet	Alias	Cmdlet
cli	Clear-Item	rvpa	Resolve-Path
clp	Clear-ItemProperty	sal	Set-Alias
clv	Clear-Variable	sasv	Start-Service
cpi	Copy-Item	sc	Set-Content
cpp	Copy-ItemProperty	select	Select-Object
cvpa	Convert-Path	si	Set-Item
diff	Compare-Object	sl	Set-Location
epal	Export-Alias	sleep	Start-Sleep
epcsv	Export-Csv	sort	Sort-Object
fc	Format-Custom	sp	Set-ItemProperty
fl	Format-List	spps	Stop-Process
foreach	ForEach-Object	spsv	Stop-Service
%	ForEach-Object	sv	Set-Variable
ft	Format-Table	tee	Tee-Object
fw	Format-Wide	where	Where-Object
gal	Get-Alias	?	Where-Object
gc	Get-Content	write	Write-Output
gci	Get-ChildItem	cat	Get-Content
gcm	Get-Command	cd	Set-Location
gdr	Get-PSDrive	clear	Clear-Host
ghy	Get-History	cp	Copy-Item
gi	Get-Item	h	Get-History
gl	Get-Location	history	Get-History
gm	Get-Member	kill	Stop-Process
gp	Get-ItemProperty	lp	Out-Printer
gps	Get-Process	ls	Get-ChildItem
group	Group-Object	mount	New-PSDrive
gsv	Get-Service	mv	Move-Item
gsnp	Get-PSSnapIn	popd	Pop-Location

TABLE 3.2 WINDOWS POWERSHELL CMDLET ALIASES (CONTINUED)

Alias	Cmdlet	Alias	Cmdlet
gu	Get-Unique	ps	Get-Process
gv	Get-Variable	pushd	Push-Location
gwmi	Get-WmiObject	pwd	Get-Location
iex	Invoke-Expression	r	Invoke-History
ihy	Invoke-History	rm	Remove-Item
ii	Invoke-Item	rmdir	Remove-Item
ipal	Import-Alias	echo	Write-Output
ipcsv	Import-Csv	cls	Clear-Host
mi	Move-Item	chdir	Set-Location
mp	Move-ItemProperty	copy	Copy-Item
nal	New-Alias	del	Remove-Item
ndr	New-PSDrive	dir	Get-ChildItem
ni	New-Item	erase	Remove-Item
nv	New-Variable	move	Move-Item
oh	Out-Host	rd	Remove-Item
rdr	Remove-PSDrive	ren	Rename-Item
ri	Remove-Item	set	Set-Variable
rni	Rename-Item	type	Get-Content
rnp	Rename-ItemProperty		

As you can see in Table 3.2, the list of aliases supported by Windows PowerShell is quite extensive. While convenient as a short-term solution for executing cmdlets, I suggest that you resist the temptation of using these aliases and instead take the time needed to learn the PowerShell's cmdlet names. This will help make your PowerShell scripts easier to maintain and support in the long run.

Windows PowerShell also lets you define your own custom aliases. This is accomplished using the Get-Alias cmdlet, which requires two arguments. The first argument is the alias to be assigned and the second argument is the name of the cmdlet for which the alias is to be associated. For example, the following statements create a new alias of ds for the Write-Host cmdlet.

```
Set-Alias ds Write-Host
```

You may recollect seeing an example of this in action earlier in this chapter when you read about how to programmatically customize Windows PowerShell.

Windows PowerShell does not perform any verification of the validity of an alias assignment when using the Set-Alias cmdlet. It is up to you to test and ensure that your new alias works as expected and that you did not mis-type the name of the target cmdlet.

BACK TO THE POWERSHELL FORTUNE TELLER GAME

Okay, it is time to turn your attention back to the chapter's main game project, the Power-Shell Fortune Teller game. This game will involve the use of a number of programming techniques, conditional logic, and looping. You will also learn how to instantiate (establish a new instance of) a new, random object in order to generate a random number.

Designing the Game

The PowerShell Fortune Teller game begins by displaying a welcome screen and then providing the player with instructions on how to formulate questions. Next, the player is prompted to ask a question. In response, the game will display a randomly generated answer based on the value of the script's randomly generated number. The specific answer displayed by the script will also vary based on the time of day, since the fortune teller gets a bit cranky in the afternoon. Once the player's question has been answered, the script will prompt the player to either ask a new question or terminate the script's execution. Thus the player is allowed to ask as many questions as he wants. Once the player indicates that he wants to terminate the script, the game ends by inviting the player to return and play again.

The development of this script will be completed in six steps, as outlined here:

1. Create a new script file and add opening comment statements.
2. Clear the screen and initialize script variables.
3. Display the opening welcome screen.
4. Display the rules for formulating questions.

5. Prompt the player to ask questions and then generate answers.

6. Invite the player to play again and terminate script execution.

Creating a New PowerShell Script

The first step in the creation of the PowerShell Fortune Teller game is to create a new PowerShell file named FortuneTeller.ps1 and add the following statements to it.

```
# *************************************************************************
#
# Script Name: FortuneTeller.ps1 (PowerShell Fortune Teller)
# Version:     1.0
# Author:      Jerry Lee Ford, Jr.
# Date:        January 1, 2007
#
# Description: This PowerShell script provides random answers to player
#              questions.
#
# *************************************************************************

#Clear the Windows command console screen
Clear-Host
```

As you can see, so far the PowerShell script file consists of comment statements that provide high-level script documentation and execute the Clear-Host cmdlet, which is called to clear the display area of the Windows command console.

Declaring and Initializing Variables

The next step in the creation of the PowerShell Fortune Teller game is to declare variables used throughout the script and to assign initial values to these variables. This is accomplished by appending the following statements to the end of the PowerShell script file.

```
#Define the variables used in this script to collect player inputs
$question = ""    #This variables will store the player's question
$status = "Play"  #This variable will be used to control game termination
$randomNo = New-Object System.Random  #This variable stores a random object
$answer = 0   #This variable stores a randomly generated number
$time = (Get-Date).Hour  #This variable stores the current hour of the day
```

Note that I have not only provided descriptive names for each variable but I have also added comments that document the purpose and use of each variable.

Displaying the Welcome Screen

The next step in the development of the PowerShell Fortune Teller game is the addition of the statements that display the game's welcome screen. These statements, shown next, should be added to the end of the script file.

```
#Display the game's opening screen
Write-Host
Write-Host
Write-Host
Write-Host
Write-Host "          W E L C O M E   T O   T H E   W I N D O W S"
Write-Host
Write-Host
Write-Host
Write-Host "          P O W E R S H E L L   F O R T U N E   T E L L E R"
Write-Host
Write-Host
Write-Host
Write-Host "                    By Jerry Lee Ford, Jr."
Write-Host
Write-Host
Write-Host
Write-Host
Write-Host
Write-Host
Write-Host
Write-Host
Write-Host
Write-Host
Write-Host " Press Enter to continue."

#Pause script execution and wait for the player to press the Enter key
Read-Host
```

The screen content is created using multiple instances of the Write-Host cmdlet. The last statement shown above uses the Read-Host cmdlet to pause script execution until the player presses the Enter key.

Displaying Game Instructions

After reading and dismissing the game's welcome screen, instructions need to be displayed that provide the player with guidance on how to formulate questions for the fortune teller. This is accomplished by added the following statements to the end of the script file.

```
#Clear the Windows command console screen
Clear-Host

#Provide the player with instructions
Write-Host
Write-Host " The fortune teller is a very busy and impatient mystic. Make"
Write-Host
Write-Host " your questions brief and simple and only expect to receive"
Write-Host
Write-host " Yes / No styled answers."
Write-Host
Write-Host
Write-Host
Write-Host
Write-Host
Write-Host
Write-Host
Write-Host
Write-Host
Write-Host
Write-Host
Write-Host
Write-Host
Write-Host
Write-Host
Write-Host
Write-Host
Write-Host
Write-Host " Press Enter to continue."

#Pause script execution and wait for the player to press the Enter key
Read-Host
```

As with the statements that generated the welcome screen, the statements that display the game's instructions clear the screen, write text output, and then pause the script's execution until the player presses the Enter key.

Controlling Gameplay

The programming logic that controls the core activities of the game is outlined next and should be appended to the end of the script file.

```
#Continue gameplay until the player decides to stop
while ($status -ne "Stop") {

  #Ask the player the first question
  while ($question -eq ""){

    Clear-Host  #Clear the Windows command console screen

    Write-Host

    $question = read-host " What is your question? "

  }

  $question = ""   #Reset variable to an empty string



  #Using the Random object, get a random number between 1 and 4
  $answer = $randomNo.Next(1, 5)



  #Select an answer based on the time and random number
  #If it is the afternoon the fortune teller will be a little cranky
  if ($time -gt 12) {
    Write-Host
    if ($answer -eq 1) { " Grrrr. The answer is no!" }
    if ($answer -eq 2) { " Grrrr. The answer is never!" }
    if ($answer -eq 3) { " Grrrr. The answer is unclear!" }
    if ($answer -eq 4) { " Grrrr. The answer is yes!" }
  }
  #If it is morning, the fortune teller will be in a good mood
  else {
    Write-Host
    if ($answer -eq 1) { " Ah. The answer is yes!" }
    if ($answer -eq 2) { " Ah. The answer is always!" }
```

```
    if ($answer -eq 3) { " Ah. The answer is uncertain!" }
    if ($answer -eq 4) { " Ah. The answer is no!" }
}


Write-Host
Write-Host
Write-Host
Write-Host
Write-Host
Write-Host
Write-Host
Write-Host
Write-Host
Write-Host
Write-Host
Write-Host
Write-Host
Write-Host
Write-Host
Write-Host
Write-Host
Write-Host
Write-Host
Write-Host " Press Enter to continue."

#Pause script execution and wait for the player to press the Enter key
Read-Host

#Clear the Windows command console screen
Clear-host

Write-Host

#Prompt the player to continue or quit
$reply = read-host " Press Enter to ask another question or type Q to quit."
if ($reply -eq "q") { $status = "Stop" }


}
```

The statements that make up this portion of the script file consist of a number of programming statements that will not be formally covered until later in Chapters 5 and 6. These statements involve conditional and looping logic. Unfortunately, it is all but impossible to develop PowerShell scripts of any real complexity without using some conditional or looping logic and there is only so much information that can be presented at one time. To make things easier to understand, I have added many comments throughout the script file. However, because this book has not yet covered these programming constructs, I will not cover them in great detail now. As a result, you may want to return and review this script once you have read Chapters 5 and 6.

The overall logic that controls gameplay, allowing the player to ask as many questions as desired, is controlled by a `while` loop that executes until the value of a variable named `$status` is set equal to `"Stop"`. Within this loop, another `while` loop is defined in order to ensure that the player enters something, as opposed to simply pressing the Enter key when prompted to ask the fortune teller a question.

Next, a random number is generated in the range of 1 to 4. Then a variable named `$time` is checked to see if its value is greater than 12. If it is, the fortune teller is said to be tired and cranky, thus resulting in the display of 1 of 4 less friendly answers (based on the game's randomly generated number). However, if it is still morning, a more positive set of answers is used when retrieving the fortune teller's answer.

Next, the selected answer is displayed and the player is prompted to either press Enter to ask another question or to type Q to signal the script that it is time to stop executing. If the player enters Q, the value of the `$status` variable is set equal to `"Stop"`, thus halting the `while` loop that controls the overall execution of the script.

Displaying the Closing Screen

Once gameplay has been finished, the player should be invited to return and ask the fortune teller more questions. This is accomplished by adding the following statements to the end of the script file.

```
#Clear the Windows command console screen
Clear-Host

#Provide the player with instructions
Write-Host
Write-Host " Very well then. Please return again to get all your questions"
Write-Host " answered."
Write-Host
```

```
Write-Host
Write-Host
Write-Host
Write-Host
Write-Host
Write-Host
Write-Host
Write-Host
Write-Host
Write-Host
Write-Host
Write-Host
Write-Host
Write-Host
Write-Host
Write-Host
Write-Host
Write-Host
Write-Host
Write-Host " Press Enter to continue."

#Pause script execution and wait for the player to press the Enter key
Read-Host

#Clear the Windows command console screen
Clear-Host
```

The player dismisses this invitation to return and play again by pressing the Enter key, after which the screen is cleared and the script file stops executing.

Okay, that's it. Assuming that you have not made any typos when keying in this code for the PowerShell Fortune Teller game, everything should work as advertised.

Summary

In this chapter you learned about the .NET Framework class library and common language runtime. You learned how Windows PowerShell cmdlets allow you to access and interact with resources exposed by the .NET Framework. You also learned how to use a number of new cmdlets, including the Get-Help cmdlet, which you can use to get additional information on any cmdlet or PowerShell topic. You also learned how to find out about object properties and methods that are not displayed by default when executing cmdlets, but that are nonetheless available behind the scenes. You learned more about working with aliases, including how to create your own custom aliases. This chapter also explained how Windows PowerShell uses object pipelines to pass structured data between cmdlets. Lastly, you learned how to create the PowerShell Fortune Teller game.

Now, before you move on to Chapter 4, I recommend that you take a few extra minutes to improve and enhance the PowerShell Fortune Teller game by implementing the following challenges.

CHALLENGES

1. Consider making the game less predictable by expanding the range of answers available to the game. You might even add a response in which the fortune teller takes offense to a question and refuses to answer.

2. Consider further altering the fortune teller's mood by making her even more cranky as the day turns into night.

Part II

Learning How to Write PowerShell Scripts

Working with Variables, Arrays, and Hashes

This is the first of four chapters designed to teach the fundamentals of the Windows PowerShell scripting language. In this chapter you will learn how to store, retrieve, and modify data. You will learn how to store individual pieces as well as collections of data. This chapter will also cover a number of other PowerShell language topics, including the use of keywords, escape characters, and string-manipulation techniques. You will also learn how to work with a number of PowerShell operators. On top of all this, you will get the opportunity to create your next Windows PowerShell computer game, the Seinfeld Trivia Quiz.

Specifically, you will learn how to

- Create and store individual pieces of data in variables
- Store and access collections of data in arrays and hashes
- Access Windows PowerShell special variables
- Execute the –Replace and Range operators
- Concatenate strings
- Format and control the display of text using escape characters

PROJECT PREVIEW: THE SEINFELD TRIVIA QUIZ

This chapter's game project is the Seinfeld Trivia Quiz, which tests the player's knowledge of the popular Seinfeld TV series. The game consists of five multiple-choice questions. When first started, the game's welcome screen appears, as shown in Figure 4.1.

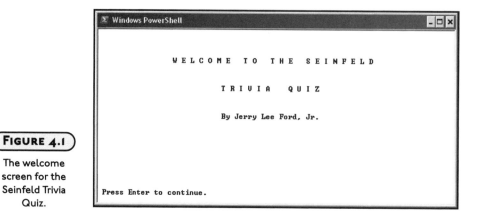

FIGURE 4.1

The welcome screen for the Seinfeld Trivia Quiz.

After the player presses Enter to dismiss the welcome screen, instructions are displayed that explain the makeup of the quiz and the grading scale, as demonstrated in Figure 4.2.

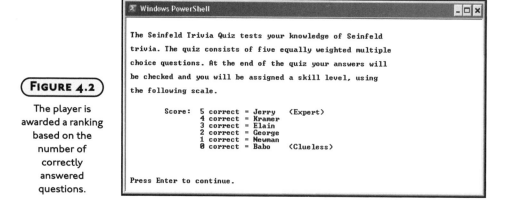

FIGURE 4.2

The player is awarded a ranking based on the number of correctly answered questions.

Next, the game displays its questions, one at a time, as demonstrated in Figure 4.3.

Once the player has finished taking the quiz and presses Enter to submit her last answer, the screen shown in Figure 4.4 appears, letting the player know that the game is about to grade the quiz.

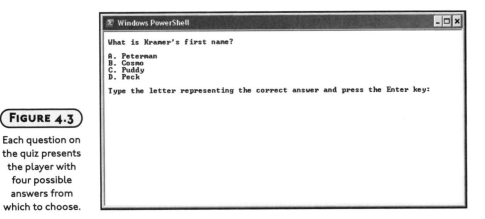

FIGURE 4.3

Each question on the quiz presents the player with four possible answers from which to choose.

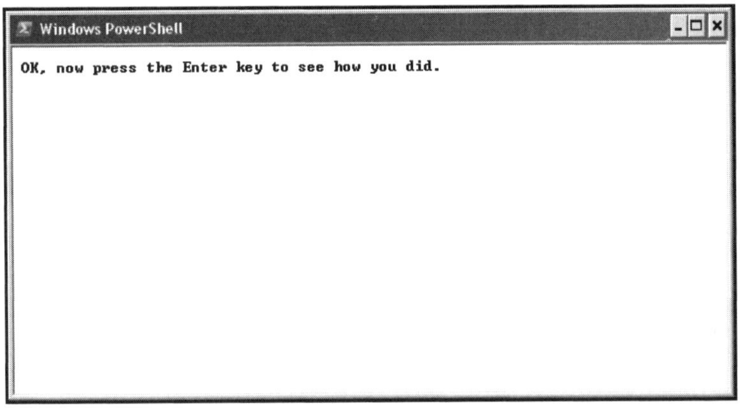

FIGURE 4.4

The game announces that it is now ready to analyze the player's quiz results.

After grading the quiz, the game informs the player how many questions were correctly answered and assigns a ranking based on that value, as demonstrated in Figure 4.5.

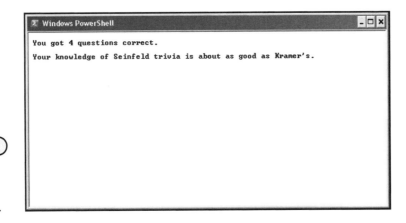

FIGURE 4.5

The player correctly answered four quiz questions.

The last screen displayed by the Seinfeld Trivia Quiz, shown in Figure 4.6, thanks the player for taking the time to complete the quiz.

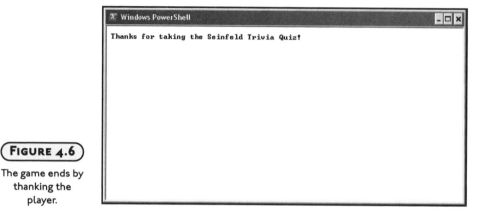

FIGURE 4.6

The game ends by thanking the player.

WINDOWS POWERSHELL LANGUAGE FEATURES

Although the primary focus of this chapter is on the storage and retrieval of data during script execution, there are a few additional topics that need to be covered to help round out your understanding of PowerShell scripting basics. These topics include:

- Reserved words
- Escape characters
- String manipulation

Windows PowerShell Reserved Words

Like any programming language, Windows PowerShell has a collection of reserved words (also referred to as *keywords*) that have a special meaning to the language and thus are not available for use as variable, array, associative array, and function names.

A *reserved word* is a keyword that Windows PowerShell has predefined as having a special purpose. An example of a PowerShell reserved word is if, which is used to set up conditional tests in order to evaluate when a condition is true or false and then control the logical execution of one or more script statements based on that result. As a reserved word, you must use the if keyword according to the strict syntactical rules defined by Windows PowerShell. Therefore, you cannot create a variable or array or any other identifier named if in your PowerShell scripts. Table 4.1 provides a listing of PowerShell reserved words.

TABLE 4.1   WINDOWS POWERSHELL RESERVED WORDS

Keyword	Keyword	Keyword	Keyword
break	elseif	if	until
continue	filter	in	where
do	foreach	return	while
else	function	switch	

Escape Characters

As you write more and more PowerShell scripts, you are going to come across situations in which you will want to exercise detailed control over how text is displayed in the Windows command console. As you have seen in previous script game examples, one way to do so is to use an extra instance of the Write-Host cmdlet and embed blank spaces inside strings, as demonstrated by the following.

```
Write-Host
Write-Host
Write-Host
Write-Host
Write-Host "          W E L C O M E    T O    T H E    W I N D O W S"
Write-Host
Write-Host
Write-Host
Write-Host "          P O W E R S H E L L    F O R T U N E    T E L L E R"
Write-Host
Write-Host
Write-Host
Write-Host "                              By Jerry Lee Ford, Jr."
Write-Host
Write-Host
Write-Host
Write-Host
Write-Host
Write-Host
Write-Host
Write-Host
```

```
Write-Host
Write-Host
Write-Host " Press Enter to continue."
```

This example required 24 lines of code. While certainly intuitive and easy to understand, using the Write-Host cmdlet in this manner consumes a lot of space and bloats your Power-Shell script code. An alternative way to exercise detailed control over your text string output is to take advantage of PowerShell's escape characters.

An *escape character* is a character that has special meaning to Windows PowerShell. Escape characters are identified by the ` character (typically located just over the Tab key on most keyboards). Using escape characters, you can insert tabs and newline feeds at any point within a text string. For example, you can insert `n at any point within a string to force an immediate newline operation, thus breaking the display of a string into two lines. Likewise, you can insert a `t within a text string to insert a logical tab. Using just these two escape characters, you could rework the previous example as demonstrated here.

```
Write-Host "`n`n`n`n`t`tW E L C O M E   T O   T H E   W I N D O W S"
Write-Host "`n`n`n`t    P O W E R S H E L L   F O R T U N E   T E L L E R"
Write-Host "`n`n`n`t`t`t  By Jerry Lee Ford, Jr."
Write-Host "`n`n`n`n`n`n`n`n`n Press Enter to continue."
```

Believe it or not, this example provides for the exact same output in just four statements that the previous example produced in 24 statements. Windows PowerShell supports a number of different escape characters, as outlined in Table 4.2.

 HINT To learn more about Windows PowerShell's escape characters, execute the following statement at the Windows PowerShell command prompt:

```
Get-Help about_escape_character
```

 TRICK When added to the end of a statement, the ` character instructs Windows PowerShell to continue the statement onto the next line, as demonstrated here:

```
Write-Host "Once upon a time there was a little girl that lived in a small" `
"house on the edge of the forest."
```

When displayed, the output produced by this statement will display just as if the statement had been written on a single line.

TABLE 4.2 WINDOWS POWERSHELL ESCAPE CHARACTERS

Escape Character	Description
`'	Single quote
`"	Double quote
`0	Null
`a	Alert
`b	Backspace
`f	Form feed
`n	Newline
`r	Carriage return
`t	Horizontal tab
`v	Vertical tab

String Manipulation

Windows PowerShell provides a number of different string-manipulation techniques that you will find helpful when developing Windows PowerShell scripts. These techniques include string concatenation, character repetition, and substring replacement.

Concatenation

Windows PowerShell allows you to use the += operator to concatenate or join together two strings, as demonstrated by the following.

```
$x = "Once upon "
$y = "a time..."
$z = $x += $y
$z
```

In this example, two strings are assigned to variables named $x and $y. The third statement uses the += operator to concatenate the values assigned to these two variables in order to create a new string, which is assigned to a variable named $z. When executed, this example generates the following output.

```
Once upon a time...
```

Windows PowerShell also allows you to concatenate two strings together using just the + operator, as demonstrated here.

```
$x = "Once upon "
$y = "a time..."
$z = $x + $y
$z
```

When executed, this example produces output that is identical to the previous example.

Repeating Character Strings

Another string-manipulation technique that you may find helpful is the ability to repeat the display of strings using the * operator, as demonstrated here.

```
$x = "Ha " * 3
$x
```

In this example, the string "Ha " is repeated three times, resulting in the output shown here.

```
Ha Ha Ha
```

This programming technique can be useful in situations where you need to generate reports in which you want to format report headings that use repeated characters to help visually separate report contents, as demonstrated here.

```
$x = "-" * 50
Write-Host $x
Get-Date
Write-Host
Write-Host "Report Title"
Write-Host
Write-Host $x
```

Here, a variable named $x is assigned a string made up of 50 - characters. This variable is displayed twice in order to provide a visual border within which a report heading, made up of a date and title, is displayed, as shown here.

```
------------------------------

Thursday, October 05, 2006 11:39:02 PM

Report Title

------------------------------
```

Replacing Parts of a String

The replace operator (-replace) lets you replace all or a portion of a string. To use the replace operator, you specify the string to be manipulated followed by the replace operator and then two operator arguments. The first argument is the part of the script that you want to replace and the second argument is the replacement string. To see the replace operator in action, take a look at the following example, which takes a string and replaces the word boy with the word girl.

```
$x = "Once upon a time there was a little boy."
$y = $x -replace "boy", "girl"
$y
```

When executed, this example displays the following output.

```
Once upon a time there was a little girl.
```

 TRICK Note that as the previous example demonstrates, you can display the contents of a variable by simply referencing its name in your script.

STORING AND RETRIEVING DATA

In any programming language, programmers need a mechanism for storing and retrieving data. You can programmatically access numerous types of data by executing cmdlets. You can then manipulate the data that is generated using other cmdlets as the data passes through the object pipeline. However, there are limits to this approach. In many circumstances, you will find that you need to be able to store data for later analysis, manipulation, and display.

Windows PowerShell's programming language provides you with several different ways of storing data, as listed here.

- **Variables.** Store individual pieces of data.
- **Arrays.** Store data as an index list.
- **Hashes.** Store data in key-value pairs.

Variables

Variables provide you with a means of storing data within your Windows PowerShell scripts. Using variables, you can store just about anything you want, including numbers, strings, and objects. If you store object data returned as output by a cmdlet, PowerShell is able to retain an awareness of the object types and therefore the properties and methods associated with the object.

Naming Your Variables

Windows PowerShell variable names are not case sensitive, meaning that if you define a variable named $username, you can later refer to it as $USERNAME and PowerShell will understand what you mean. Windows PowerShell variable names can include letters, numbers, and the underscore character (_). Windows PowerShell variable names must begin with the $ character. Examples of valid variable names include:

- $userName
- $total
- $1stName
- $game_winner

Examples of invalid variable names include:

- $user Name
- $total!
- $#!,).@%&

The first example is invalid because it includes a blank space. The second example is invalid because it includes the ! character. Lastly, the third example is invalid because it contains a whole slew of unsupported characters. If you forget and include an invalid variable in a PowerShell script, your script will most likely terminate with an error. For example, the following variable assignment statement is invalid because it contains a number of invalid characters.

```
$#!,).@%& = "Winner"
```

If you were to try and use this variable name in a PowerShell script, the script will terminate and display the following error.

```
Invalid variable reference. '$' was not followed by a valid variable name character.
Consider using ${} to delimit the name.
At C:\MyScripts\xxx.ps1:3 char:1
+ $ <<<< #!,).@%& = "Winner"
```

TRICK If you find yourself with a strong desire to include special characters within your variable's name, you may do so by enclosing the variable name inside matching {} characters, as demonstrated here.

```
${bang#!} = "Winner"
```

By enclosing variable names within {} brackets, you can include an assortment of different characters, such as #, $, %, and *, as well as periods, commas, and even blank spaces.

Defining and Initializing Variables

Windows PowerShell supports a range of data types that corresponds to data types supported by the .NET Framework. For example, Windows PowerShell supports integers and floating-point numbers, which you can assign to variables, as demonstrated by the following.

```
$x = 5
$y = 5.5
$z = "Winner"
```

Windows PowerShell automatically recognizes the first assignment shown above as an integer, the second assignment as a floating-point number, and the third assignment as a string.

 TRAP I strongly recommend that you assign an initial default value to any variable that you declare within your Windows PowerShell scripts. If a script statement attempts to access a variable that has not been assigned a value, an error is not generated. Instead, your script will keep running and you'll end up with unpredictable results.

Variable Interpolation

Up to this point in the book, all of the strings that you have seen have been placed inside matching sets of double quotation marks. However, you are also allowed to define strings using matching sets of single quotation marks. The difference between the two is that variable interpolation occurs when a variable is embedded inside a string enclosed within double quotations marks but does not occur within a string enclosed within single quotation marks. To see how this works, consider the following example.

```
$x = "red"
Write-Host "The little boy held on tightly to his $x balloon"
```

When executed, the following output is displayed.

```
The little boy held on tightly to his red balloon
```

As you can see, Windows PowerShell automatically substituted the value of $x when generating text output. However, if you were to rework this example by placing the string inside single quotation marks, as shown next, variable interpolation does not occur.

```
$x = "red"
Write-Host 'The little boy held on tightly to his $x balloon'
```

If you run this example, the following output will be displayed.

```
The little boy held on tightly to his $x balloon
```

In most cases, using double quotes to define strings is all you will need.

Assigning Variable Values Using Expressions

You can also assign variable values using expressions. Here, the value of 1 + 4 (i.e., 5) is assigned to a variable named $x.

```
$x = 1 + 4     # $x equals 5
```

In addition to the + operator, Windows PowerShell supports a wide range of arithmetic operators, as shown in Table 4.3.

TABLE 4.3 WINDOWS POWERSHELL ARITHMETIC OPERATORS	
Operator	**Description**
+	Adds two numbers together
-	Subtracts one number from another
*	Multiplies two numbers together
/	Divides one number by another
%	Retrieves the remainder of a division operation (modulus)

Precedence

In Windows PowerShell scripting, like in any other programming language, mathematical operations are executed according to a specific order of precedence, which occurs on a left-to-right basis. Specifically, the - unary operator, which negates a number, is evaluated first. Next, PowerShell performs multiplication and division and then remaindering. Finally, addition and subtraction are performed. For example, consider the following expression.

 HINT *An expression is a statement that is evaluated and produces a result.*

```
$x = 5 * 4 / 2 * 5 - 5 * 5
```

When executed by PowerShell, the value assigned to $x is 25, which is calculated as follows:

1. Multiplication and division occurs first, so 5 * 4 = 20, which is then divided by 2, resulting in a value of 10. This value is then multiplied by 5 to get a new value of 50.

2. Since multiplication and division occur before addition and subtraction, the subtraction operation, which appears next in the equation, is skipped and the multiplication operation at the end of the statement is executed, resulting in a value of 25.

3. Finally, 25 is subtracted from 50 to produce a value of 25.

An expression like this can be difficult to read. To help clarify things, you can use parentheses to visually group different parts of the expression.

```
$x = (5 * 4 / 2 * 5) - (5 * 5)
```

In addition to helping to visually organize the expression, you can also use parentheses to alter the order in which the contents of the expression are executed by overriding the order of precedence. Take, for example, the following statement:

```
$x = 5 * 4 / (2 * 5 - 5) * 5
```

As you can see, this statement is almost identical to the previous example, except that parentheses have altered the order in which the expression is evaluated. As a result, the expression evaluates to a value of 20, which is computed as follows:

1. The multiplication of 2 * 5 occurs first, resulting in a value of 10, from which 5 is then subtracted.

2. Next, starting at the beginning of the expression, 5 is multiplied by 4, resulting in a value of 20.

3. 20 is then divided by the value computed in the first step (i.e., 5), resulting in a value of 4. The value of 4 is then multiplied by the last number in the expression, resulting in a value of 20.

 TRICK Two arithmetic operators (+ and *) are overloaded, allowing them to work for strings as well as numbers. Thus, as you have already seen, you can use the + operator to concatenate two strings together. You can also use the * operator to repeat a string a specified number of times as was demonstrated earlier in this chapter.

PowerShell Assignment Operators

Up to this point in the book, you have seen the equal (=) operator used to make all assignments. However, Windows PowerShell supports a host of different assignment operators, as shown in Table 4.4.

TABLE 4.4 WINDOWS POWERSHELL ASSIGNMENT OPERATORS

Operator	Description
=	Assigns a value to a variable
+=	Adds a value to a variable
-=	Subtracts a value from a variable
*=	Multiplies a variable value
/=	Divides a variable value
%=	Assigns the remainder of a division

As an example of how to work with these operators, consider the following example.

```
$x = 5
$x +=5
```

Here, the value of $x is equal to 5 and then incremented by 5, resulting in a final value of 10.

In addition to the assignment operators shown in Table 4.4, Windows PowerShell also supports two additional operators that you can use to automatically increment and decrement the value of a variable by 1.

- ++ Automatically increments a value by 1.
- — Automatically decrements a value by 1.

As an example of how these two operators work, consider the following statements.

```
$x = 5
$y = $x++
```

HINT In the previous example, $x++ is functionally equivalent to $x = $x + 1.

Here, a variable named $x is set equal to 5. Next, a variable named $y is assigned the value assigned to $x, after $x is incremented by 1. Thus $y ends up assigned a value of 6.

Special Variables

Windows PowerShell provides you with access to a number of variables that are always available to your PowerShell scripts. These variables provide access to commonly used information. By making references these special variables, you save yourself the effort of having to create and maintain your own version of these variables. Table 4.5. lists a number of commonly used special variables.

TABLE 4.5 WINDOWS POWERSHELL SPECIAL VARIABLES

Special Character	Description
$_	Represents the current pipeline object when used in script blocks such as the Foreach-Object and the Where-Object blocks
$Error	Provides access to information about recent errors
$HOME	Represents the home directory of the current user
$PSHome	Indicates the name of the folder where Windows PowerShell is installed
$null	Represents a null object

You have seen the $_ special variable used a couple times already in this book. As another example of how to use Windows PowerShell's special variables, consider the following example.

```
Set-Location $home
$x = Get-ChildItem
$x
```

When executed, this example changes the current working directory to the home directory of the person who runs the script and then assigns a list of all of contents of that folder to a variable named $x.

HINT To view a listing of all Windows PowerShell's special variables and see their definitions, use the Get-Help cmdlet and pass it an argument of about_automatic _variables, as shown here.

```
Get-Help about_automatic_variables
```

Variable Scope

Within Windows PowerShell scripts, variable access depends on the location at which a variable is defined. Within Windows PowerShell, access is governed by scope. PowerShell supports four different scopes, each of which can be referenced by one of the following labels.

- **Local scope.** Refers to the current scope, which can be global, private, or script.
- **Global scope.** A scope that is established whenever a new PowerShell session is started.
- **Private scope.** A scope that is not visible or accessible to other scopes.
- **Script scope.** A scope that is established whenever a script is executed and which ends when the script stops executing.

Whenever you start up a new Windows PowerShell session, you establish a global scope. Any variable created from the command prompt during the current session is global in scope. Global variables can be accessed from within the current scope (e.g., from the command line as well as from child scopes). When you execute a PowerShell script, a new script scope is created. This scope is a child scope to the global scope.

Variables defined within your PowerShell scripts (outside of any functions) are local variables and can be accessed from anywhere within the script. Within the PowerShell script, you can define functions in order to improve the overall organization of the script and to further refine the scope. Variables defined within a function are local to the function and the function's scope is a child scope of the script's script scope.

 A *function* is a collection of statements that can be called upon to execute as a unit. Functions are covered in Chapter 7, "Organizing Scripts Using Functions."

By default, variables created in a child scope can be seen and accessed in a parent scope, unless the variables are defined as private, in which case the variables can only be accessed from within their own scope.

So far all of the variables that you have worked with in this book's PowerShell game scripts have been local in scope and as such have been accessible throughout the entire script. However, as you will see in Chapter 7, you can define variables within functions and mark them as private, limiting access to just within the function itself.

Arrays

As has been already stated, variables can be used to store numbers, strings, and objects of any type. Variables can also be used to store arrays. An *array* is an indexed list of values.

Each element stored in an array is assigned a unique numeric index number, which can later be used to retrieve its value. In Windows PowerShell, array indexes start at zero, so the first element in an array has an index of 0 and the second element has an index of 1 and so on.

Creating an Array

You can create a new empty array by assigning an empty array (represented as @( )) to a variable, as demonstrated here.

```
$names = @( )
```

You can later add new elements to the array by assigning each element using the = operator.

```
$names[0] = "Alexander"
$names[1] = "William"
$names[2] = "Molly"
```

Once populated, you can refer to any array element by referencing its index number, as demonstrated here.

```
Write-Host $names[1] "is a great kid."
```

In this example, $x is assigned a value of Molly. Because arrays are indexed, you can process all the elements stored in an array using a loop. You will find examples of how to do this in Chapter 6, "Using Loops to Process Data."

 TRICK In addition to referencing an array element by its index number, Windows PowerShell also allows you to use negative numbers to reference the elements stored at the end of an array. An index value of -1 would refer to the last elements stored in the array; a value of -2 would represent the second to last element, and so on.

Alternatively, you can populate an array with data at creation time, as demonstrated by the following.

```
$numbers = @(1, 2, 3, 4, 5)
Write-Host $numbers
```

Here, an array named $numbers has been defined and populated with five numeric values. Note that the array is identified by the @ character and the elements assigned to the array are provided as a comma-separated list enclosed inside matching parentheses. When executed, this example produces the following output.

```
1 2 3 4 5
```

TRICK If you want, you can use the range operator (. .) to populate an array with a range of values. For example, the following statement can be used to create an array named $numbers and assign it 1, 2, 3, 4, 5 as its initial elements.

```
$numbers = @(1..5)
```

Modifying Element Values

You can modify the value of any element in an array by specifying its index number, as demonstrated by the following.

```
$numbers = @(1, 2, 3, 4, 5)
$numbers[2] = 9
$numbers
```

When executed, this example produces the following output

```
1
2
9
4
5
```

As you can see, the value stored in the array's third element has been changed to 9. (Remember that array indexes begin at 0 and not 1.)

Keeping Track of Array Size

Arrays have a Count property that you can use to determine the number of elements in an array, as demonstrated here.

```
$names = @("Alexander", "William", "Molly")
$total = $names.Count
$total
```

When executed, $total is assigned a value of 3.

 HINT Arrays also have a length property that you can use to retrieve the number of elements in an array, as demonstrated next.

```
$names = @("Alexander", "William", "Molly")
$total = $names.Length
$total
```

Combining Arrays

Windows PowerShell also allows you to combine two or more arrays to create a new larger array using the + operator, as demonstrated by the following.

```
$lowNumbers = @(1, 2, 3)
$highNumbers= @(4, 5, 6)

$numbers = $lowNumbers + $highNumbers

$numbers
```

In this example, two arrays, named $lowNumbers and $highNumbers, have been defined. Then using the + operator, these two arrays are combined to create a new array named $numbers, whose elements are 1, 2, 3, 4, 5, and 6.

Deleting and Inserting Array Elements

There is no direct way to insert an element into a particular location in an array. However, using the range operator and the + operator, you can work around this shortcoming, as demonstrated here.

```
$numbers = @(1, 2, 3, 4, 5, 6, 7)
$numbers = $numbers[0..2 + 4..6]
$numbers
```

In this example, the first statement defines an array named $numbers and assigns it a range of values. The second statement reassigns the contents of the $numbers array by using the range operator and the + operator to generate a new list of elements consisting of the first three and last three elements in the original array. When executed, this example produces the following output.

```
1
2
3
5
6
7
```

There is no direct way to insert an element into the beginning or middle of an array. However, by adapting the aforementioned technique, you can insert a number at any given location within an array, as demonstrated here.

```
$numbers = @(1, 2, 3, 4, 5, 6, 7)
$numbers = $numbers[0..3] + 99 + $numbers[4..6]
$numbers
```

In this example, the number 99 is inserted into the middle of the array.

Associative Arrays

One shortcoming of arrays is that as they grow bigger, it becomes difficult to keep track of where individual array elements are stored. As a result, to find a given value, you usually have to set up a loop to search the array, examining every element in order to find the one you want. An *associative array*, sometimes referred to as a *hash* or *dictionary*, provides a more efficient and faster alternative, allowing you to store data in key-value pairs.

Creating an Associative Array

One way to create an associative array is to define it as an empty associative array, as demonstrated next.

```
$ids = @{}
```

As you can see, the variable used to store the hash is just a regular variable, and the empty hash table is represented by @{}.

Once defined, you can add as many key-value pairs to it as necessary, as demonstrated by the following.

```
$ids[12345] = "William"
$ids[23456] = "Alexander"
$ids[34567] = "Molly"
$ids[22334] = "Mary"
$ids[55555] = "Jerry"
```

Each of these statements adds a new entry into the associative array. The value specified inside the brackets is the key and the value specified to the right side of the equals sign is the value.

Accessing Data Stored in Associative Arrays

Once created and populated with data, you can retrieve a value from the associative array, as demonstrated here.

```
$x= $ids[34567]
```

Here, a value of Molly is retrieved from the associative array and assigned to a variable named $x.

Associative arrays can be used to store any amount of data. Associative array keys and values can be of any length. Associative array elements are stored as values and must be enclosed inside quotation marks if they contain blank spaces. Stored values are retrieved by referencing their associated key. Associated arrays can store any type of data. Data retrieval from associative arrays is relatively fast and does not increase as more values are added.

Populating Associative Arrays at Creation Time

Associative arrays can also be populated at creation time, as demonstrated here.

```
$nicknames = @{Alexander = "X-Man"; William = "William-D"; Molly = "Might-One"}
$x = $nicknames["Alexander"]
```

As you can see, three separate key-value pairs have been defined. Key-value pairs are separated by semicolons and enclosed inside matching brackets and preceded by the @ character. When executed, $x is assigned a value of Alexander.

If you want, you can display the contents of an associative array from within your Power-Shell scripts, as demonstrated by the following.

```
$nicknames = @{Alexander = "X-Man"; William = "William-D"; Molly = "Might-One"}
$nicknames
```

When executed, this example will produce the following output.

```
Name              Value
---               ----

Alexander         X-Man
Molly             Might-One
William           William-D
```

HINT   Like arrays, you can combine the contents of associative arrays using the + operator, as demonstrated here.

```
$kidNames = @{Alexander = "X-Man"; William = "William-D"; Molly = "Might-One"}
$parentNames = @{Jerry = "Daddy"; Mary = "Mommy"}

$familyNames = $kidNames + $parentNames

$familyNames
```

When executed, this example produces the following output.

```
Name                          Value
---                           ---
William                       William-D
Alexander                     X-Man
Jerry                         Daddy
Molly                         Might-One
Mary                          Mommy
```

Deleting a Key-Value Pair

Associative arrays provide you with access to methods that allow you to manipulate their contents. For example, you can remove an entry from an associative array using the `Remove` method, as demonstrated here.

```
$nicknames = @{Alexander = "X-Man"; William = "William-D"; Molly = "Might-One"}
$nicknames.Remove("Alexander")
$nicknames
```

When executed, this example will produce the following output.

```
Name                          Value
---                           ---
Molly                         Might-One
William                       William-D
```

Removing Associative Array Contents

Using the `Clear` method, you can remove the contents of an associative array, as demonstrated by the following.

```
$nicknames.Clear()
```

> **HINT**   To learn more about hashes, use the Get-Help cmdlet to look up about_Associative_Array.

BACK TO THE SEINFELD TRIVIA QUIZ

Okay, let's turn our attention back to the development of this chapter's main game project, the Seinfeld Trivia Quiz. The development of this game will demonstrate how to create an interactive online quiz that presents the player with a series of questions that are then analyzed and graded. The primary point of focus for you as you create this game should be on the use of variables to store and analyze data collected from the player. In addition, you should take note of the use of Windows PowerShell escape characters in the generation of display output.

Designing the Game

The Seinfeld Trivia Quiz will begin by displaying a welcome screen and then displaying instructions for taking the quiz. Next, it will present a series of five multiple-choice questions. The game should validate player answers for each question before accepting them and store each answer for later analysis. Once the player has finished taking the quiz, the player's answers should be graded and a ranking should be assigned to the player based on how well she did.

The overall steps involved in developing the Seinfeld Trivia Quiz are as follows:

1. Create a new script file and add opening comment statements.
2. Define variables used in the script to store player answers and keep track of the number of correctly answered questions.
3. Display a welcome screen.
4. Display instructions for gameplay and explain the grading scale.
5. Present the player with the first quiz question.
6. Display the rest of the quiz questions.
7. Let the player know when all questions have been answered
8. Analyze the answers provided for each quiz question.
9. Assign a ranking based on the number of correctly answered questions.
10. Thank the player for taking time to take the quiz.

Creating a New Script

The first step is creating a new PowerShell file named SeinfeldTrivia.ps1 and adding the following statements to it.

```
# *************************************************************************
#
# Script Name:    SeinfeldTrivia.ps1 (The Seinfield Trivia Quiz)
# Version:        1.0
# Author:         Jerry Lee Ford, Jr.
# Date:           January 1, 2007
#
# Description:    This PowerShell script tests the player's knowledge
#                 of Seinfeld trivia through the administration of
#                 a computer quiz made up of 5 questions.
#
# *************************************************************************


#Clear the Windows command console screen
Clear-Host
```

As with previous game scripts, this script file has been generated using the Windows Power-Shell template that was developed back in Chapter 2, "Interacting with the Windows PowerShell Command Line." In addition, the script's first statement has been added, which executes the Clear-Host cmdlet in order to clear the display area of the Windows command console.

Defining and Initializing Variables

The next step in the creation of the Seinfeld Trivia Quiz is to define variables used throughout the script and to assign their initial values. This is accomplished by adding the following statements to the end of the PowerShell script file.

```
#Define the variables used in this script to store player answers
$question1 = ""
$question2 = ""
$question3 = ""
$question4 = ""
$question5 = ""


#Define a variable to keep track of the number of correctly answered
#quiz questions
$noCorrect = 0
```

The first set of statements shown above defines five variables that will be used to store answers provided by the player in response to quiz questions. The last statement defines a variable named $noCorrrect, which will be used to keep track of the number of questions that the player answers correctly.

Displaying the Welcome Screen

The next step in the development of the Seinfeld Trivia Quiz is the display of the game's welcome screen. This is accomplished by appending the following statements to the end of the script file.

```
#Display the game's opening screen
Write-Host "`n`n`n`n`t`t W E L C O M E    T O    T H E    S E I N F E L D"
Write-Host "`n`n`n`t`t`t    T R I V I A    Q U I Z"
Write-Host "`n`n`n`t`t`t    By Jerry Lee Ford, Jr."
Write-Host "`n`n`n`n`n`n`n`n`n Press Enter to continue."

#Pause script execution and wait for the player to press the Enter key
Read-Host
```

As you can see, the game's welcome screen is created using a series of Write-Host cmdlets. In order to control the string formatting, a series of escape characters has been embedded within each statement. Specifically, instances of the `n escape character have been added to generate newline commands, and the `t escape character has been used to insert tab commands. The last statement shown above uses the Read-Host cmdlet to pause script execution until the player presses the Enter key.

Displaying Instructions

After reading and dismissing the game's welcome screen, instructions for taking the quiz and an explanation of its ranking system need to be displayed. This is accomplished by appending the following statements to the end of the script file.

```
#Clear the Windows command console screen
Clear-Host

#Provide the player with instructions
Write-Host "`n`n The Seinfeld Trivia Quiz tests your knowledge of Seinfeld`n"
Write-Host " trivia. The quiz consists of five equally weighted multiple`n"
Write-Host " choice questions. At the end of the quiz your answers will`n"
Write-Host " be checked and you will be assigned a skill level, using`n"
Write-Host " the following scale.`n`n"
Write-Host " `t Score:  5 correct = Jerry    (Expert)"
```

```
Write-Host " `t`t 4 correct = Kramer"
Write-Host " `t`t 3 correct = Elaine"
Write-Host " `t`t 2 correct = George"
Write-Host " `t`t 1 correct = Newman"
Write-Host " `t`t 0 correct = Babo    (Clueless)"
Write-Host "`n`n`n`n Press Enter to continue."


#Pause script execution and wait for the player to press the Enter key
Read-Host
```

The statements shown above clear the screen and display text output using a series of Write-Host cmdlets. The script is then paused using the Read-Host cmdlet, forcing the player to press the Enter key in order to continue the quiz.

Displaying the First Quiz Question

The next step in the creation of the Seinfeld Trivia Quiz is the presentation of the first quiz question and the collection of the player's answer. The code statements required to present the game's first question are outlined next and should be appended to the end of the script file.

```
#Ask the player the first question
while (($question1 -ne "a") -and ($question1 -ne "b") `
  -and ($question1 -ne "c") -and ($question1 -ne "d")) {

  Clear-Host  #Clear the Windows command console screen

  Write-Host
  Write-Host " What is Kramer's first name?"
  Write-Host
  Write-Host " A. Peterman"
  Write-Host " B. Cosmo"
  Write-Host " C. Puddy"
  Write-Host " D. Peck"
  Write-Host
  $question1 = Read-Host " Type the letter representing the correct" `
    " answer and press the Enter key"

}
```

The overall logic of this portion of the script file is controlled by a while loop. Within the while loop, the Read-Host cmdlet is used to prompt the player to provide an answer to the first quiz question. The player's answer is stored in a variable named $question1. The loop is set up to execute until the player submits a valid answer to the first quiz question. Valid answers are a, A, b, B, c, C, d, or D. (Remember, by default Windows PowerShell is not case-sensitive.) If the player provides a valid answer, the loop stops executing and the script continues running. However, if the player fails to provide a valid response, the loop repeats itself, prompting the player to answer the question.

> The logic that makes up this portion of the script file consists of a number of programming statements that are not formally introduced until Chapters 5 and 6. Since this book has not yet covered these programming constructs, I will not cover them in detail now. These statements require the implementation of conditional and looping logic. For now, to make things a little easier to understand, I have added numerous comment statements to document what is occurring in this portion of the script file. I suggest that you return and review this portion of the script file once you have read Chapters 5 and 6.

Displaying the Remaining Quiz Questions

The statements that present the next four quiz questions and collect the player's answers are presented below and should be appended to the end of the script file.

```
#Clear the Windows command console screen
Clear-Host

#Ask the player the second question
while (($question2 -ne "a") -and ($question2 -ne "b") `
  -and ($question2 -ne "c") -and ($question2 -ne "d")) {

  Clear-Host  #Clear the Windows command console screen

  Write-Host
  Write-Host " What was George's favorite pretend career?"
  Write-Host
  Write-Host " A. Bra salesman"
  Write-Host " B. Real estate"
  Write-Host " C. City planner"
  Write-Host " D. Architect"
  Write-Host
```

```
  $question2 = Read-Host " Type the letter representing the correct" `
    "answer and press the Enter key"


}



#Clear the Windows command console screen
Clear-Host

#Ask the player the third question
while (($question3 -ne "a") -and ($question3 -ne "b") `
  -and ($question3 -ne "c") -and ($question3 -ne "d")) {

  Clear-Host  #Clear the Windows command console screen

  Write-Host
  Write-Host " For whom did Elaine buy white socks?"
  Write-Host
  Write-Host " A. Mr. Lippman"
  Write-Host " B. Mr. Peterman"
  Write-Host " C. Mr. Pitt"
  Write-Host " D. Puddy"
  Write-Host
  $question3 = Read-Host " Type the letter representing the correct" `
    "answer and press the Enter key"

}



#Clear the Windows command console screen
Clear-Host

#Ask the player the fourth question
while (($question4 -ne "a") -and ($question4 -ne "b") `
  -and ($question4 -ne "c") -and ($question4 -ne "d")) {

  Clear-Host  #Clear the Windows command console screen
```

```
Write-Host
Write-Host " What is Kramer scared of?"
Write-Host
Write-Host " A. Swimming"
Write-Host " B. Fried Chicken"
Write-Host " C. Clowns"
Write-Host " D. The dentist"
Write-Host
$question4 = Read-Host " Type the letter representing the correct" `
   "answer and press the Enter key"

}


#Clear the Windows command console screen
Clear-Host

#Ask the player the fifth question
while (($question5 -ne "a") -and ($question5 -ne "b") `
  -and ($question5 -ne "c") -and ($question5 -ne "d")) {

  Clear-Host  #Clear the Windows command console screen

  Write-Host
  Write-Host " Where do Jerry's parents live?"
  Write-Host
  Write-Host " A. Kansas"
  Write-Host " B. New York"
  Write-Host " C. California"
  Write-Host " D. Florida"
  Write-Host
  $question5 = Read-Host " Type the letter representing the correct" `
     "answer and press the Enter key"

}
```

As you can see, the presentation of the remaining quiz questions follows the same pattern as the first question, except for variations in the text strings that are displayed.

Let the Player Know the Quiz Is Complete

Once the player has finished answering each of the quiz's five questions, the script should pause to let the player know that the quiz will now be graded. This is accomplished by adding the following statements to the end of the script file.

```
#Clear the Windows command console screen
Clear-Host


Write-Host
Write-Host " OK, now press the Enter key to see how you did."


#Pause script execution and wait for the player to press the Enter key
Read-Host
```

As you can see, these statements use the Clear-Host cmdlet to clear the Windows command console screen, the Write-Host cmdlet to display text, and the Read-Host cmdlet to pause script execution until the player presses the Enter key.

Analyzing Player Answers

At this point, it is time to analyze each answer provided by the player to determine if it is right or wrong. This is accomplished by appending the following statements to the end of the script file.

```
#Clear the Windows command console screen
Clear-Host


#Grade the answers for each quiz question
if ($question1 -eq "b") { $noCorrect++ }   #The answer to question 1 is "B"
if ($question2 -eq "d") { $noCorrect++ }   #The answer to question 2 is "D"
if ($question3 -eq "c") { $noCorrect++ }   #The answer to question 3 is "C"
if ($question4 -eq "c") { $noCorrect++ }   #The answer to question 4 is "C"
if ($question5 -eq "d") { $noCorrect++ }   #The answer to question 5 is "D"
```

Each of the five if statements shown above is designed to address one of the quiz's questions. The first statement examines the player's first answer, which is stored in $question1, to see if it is equal to b. If it is, the value of the variable named $noCorrect is incremented by 1 using the ++ operator. The next four if statements are set up to analyze the player's answers to the remaining quiz questions.

Assigning a Ranking

Once the number of correctly answered quiz questions has been tabulated, the script needs to assign the player a ranking based on the resulting value. Specifically, the ranking assignment is made by comparing the value of $noCorrect to the values outlined in Table 4.6.

TABLE 4.6 RANK ASSIGNMENTS FOR THE SEINFELD TRIVIA QUIZ

Assignment	Description
Babo	Zero correct answers
Newman	One correct answer
George	Two correct answers
Elaine	Three correct answers
Kramer	Four correct answers
Jerry	Five correct answers

```
#Assign a ranking based on quiz score
if ($noCorrect -eq 0) {
  Write-Host
  Write-Host " You did not get any questions correct."
  Write-Host
  Write-Host " Your knowledge of Seinfeld trivia is no better than Babo's."
}

if ($noCorrect -eq 1) {
  Write-Host
  Write-Host " You got 1 question correct."
  Write-Host
  Write-Host " Your knowledge of Seinfeld trivia is no better than" `
    "Newman's."
}

if ($noCorrect -eq 2) {
  Write-Host
  Write-Host " You got 2 questions correct."
```

```
  Write-Host
  Write-Host " Your knowledge of Seinfeld trivia is approximately that" `
    "of George's."
}

if ($noCorrect -eq 3) {
  Write-Host
  Write-Host " You got 3 questions correct."
  Write-Host
  Write-Host " Your knowledge of Seinfeld trivia is approximately that" `
    "of Elaine's."
}

if ($noCorrect -eq 4) {
  Write-Host
  Write-Host " You got 4 questions correct."
  Write-Host
  Write-Host " Your knowledge of Seinfeld trivia is about as good as" `
    "Kramer's."
}

if ($noCorrect -eq 5) {
  Write-Host
  Write-Host " You got 5 questions correct."
  Write-Host
  Write-Host " Your knowledge of Seinfeld trivia is every bit as good" `
    "as Jerry's."
}


#Pause script execution and wait for the player to press the Enter key
Read-Host
```

The value of $noCorrect can only be equal to one of the values outlined in the five if statements mentioned previously. The matching if statement displays a series of text strings showing how many questions the player correctly answered and the ranking assigned as a result. The code statements embedded within the four non-matching if statements are ignored and never executed.

Finishing the Quiz

Once gameplay has been finished, the Seinfeld Trivia Quiz ends by thanking the player for taking the time to complete the quiz. This is accomplished by adding the following statements to the end of the script file.

```
#Clear the Windows command console screen
Clear-Host

#Provide the player with instructions
Write-Host
Write-Host " Thanks for taking the Seinfeld Trivia Quiz!"

#Pause script execution and wait for the player to press the Enter key
Read-Host


#Clear the Windows command console screen
Clear-Host
```

The player dismisses this screen by pressing the Enter key. The Windows command console screen is then cleared and the script file stops executing.

The Final Result

Okay, this should be everything you need to finish the development of the Seinfeld Trivia Quiz. Assuming that you have not made any typos when keying in the script file, everything should work as expected. In the event that an error does occur, then you have made a typo or two somewhere in the script file. In order to track down your errors, begin by analyzing the error message that was displayed when you tried to run your script. Hopefully, there will be enough information provided to help you track down the error. It may be that you made a typo or left out a statement somewhere along the way when keying in the script's statements. If your script file contains more than one error, you may have to go through several iterations before you eliminate all your errors.

SUMMARY

This chapter showed you how to store, retrieve, and modify data. You learned how to work with variables, arrays, and hashes. You also learned how to work with special built-in Windows PowerShell variables. You learned how to work with the -Replace operator to perform string substitution operations and the Range operator to generate a list of values. In addition, you learned how to concatenate strings, variables, and hashes. You also learned how to use Windows PowerShell escape characters to streamline and control the formatting of text output. Lastly, you learned how to create a new Windows PowerShell computer game, the Seinfeld Trivia Quiz.

Before you move on to the next chapter, take a few minutes to improve the Seinfeld Trivia Quiz by completing the following list of challenges.

CHALLENGES

1. Currently, the Seinfeld Trivia Quiz is limited to five questions. Make the quiz more challenging by adding questions of your own.

2. Rather than limiting the quiz to just multiple-choice questions, add differently formatted questions, such as true/false and fill in the blank.

3. As currently written, the game displays the number of quiz questions that the player correctly answered. However, additional detail regarding question results would provide the player with better feedback. Consider displaying a report at the end of the game that displays each question, the player's answer, and the correct answer.

CHAPTER 5

IMPLEMENTING CONDITIONAL LOGIC

The Windows PowerShell scripting language, just like every programming language, includes language statements that provide you with the ability to test and evaluate different conditions. Conditional logic is a fundamental component of programming logic and it is all but impossible to develop a PowerShell script of any level of complexity without using it. Conditional logic facilitates the evaluation of user, system, and file input against each other and against system resources. Based on the results of conditional tests, your PowerShell scripts can exercise tight control over which statements are executed, thus creating create dynamic scripts that adjust their execution according to the data they encounter.

In this chapter you will learn how to:

- Implement conditional logic using variations of the `if` statement
- Embed `if` statements inside one another to build more complex logic
- Use the `switch` statement to create logical tests that evaluate multiple conditions
- Work with different types of comparison and logical operators

PROJECT PREVIEW: THE GUESS MY NUMBER GAME

In this chapter, you will learn how to create a new Windows PowerShell game called the Guess My Number game. This game will challenge the player to guess a randomly generated number in the range of 1 to 100 in as few tries as possible. As Figure 5.1 shows, the game begins by displaying a welcome screen.

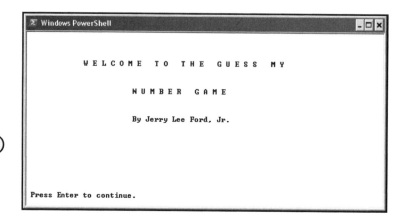

FIGURE 5.1

The opening screen for the Guess My Number game.

The player dismisses the welcome screen by pressing the Enter key. Next, the game displays the message shown in Figure 5.2, prompting the player to make an initial guess.

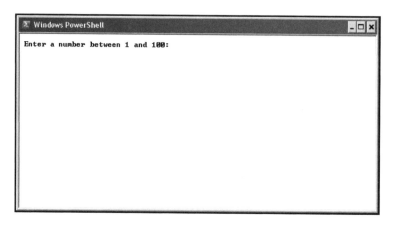

FIGURE 5.2

The game generates random numbers in the range of 1 to 100.

After each guess, the game analyzes the player's input to see if it was too high, too low, or if the player correctly guessed the game's secret number. Figure 5.3 shows the message displayed by the game when the player's guess is too low.

FIGURE 5.3

The game
provides the
player with clues
that assist in
homing in on the
secret number.

The game congratulates the player once the secret number is finally guessed, as demonstrated in Figure 5.4.

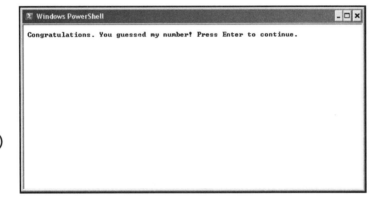

FIGURE 5.4

The player has
guessed the
secret number.

Next, game statistics are displayed that remind the player of the value of the secret number and then show how many guesses it took before the player was able to guess it, as demonstrated in Figure 5.5.

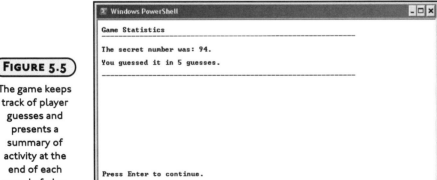

FIGURE 5.5

The game keeps
track of player
guesses and
presents a
summary of
activity at the
end of each
round of play.

After pressing the Enter key to dismiss the display of game statistics, the game invites the player to play another round, as shown in Figure 5.6.

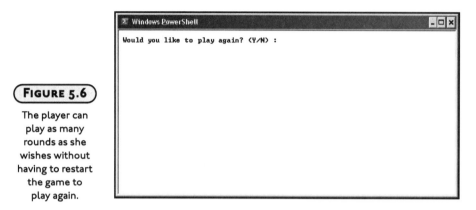

<blockquote>
Would you like to play again? (Y/N) :
</blockquote>

FIGURE 5.6

The player can play as many rounds as she wishes without having to restart the game to play again.

If the player enters Y, a new round of play is started. If the player enters N, the game ends and the player is returned to the Windows PowerShell command prompt. Any other input is rejected and the player is again prompted to make a decision as to whether to continue playing.

COMPARING VALUES

Windows PowerShell provides you with the ability to compare different resources, such as numbers and strings. To demonstrate this ability, start a new PowerShell session, type **5 -eq 5**, and press Enter, as demonstrated below.

```
PS C:\> 5 -eq 5
True
```

-eq is the PowerShell equals operator and is used in this example to determine whether two numbers are equal. Once evaluated, Windows PowerShell displays the result of its evaluation in the form of a Boolean true or false value. All comparison operations evaluate to a value of true or false. The next example demonstrates the results returned from the comparison between two unequal values.

```
PS C:\> 5 -eq 10
False
```

You can also compare different types of values such as strings and numbers, as demonstrated by the following.

```
PS C:\> 5 -eq "X"
False
```

In order to perform this evaluation, Windows PowerShell has to convert the values being compared to the same type. When faced with this situation, PowerShell attempts to convert the second value to the same type as the first value. A good example of how this type of conversion can result in a true value is provided here.

```
PS C:\> 5 -eq "5"
True
```

In this example, PowerShell converted the string "5" to its numeric equivalent. Windows PowerShell allows you to compare expressions of various levels of complexity, as demonstrated here.

```
PS C:\> 5 + 7 -eq 3 + 3 + 3 + 3
True
```

Once executed, the value of the expression on the left side of the operator evaluates to 12 as does the value of the expression on the right operator.

TRICK If you find yourself working from the Windows PowerShell command line and in need of doing a quick calculation or two, there is no need to stop what you are doing just so you can open up the calculator application and crunch a few numbers. Instead, you can save yourself a little time by using Windows PowerShell as your calculator. For example, if all you need it to do is multiply a couple numbers, just type them in using the appropriate PowerShell arithmetic operator, as demonstrated here.

```
PS C:\> 5 * 5
25
PS C:\>
```

Here, the expression 5 * 5 has been typed in at the PowerShell command prompt. When the Enter key is pressed, PowerShell resolves the expression and displays the result. As the following example demonstrates, you can key in more complex mathematic expressions if need be.

```
PS C:\> 20 * 5 / (10 + 15) * 3
12
PS C:\>
```

COMBINING PIPELINES AND OPERATORS

In addition to comparing strings and numbers, you can compare object data against different values as it passes through the PowerShell object pipeline. This provides you with the ability to select the data that you want to continue sending through the pipeline, thus discarding the data you do not need to process. For example, using the -eq operator, you can pull out the name of any currently executing processes, as demonstrated here.

```
PS C:\> Get-Process | Where-Object {$_.Processname -eq "Winword"}

Handles     NPM(K)      PM(K)       WS(K)       VM(M)       CPU(s)      Id ProcessName
-------     ------      -----       -----       -----       ------      -- -----------
237         11          7540        18992       110         5,286.61    1620 WINWORD

PS C:\>
```

As you can see, the Get-Process cmdlet has been executed. It generates a list of active processes running on the computer. This list is then piped to the Where-Object cmdlet, which evaluates each process looking for one named Winword. If found, information about the process is displayed.

This type of evaluation is not limited to just the Get-Process cmdlet. It can be applied to the output of any cmdlet. For example, this next set of statements processes the output generated by the Get-ChildItem cmdlet, looking for a particular folder.

```
PS C:\> Get-ChildItem | Where-Object {$_.Name -eq "MyScript"}

    Directory: Microsoft.PowerShell.Core\FileSystem::C:\

Mode            LastWriteTime               Length Name
----            -------------               ------ ----
d---            3/28/2006    1:56 PM               MyScripts

PS C:\>
```

IMPLEMENTING CONDITIONAL LOGIC

Comparison operations are a critical feature of PowerShell scripting and are required in all but the simplest PowerShell scripts. However, to be useful, you need to include comparisons as part of conditional statements. Windows PowerShell supports two different conditional logic statements, as outlined below.

- **if.** This statement evaluates a comparison and then executes or skips the execution of statements located in an associated code block.
- **switch.** This statement supports the execution of multiple comparison operations, each of which has the ability to execute statements embedded inside associated code blocks.

Comparing Data Using the if Statement

The if statement is used to test the value of a condition and to conditionally execute statements located in an associated code block based on the results of that evaluation. You have already seen the if statement in action on numerous occasions in this book. Its syntax is outlined here.

```
if (condition) {code block}
elseif (condition) {code block}
   .
   .
   .
else {code block}
```

condition is a placeholder representing an expression that evaluates to a Boolean value of true or false. *code block* is a placeholder representing any number of statements that are executed based on the results of the test. The if statement is very flexible and supports a number of different variations.

elseif is an optional statement that you can include to test an alternative condition. Windows PowerShell allows you to include as many elseif statements as you want. *else* is also an optional statement that, when added, executes its associated control block whenever none of the preceding conditional tests evaluate as being true.

The if, elseif, and else statements let you execute statements stored in code blocks based on the evaluation of a test, such as a variable, pipeline object, or an expression. If you create an if statement that contains multiple elseif evaluations, the code block belonging to the first test that evaluates to true is executed and the remaining statements in the if statement are skipped.

Formulating if Statements

To help you understand the basic concept behind the if statement, let's look at an example. Suppose you had trouble remembering to pay the rent, which is due on the 15th of every month. To help remind yourself, you might add a few lines of code to a PowerShell script that you run every day that checks the date and displays a message if it is the 15th of the month. In plain English, the logic required to develop this new logic is outlined here.

```
Get the date
if (Today is the 15th of the month)
{
  It is time to pay rent
```

```
}
else
{
   It is ok to go out to eat
}
```

As you can see, this pseudocode of an if statement very clearly outlines the logic involved using a combination of English and if statement syntax. To help highlight key syntactical elements, I have bolded key elements that make up the statements.

> **HINT**   *Pseudocode* is a term used to describe an English-like outline or sketch of some or all of the programming logic required to develop a script. By outlining the logic required to develop a script using pseudocode, programmers provide themselves with a roadmap that helps to guide the overall design of their scripts. This helps you to ensure that you know what you are going to do before you start doing it and can be used to help prevent errors and delays that can occur when you start working without a plan.

Using this pseudocode outline as a guide, you can then translate the English-like statements into PowerShell statements.

```
$today = Get-Date

if ($today.day -eq 15)
{
   Write-Host "Remember to pay the rent today."
}
else
{
   Write-Host "It is OK to go out to eat!"
}
```

In this example, a variable named $today is assigned a value representing the current date, which is retrieved by executing the Get-Date cmdlet. Next, an if statement has been set up that evaluates the expression $today.day -eq 15. The first part of this expression retrieves the day property associated with the current date. This value is then compared to a value of 15 to see if the two values are equal. If they are, the statement stored in the if statement's code block is executed. If these two values are not equal, the statement embedded in the optional else statement's code block is executed.

Single Line if Statements

In its simplest form, the if statement consists of a single statement:

```
if ($x -eq 10) {Write-Host "Game over!"}
```

In this example, the value of $x is tested to see if it is equal to 10. If this text evaluates to true, the Write-Host cmdlet located inside the if statement's code block is executed. This form of the if statement is best applied to simple conditional tests that contain a single statement in its code block. For situations where more than one statement must be executed inside the code block, the multiline form of the if statements should be used.

Multiline if Statements

Often, you will want to execute a number of statements based on the evaluation of a conditional test. In these situations, you can apply an if statement, as demonstrated here.

```
if ($x -eq 10) {
  Clear-Host
  Display-Host "Game over! Press Enter to continue."
  Read-Host
}
```

As this example demonstrates, you can embed any number of statements in an if statement's code block. In this example, if the value of $x is equal to 10, all of the statements inside the code block's opening and closing brackets are executed. If, however, the value of $x is not equal to 10, the statements located inside the code block are skipped.

Providing an Alternative Course of Action

The if statement is extremely flexible. By including an optional else statement, you can add additional logic that provides for an alternative course of action in the event the tested condition evaluates as false. For example, you might use the else statement to modify the previous example as shown here.

```
if ($x -eq 10) {
  Clear-Host
  Display-Host "Game over! Press Enter to continue."
  Read-Host
}
else {
  Clear-Host
```

```
Display-Host "Press Enter to try again."
   Read-Host
}
```

Figure 5.7 provides a flowchart overview of the logic implemented in the previous example.

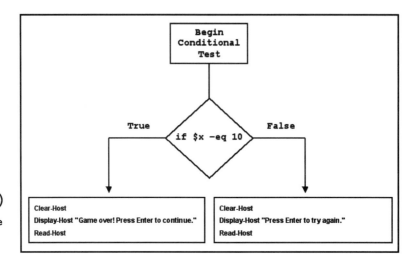

 A *flowchart* is a tool used by programmers to graphically depict the logical flow of all or part of a script. By creating a flowchart, you can visually lay out the overall logical flow of your PowerShell scripts. Once created, you can use a flowchart to help guide the development of the script.

Testing Different Conditions

The if statement can also be expanded by including one or more optional elseif statements. Each elseif statement provides you with the ability to test for different conditions, as demonstrated here.

```
if ($x -eq 10) {
  Clear-Host
  Write-Host "Game over! Press Enter to continue."
  Read-Host
}
elseif ($x -eq 20) {
  Clear-Host
  Write-Host "Invalid guess. Press Enter to try again."
  Read-Host
```

```
}
elseif ($x -eq 30) {
  Clear-Host
  Write-Host "Invalid input. Press Enter to try again."
  Read-Host
}
else {
  Clear-Host
  Write-Host "Unknown error. Press Enter to try again."
  Read-Host
}
```

Here, three separate conditions are evaluated. Windows PowerShell begins this example by testing the value of the first condition ($x -eq 10). If this test evaluates as being true, the three statements in its code block are executed and the rest of the statements in the if statement are skipped. If the condition evaluates as being false, the condition associated with the first elseif statement is executed. If it evaluates as being true, the statements in its code block are executed and the rest of the statements in the if statement are skipped. Otherwise, the elseif statement's code block is skipped and the next elseif statement condition is evaluated. If its condition evaluates as true, its code block executes and the rest of the statements in the if statement are skipped. If none of the previous tested conditions evaluate as being true, the code block associated with the else statement is executed.

 HINT If you find yourself creating if statements that consist of numerous elseif statements that evaluate against the same value, you may be better off using a switch statement, discussed in the next section.

Nesting if Statements

Windows PowerShell lets you nest, or embed, one if statement within another in order to develop complex conditional tests. Nested if statements allow you to build programming logic that begins by testing for one condition before deciding whether to further analyze things by performing additional tests.

As an example of the usefulness of nesting if statements, consider the following (which was extracted from the Fortune Teller game that you developed in Chapter 3, "Object-Based Scripting with .NET").

```
#Select an answer based on the time and random number
#If it is the afternoon, the fortune teller will be a little cranky
```

```
if ($time -gt 12) {
  Write-Host
  if ($answer -eq 1) { " Grrrr. The answer is no!" }
  if ($answer -eq 2) { " Grrrr. The answer is never!" }
  if ($answer -eq 3) { " Grrrr. The answer is unclear!" }
  if ($answer -eq 4) { " Grrrr. The answer is yes!" }
}
#If it is morning, the fortune teller will be in a good mood
else {
  Write-Host
  if ($answer -eq 1) { " Ah. The answer is yes!" }
  if ($answer -eq 2) { " Ah. The answer is always!" }
  if ($answer -eq 3) { " Ah. The answer is uncertain!" }
  if ($answer -eq 4) { " Ah. The answer is no!" }
}
```

In this example, the if statement checks to see if $time is greater than 12. If it is, a series of four if statements, embedded in its code block, are executed, each of which evaluates the value of a variable named $answer, in order to determine which answer to return to the player. If the opening if statement evaluates as being false, an else statement executes instead. Note that four if statements have been embedded within the else statement's code block as well.

Making Multiple Comparisons Using the switch Statement

if statements provide you with the ability to compare two conditions. By adding elseif statements, you can create if statements that perform additional tests. As the number of additional tests increases, they can become difficult to formulate and understand. Windows PowerShell provides you with access to the switch statement as an alternative. The switch statement is used to define a collection of different test and code blocks, each of which evaluates against the same expression.

The syntax implemented by the switch statement is outlined here.

```
switch (expression)
{
  {test} {code block}
  value {code block}
  default {code block}
}
```

The switch statement begins by defining the expression against which all comparisons inside its code block are evaluated. The switch statement supports any of three different types of comparison operations, as outlined here.

- **Test.** An expression whose value is evaluated.
- **Value.** A literal value, such as a string or number.
- **Default.** Specifies a default code block that is executed if none of the previously defined comparisons evaluate as being true.

Unlike the if statement, switch statements do not stop executing once a matching value has been found. Instead, every test specified within a switch statement is evaluated, thus potentially resulting in some or all of the embedded code blocks being executed. The optional default component and its associated code block are only executed in the event that none of the previously defined tests evaluate as being true.

To get a good idea of how to work with the switch statement, consider the following example.

```
$today = get-date

switch ($today.Day)
{
  1 {Write-Host "Payday!"}
  5 {Write-Host "It is time to water the plants."}
  10 {Write-Host "Remember to pay the bills."}
  15 {Write-Host "Payday!"}
  20 {Write-Host "It is time to water the plants."}
  25 {Write-Host "It is time to clean the garage again."}
  default {Write-Host "There are no calendar entries to remember today."}
}
```

Here, a series of six conditional tests have been defined, each of which is compared to the value of $today.Day. Because each of the values being compared is distinct, only one can result in a match. However, if you were to rework this example by adding additional tests as shown next, multiple matches could occur and, as has been stated, the switch statement will execute the code block belonging to any matching statements.

```
$today = get-date

switch ($today.Day)
{
```

```
 1 {Write-Host "Payday!"}
 1 {Write-Host "It is time to water the plants."}
 5 {Write-Host "It is time to water the plants."}
10 {Write-Host "Remember to pay the bills."}
10 {Write-Host "It is time to water the plants."}
15 {Write-Host "Payday!"}
15 {Write-Host "It is time to water the plants."}
20 {Write-Host "It is time to water the plants."}
25 {Write-Host "It is time to clean the garage again."}
25 {Write-Host "It is time to water the plants."}
default {Write-Host "There are no calendar entries to remember today."}
}
```

As you can see, for all but two dates, multiple matches can occur, resulting in the execution of multiple code blocks. Even though these examples shown here have included single statements inside each switch statement code block, there is no limit to the number of statements that you can include.

WINDOWS POWERSHELL OPERATORS

So far, you have seen the equals (-eg) operator used extensively in this chapter as a means of comparing different values. Windows PowerShell provides a host of additional operators that provide you with the ability to test different relationships between values and to reverse the logic of comparison operators.

Comparison Operators

Windows PowerShell supports a number of additional comparison operators in addition to the -eq operator, allowing you to perform comparisons that provide you with the ability to test different values in different ways. For example, you can also compare whether a value is greater than or less than another value. Table 5.1 lists Windows PowerShell comparison operators.

Unlike arithmetic operators, Windows PowerShell does not process comparison operators according to a predefined order or precedence. Instead, each comparison operation is performed in the order in which you define it, starting from left to right. You will see several examples of these operators in action a little later when you work on the Guess My Number game.

TABLE 5.1 WINDOWS POWERSHELL COMPARISON OPERATORS

Operator	Description
-eq	Equal to
-lt	Less than
-gt	Greater than
-ge	Greater than or equal to
-le	Less than or equal to
-ne	Not equal to

Logical Operators

Windows PowerShell provides a small set of logical operators that provides you with the ability to modify the logical evaluation of a comparison. Table 5.2 lists Windows PowerShell logical operators.

TABLE 5.2 WINDOWS POWERSHELL LOGICAL OPERATORS

Operator	Description
-not	Not
!	Not
-and	And
-or	Or

The -not and ! operators can be used to reverse the logic of any comparison operation, as demonstrated here.

```
$x = 1
$y = 2
if (-not ($x -eq $y)) {Write-Host 'The value of $X does not equal $y.'}
if (! ($x -eq $y)) {Write-Host 'The value of $X does not equal $y.'}
```

As you can see, to use either the -not or ! operator, you must place it just before the expression or value to be tested. When executed, these operators reverse the logic of a comparison operation.

TRAP Take note of the location and placement of the parentheses in the previous examples. The inclusion of the -not and ! operators require that you add an additional set of parentheses in order to meet the syntax requirement of the if statement, which requires that whatever is being tested be enclosed inside parentheses.

The -and operator, on the other hand, is used to create a comparison operation that checks to see whether two different expressions or values both evaluate to true, as demonstrated by the following.

```
$x = 1
$y = 2
if (($x -eq 1) -and ($y -eq 2)) {Write-Host 'The variables equal the expected values.'}
```

In this example, the statement inside the if statement's code block is executed only if both expressions being tested by the if statement evaluate to true. Since both of the expressions evaluated in the previous example evaluate as being true, the statement located inside the if statement's code block is executed.

To help speed up the logical processing of the -and operator, Windows PowerShell implements a process called short-circuiting, whereby the second expression is evaluated only in the event the first expression proves true. If the first expression proves to be false, there is no point to evaluating the second expression, since the end result of the -and logical comparison will result in a value of false regardless of the result of the value of the second expression.

The -or operator is also short-circuited. This operator checks to see whether either of two different expressions or values evaluates to true, as demonstrated here.

```
$x = 1
$y = 2
if (($x -eq 1) -and ($y -eq 3)) {Write-Host 'At least one value matched..'}
```

In the previous example, the first expression evaluates as true and the second expression evaluates as false. As long as one of the tested expressions evaluates as true, the statement located inside the if statement's code block is executed.

String Comparison Operators

While you can certainly use the six comparison operators listed in Table 5.1 to compare strings, the result is a case-insensitive comparison. As a result, PowerShell will evaluate strings such as "abc" and "ABC" as being equal, even though that was not your intention. If string case is important in your comparison operators, you can instead use any of the case-sensitive string-comparison operators listed in Table 5.3.

TABLE 5.3 WINDOWS POWERSHELL STRING COMPARISON OPERATORS

Operator	Description	Case-Sensitive
-ieq	Equal to	No
-ilt	Less than	No
-igt	Greater than	No
-ige	Greater than or equal to	No
-ile	Less than or equal to	No
-ine	Not equal	No
-ceq	Equal to	Yes
-clt	Less than	Yes
-cgt	Greater than	Yes
-cge	Greater than or equal to	Yes
-cle	Less than or equal to	Yes
-cne	Not equal to	Yes

As you can see, Table 5.3 contains two different categories of operators: those that perform case-sensitive comparison and those that do not. As an example of the difference between these two categories of string comparison operators, consider the following example.

```
$x = "abc"
$y = "ABC"
if ($x -ieq $y) {Write-Host 'A case-insensitive match has occurred!'}
if ($x -ceq $y) {Write-Host 'A case-sensitive match has occurred!'}
```

In this example, the first if statement performs a case-insensitive comparison, which results in an evaluation of true. However, the second if statement performs a case-sensitive comparison, which results in a value of false.

BACK TO THE GUESS MY NUMBER GAME

Okay, let's turn your attention back to the chapter's main game project, the Guess My Number game. Through the development of this game, you will get ample opportunity to focus on the use of conditional logic in order to control the logical execution of Windows PowerShell scripts.

Designing the Game

The Guess My Number game begins by displaying the game's welcome screen and then prompts the player to guess the game's randomly generated number, which is in the range of 1 to 100. Each guess made by the player is evaluated to see if it is too high, too low, or if the player has guessed the number. The game displays hints to help guide the player's next guess when the player's previous guess is too high or too low. Game statistics are displayed after the player guesses the game's secret number and then the player is invited to play another round.

The Guess My Number game will be completed in 12 steps, as outlined here:

1. Create a new script file and add opening comment statements.
2. Define and initialize the game's variables.
3. Display the opening welcome screen.
4. Set up a loop to control overall gameplay.
5. Generate the game's secret number.
6. Set up a loop to collect and analyze player guesses.
7. Collect the player's input.
8. Analyze player input.
9. Display the game's statistics.
10. Prompt the player to play another game.
11. Analyze the player's answer.
12. Clear the screen prior to terminating.

Creating a New Script

The first step in creating the Guess My Number game is to create a new PowerShell file named GuessMyNumber.ps1 and add the following statements to it.

```
# **********************************************************************
#
# Script Name: GuessMyNumber.ps1 (The Guess My Number Game)
# Version:     1.0
# Author:      Jerry Lee Ford, Jr.
# Date:        January 1, 2007
#
# Description: This PowerShell script challenges the player to attempt
#              to guess a randomly generated number in the range of
#              1 to 100 in as few guesses as possible.
#
# **********************************************************************

#Clear the Windows command console screen
Clear-Host
```

As was the case with previous game scripts, you should begin this script using the Windows PowerShell template developed in Chapter 2, "Interacting with the Windows PowerShell Command Line." In addition, you'll notice that I have added the script's first statement, which executes the Clear-Host cmdlet in order to clear the display area.

Define and Initialize Game Variables

The next step in the development of the Guess My Number game is to define and initialize variables used throughout the script. This is accomplished by appending the statements shown below to the end of the script file.

```
#Define variables used in this script
$number = 0                              #Keeps track of the game's secret number
$noOfGuesses = 0                         #Keeps track of the number of guesses made
$randomNo = New-Object System.Random     #This variable stores a random object
$playGame = "Yes"                        #Controls when to quit the game
$status = "Play"                         #Controls the current round of play
$guess = 0                               #Stores the player's guess
$reply = ""                              #Stores the player's response when asked to
                                         play again
```

Comments have been provided for each of the seven variables defined in order to document and explain their purpose.

Displaying the Welcome Screen

Next, let's set up the game's welcome screen by adding the following statements to the end of the script file.

```
#Display the game's opening screen
Write-Host "`n`n`n`n`t    W E L C O M E    T O    T H E    G U E S S    M Y"
Write-Host "`n`n`n`t`t`tN U M B E R    G A M E"
Write-Host "`n`n`n`t`t`tBy Jerry Lee Ford, Jr."
Write-Host "`n`n`n`n`n`n`n`n`n Press Enter to continue."

#Pause the game until the player presses the Enter key
Read-Host
```

As you can see, the game's welcome screen consists of a series of Write-Host cmdlets whose text is formatted using the `n and `t escape characters. The `n escape character generates newline commands and the `t escape character inserts tab commands. The last statement uses the Read-Host cmdlet to pause script execution and wait until the player presses the Enter key.

Setting Up a Loop to Control Gameplay

The overall execution of the game is controlled by a while loop that executes until the player decides to terminate the game. This is accomplished by adding the following statements to the end of the script file.

```
#Loop until the player decides to quit the game
while ($playGame -ne "No") {



}
```

As you can see, the while loop's execution is controlled by the value assigned to the $playGame variable, which is set equal to No later in the script once the player decides to stop playing the game. Except for the execution of the Clear-Host cmdlet at the very end of the script file, all of the remaining code statements that make up the Guess My Number game are going to be embedded within this while loop.

Generating a Random Number

The next task to be completed is the generation of the game's secret number, which is generated using the random object's Next method. This is accomplished by adding the following statement to the beginning of the while loop that you defined in the previous section.

```
#Generate the game's random number (between 1 - 100)
$number = $randomNo.Next(1, 101)
```

Setting Up a Loop to Collect and Analyze Player Guesses

The next step is to clear the screen and prompt the player to make a guess, which is accomplished by adding the following statements just after the previous statements.

```
#Clear the Windows command console screen
Clear-Host
```

```
#Loop until the player guesses the secret number
while ($status -ne "Stop") {



}
```

This while loop will be used to control player input and ensure that the input is acceptable. The loops will execute until the value of $status is set equal to Stop. The code statements outlined in the next two sections will be embedded within this loop.

Collecting Player Input

The code statement shown next must be keyed in to the previous while loop and is responsible for collecting the user's input.

```
#Prompt the player to guess a number
while ($guess -eq "") {

  Clear-Host  #Clear the Windows command console screen

  Write-Host

  #Collect the player's guess
  $guess = Read-Host " Enter a number between 1 and 100"

}
```

The loop is designed to repeat in the event the player presses the Enter key without entering any input. Within this loop, the screen is cleared and the Read-Host cmdlet is used to prompt the player to take a guess. The player's answer is then stored in a variable named $guess.

Analyzing Player Input

Now that you have added the code statements required to collect the player's guess, you need to add the following statements immediately after the preceding section's statements.

```
#Keep track of the number of guesses made so far
$noOfGuesses++


if ($guess -lt $number) {  #The player's guess was too low

  Clear-Host  #Clear the Windows command console screen
  Write-Host "`n Sorry. Your guess was too low. Press Enter to" `
    "guess again."
  $guess = ""  #Reset the player's guess
  Read-Host  #Pause the game until the player presses the Enter key

}
elseif ($guess -gt $number) {  #The player's guess was too high

  Clear-Host  #Clear the Windows command console screen
  Write-Host "`n Sorry. Your guess was too high. Press Enter to" `
    "guess again."
  $guess = ""  #Reset the player's guess
  Read-Host  #Pause the game until the player presses the Enter key

}
else {  #The player has guessed the game's secret number

  Clear-Host  #Clear the Windows command console screen
  Write-Host "`n Congratulations. You guessed my number! Press Enter" `
    "to continue."
  $status = "Stop"  #Reset the player's guess
  Read-Host  #Pause the game until the player presses the Enter key

}
```

The first statement increments the value of $noOfGuesses in order to keep track of the number of guesses that the player has made thus far in the game. The rest of the statements are organized by an if statement. The if statement is set up to test whether the value of the player's guess, stored in $guess, is less than the game's random number's which is stored in

$number. If $guess is less than $number, then a message is displayed informing the player that her guess was too low and $guess is set equal to an empty string ("") in order to ready it for the player's next guess.

Next, an elseif statement has been set up to respond in the event the player's guess was too high. Lastly, an else statement is defined that executes when the player correctly guesses the game's secret number. Note that if this is the case, the $status variable is assigned a value of Stop in order to signal that the current round of play is over.

Displaying Game Statistics

The next set of program statements needs to be added to the end of the game's main controlling while loop.

```
#Clear the Windows command console screen
Clear-Host

#Display the game's opening screen
Write-Host "`n Game Statistics"
Write-Host " ---------------------------------"
Write-Host "`n The secret number was: $number."
Write-Host "`n You guessed it in $noOfGuesses guesses.`n"
Write-Host " ---------------------------------"
Write-Host "`n`n`n`n`n`n`n`n`n`n`n`n`n`n Press Enter to continue."

#Pause the game until the player presses the Enter key
Read-Host
```

As you can see, these statements are responsible for clearing the Windows command console and then displaying game statistics. These statistics are stored in the $number and $noOfGuesses variables.

Prompting the Player to Play Again

At this point, it is time to prompt the player to play another game and to validate the player's response. This is accomplished by appending the following statements to the end of the game's while loop, just beneath the previous sets of statements.

```
#Clear the Windows command console screen
Clear-Host

$reply = ""  #Stores the player's response when asked to play again
```

```
#Prompt the player to play another round
while ($reply -eq "") {

  Clear-Host  #Clear the Windows command console screen

  Write-Host

  #Collect the player's answer
  $reply = Read-Host " Would you like to play again? (Y/N) "

  #Validate player input, allowing only Y and N as acceptable responses
  if (($reply -ne "Y") -and ($reply -ne "N")) {

    $reply = ""  #Reset the variable to its default value

  }

}
```

After clearing the screen, a variable named $reply is defined. This variable is used to store the player's response when prompted to play another game. The Read-Host cmdlet is used to prompt the player to play again. An if statement is then set up to validate the player's input, ensuring that only a response of Y or N has been provided. A value of Y indicates that the player would like to play another game, whereas a value of N indicates that the player is ready to terminate gameplay.

Analyzing the Player's Response

Once valid input has been received, the game needs to respond by either resetting game variables to their default settings to prepare the game for a new round of play or by setting $playGame equal to No, thus terminating the game's main while loop upon its next iteration. This is accomplished by adding the following statements to the end of the game's main while loop.

```
#The player has elected to play again
if ($reply -eq "Y") {

  #Reset variables to their default values
  $number = 0
  $noOfGuesses = 0
```

```
   $status = "Play"
   $guess = 0

}
else {    #The player has decided to quit playing

  $playGame = "No"  #Modify variable indicating that it is time to
                    #terminate gameplay

}
```

Clearing the Screen

Finally, to finish the development of the game, add the following statements to the end of the script file, just after the end of its main `while` loop.

```
#Clear the Windows command console screen
Clear-Host
```

After executing the `Clear-Host` cmdlet, the script will end, returning the player back to the Windows PowerShell command prompt.

The Final Result

Ordinarily, I would write a script like Guess My Number using functions to help organize and modularize the script's logic into discrete units. However, because I have not covered that topic yet, I had to take a different approach, which involved developing some fairly complex programming logic that was embedded inside a series of `while` loops.

When laying out the code of this game, I chose to take the approach of having you first define each `while` loop and then come back and add in its code statements as separate steps. This helped to break the game's code statements into smaller groupings but also required that you be extra careful when following behind and keying in the code statements. To help make sure that you understand what the final result should look like, I have laid out the entire script for you here:

```
# ***********************************************************************
#
# Script Name: GuessMyNumber.ps1 (The Guess My Number Game)
# Version:     1.0
# Author:      Jerry Lee Ford, Jr.
# Date:        January 1, 2007
```

```
#
# Description: This PowerShell script challenges the player to attempt
#              to guess a randomly generated number in the range of
#              1 to 100 in as few guesses as possible.
#
# ************************************************************************


#Clear the Windows command console screen
Clear-Host

#Define variables used in this script
$number = 0           #Keeps track of the game's secret number
$noOfGuesses = 0      #Keeps track of the number of guesses made
$randomNo = New-Object System.Random

1  #This variable stores a random object
$playGame = "Yes"     #Controls when to quit the game
$status = "Play"      #Controls the current round of play
$guess = 0            #Stores the player's guess
$reply = ""           #Stores the player's response when asked to play again

#Display the game's opening screen
Write-Host "`n`n`n`n`t   W E L C O M E   T O   T H E   G U E S S   M Y"
Write-Host "`n`n`n`t`t`tN U M B E R   G A M E"
Write-Host "`n`n`n`t`t`tBy Jerry Lee Ford, Jr."
Write-Host "`n`n`n`n`n`n`n`n`n Press Enter to continue."

#Pause the game until the player presses the Enter key
Read-Host

#Loop until the player decides to quit the game
while ($playGame -ne "No") {

  #Generate the game's random number (between 1 - 100)
  $number = $randomNo.Next(1, 101)

  #Clear the Windows command console screen
  Clear-Host
```

```
#Loop until the player guesses the secret number
while ($status -ne "Stop") {

  #Prompt the player to guess a number
  while ($guess -eq "") {

    Clear-Host  #Clear the Windows command console screen

    Write-Host

    #Collect the player's guess
    $guess = Read-Host " Enter a number between 1 and 100"

  }

  #Keep track of the number of guesses made so far
  $noOfGuesses++

  if ($guess -lt $number) {  #The player's guess was too low

    Clear-Host  #Clear the Windows command console screen
    Write-Host "`n Sorry. Your guess was too low. Press Enter to" `
      "guess again."
    $guess = ""  #Reset the player's guess
    Read-Host  #Pause the game until the player presses the Enter key

  }
  elseif ($guess -gt $number) {  #The player's guess was too high

    Clear-Host  #Clear the Windows command console screen
    Write-Host "`n Sorry. Your guess was too high. Press Enter to" `
      "guess again."
    $guess = ""  #Reset the player's guess
    Read-Host  #Pause the game until the player presses the Enter key

  }
  else {  #The player has guessed the game's secret number
```

```
         Clear-Host  #Clear the Windows command console screen
         Write-Host "`n Congratulations. You guessed my number! Press Enter" `
           "to continue."
         $status = "Stop"  #Reset the player's guess
         Read-Host  #Pause the game until the player presses the Enter key


      }


   }


   #Clear the Windows command console screen
   Clear-Host


   #Display the game's opening screen
   Write-Host "`n Game Statistics"
   Write-Host " ————————————————————————————"
   Write-Host "`n The secret number was: $number."
   Write-Host "`n You guessed it in $noOfGuesses guesses.`n"
Write-Host " ————————————————————————————"
   Write-Host "`n`n`n`n`n`n`n`n`n`n`n`n`n Press Enter to continue."


   #Pause the game until the player presses the Enter key
   Read-Host


   #Clear the Windows command console screen
   Clear-Host


   $reply = ""  #Stores the player's response when asked to play again


   #Prompt the player to play another round
   while ($reply -eq "") {

      Clear-Host  #Clear the Windows command console screen

      Write-Host

      #Collect the player's answer
```

```
$reply = Read-Host " Would you like to play again? (Y/N) "


    #Validate player input, allowing only Y and N as acceptable responses
    if (($reply -ne "Y") -and ($reply -ne "N")) {

        $reply = ""  #Reset the variable to its default value


    }


}


#The player has elected to play again
if ($reply -eq "Y") {

    #Reset variables to their default values
    $number = 0
    $noOfGuesses = 0
    $status = "Play"
    $guess = 0


}
else {    #The player has decided to quit playing

    $playGame = "No"  #Modify variable indicating that it is time to
                        #terminate gameplay


}


}


#Clear the Windows command console screen
Clear-Host
```

Well, that's it. As long as you did not make any typos when keying it in, your version of the Guess My Number game should be ready to run.

SUMMARY

In this chapter you learned how to work with the if and switch statements to develop conditional logic that controls the execution of groups of statements within your Windows PowerShell scripts. Conditional logic facilitates the evaluation of user, system, and file input against each other and against system resources. You also learned how to work with a host of different PowerShell operators, including the logical -and and -or operators which further facilitate the development of conditional logic.

Now, before you move on to Chapter 6, "Using Loops to Process Data," why don't you set aside a little extra time to work on and improve the Guess My Number game by tackling the following list of challenges?

CHALLENGES

1. As it is currently written, the Guess My Number game provides somewhat cryptic messages when interacting with the user. Consider making the game more intuitive by adding additional instructions and guidance.

2. Consider tracking and displaying additional game statistics. For example, you might create a new variable that keeps track of the total number of games played. You might also keep track of the number of low versus high guesses in order to help players detect any trends in their methods of play (e.g., a tendency to guess too low too often).

3. Consider modifying the game to allow the player to quit at any time, instead of just at the end of the current round of play. For example, in addition to looking for a number in the range of 1 to 100, you might also look for the user to instead type a Q, signaling a desire to quit.

4. Rather than arbitrarily using a range of 1 to 100, consider giving the player the option of specifying a different range. For example, you might offer to allow the player to select from three different ranges, such as 1 to 10, 1 to 100 or 1 to 1,000.

USING LOOPS TO PROCESS DATA

As you have certainly noticed already in previous chapters, loops are an essential element in most scripts, allowing you to develop programming logic that repeats a series of statements over and over again using a minimal amount of code. Without loops, it would be all but impossible to develop Windows PowerShell scripts that are designed to process large amounts of data. Loops also provide you with a mechanism for processing collections of data passed through the object pipeline or stored in arrays. Windows PowerShell provides you with the ability to set up many different types of loops and also provides you with commands for breaking out of loops when necessary. This chapter will not only teach you how to implement loops but also guide you through the creation of your next Windows PowerShell script, the Rock, Paper, Scissors game.

Specifically, you will learn the following:

- How to set up do while and do until loops
- How to set up for and foreach loops
- How to create while loops
- How to use the Continue and Break keywords to alter loop execution

PROJECT PREVIEW: THE ROCK, PAPER, SCISSORS GAME

This chapter's game project is based on the classic children's Rock, Paper, Scissors game. In this game, the player goes head to head against the computer. As with the previous games that you have seen in this book, the Rock, Paper, Scissors game begins by displaying a welcome screen, as shown in Figure 6.1.

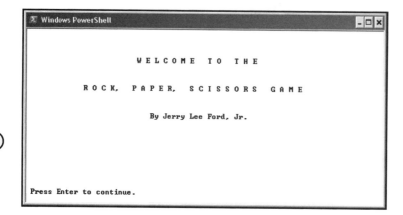

FIGURE 6.1

The welcome screen for the Rock, Paper, Scissors game.

After dismissing the welcome screen, the player is prompted to make a move by specifying R for rock, P for paper, or S for scissors, as shown in Figure 6.2. Alternatively, the player can quit the game at any time by entering Q.

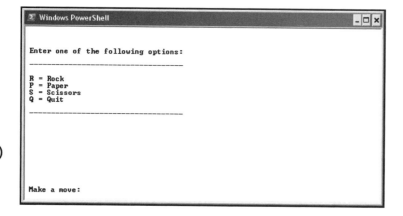

FIGURE 6.2

Four options are available to the player.

As soon as the player makes a move, the game generates the computer's move and then determines the winner of the current round of play, as demonstrated in Figure 6.3.

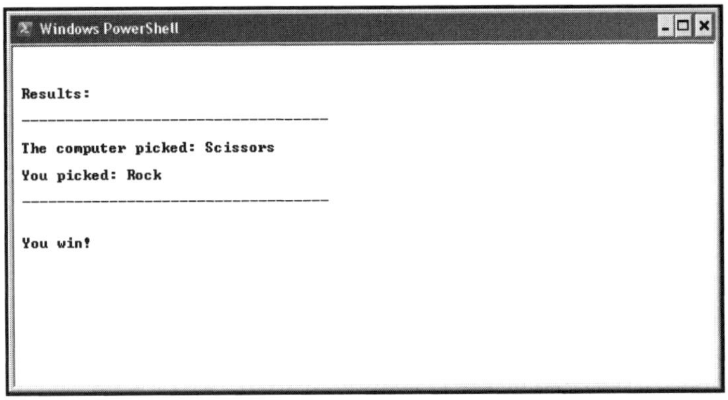

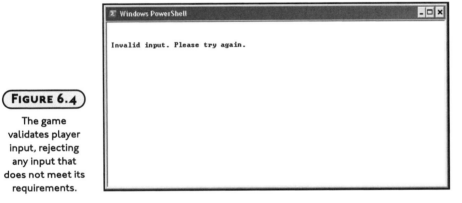

FIGURE 6.3

All games result in a win, loss, or tie.

If the player enters anything other than R, P, S, or Q, the message shown in Figure 6.4 is displayed. After dismissing the message, the player is again prompted to make a move.

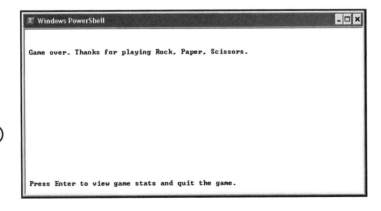

FIGURE 6.4

The game validates player input, rejecting any input that does not meet its requirements.

Game play ends when the player enters Q. In response, the game displays the screen shown in Figure 6.5, thanking the player for playing.

FIGURE 6.5

The player has decided to stop playing Rock, Paper, Scissors.

Finally, just before ending, the game displays statistics that it has been accumulating as demonstrated in Figure 6.6.

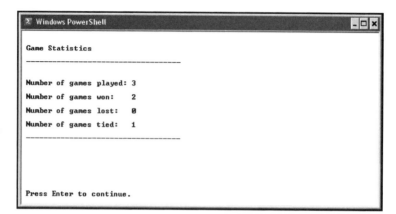

```
Game Statistics
-----------------------------------------

Number of games played: 3
Number of games won:     2
Number of games lost:    0
Number of games tied:    1
-----------------------------------------



Press Enter to continue.
```

FIGURE 6.6

The game keeps track of wins, losses, ties, and the number of games played.

WORKING WITH LOOPS

In order to effectively repeat a series of commands or to process large amounts of data, you need the ability to create loops. A *loop* is a set of programming statements that can be repeatedly executed as a unit. A loop allows you to write a few lines of code and execute them over and over in order to perform a great deal of work. Loops help to reduce the number of code statements required to write a PowerShell script and, by centralizing a specific set of programming logic, help to make your scripts more manageable.

Loops are a good tool for processing the contents of arrays and collections of data returned by cmdlets. As you have already seen, loops can also be set up to repeatedly prompt a user to supply valid input and to repeatedly execute a collection of statements until a specific result is achieved. Windows PowerShell provides you with access to a number of different types of loops, including:

- `do while`. Iterates as long as a specified condition is true
- `do until`. Iterates until a specified condition is true
- `for`. Iterates a set number of times
- `foreach`. Iterates through all of the elements stored in a collection or array
- `while`. Iterates as long as a specified condition is true

You will learn how to work with each of these types of loops in the sections that follow.

In addition to the language looping statements listed previously, Windows PowerShell also provides you with access to the Where-Object and Foreach-Object cmdlets. As you have already seen, these cmdlets let you loop through and process lists of data as they pass through the object pipeline.

Setting Up do while Loops

do while loops execute as long as, or while, the tested condition remains true. Because the condition being tested is evaluated at the end of the loop, you can count on the loop always executing at least one time. The syntax of the do while loop is as follows.

```
do {
    code block
} while (condition)
```

condition is an expression that is tested at the end of each iteration of the loop. An example of how to work with the do while loop is provided here.

```
$i = 1

do {
    Write-Host $i
    $i++
} while ($i -le 10)
```

In this example, a variable named $i is set equal to 1 and then used within the do while loop that follows. Inside the loop, the value of $i is displayed and then incremented by 1. The conditional test, located at the end of the loop, is then evaluated, and as long as the value of $i remains less than 10, the loop continues executing. When run, this example displays the following results.

```
1
2
3
4
5
6
7
8
9
10
```

One of the things that you need to watch out for when developing your PowerShell scripts is an endless loop. An *endless loop* is a loop that never terminates and thus runs forever, draining the computer's resources. An endless loop occurs when you create a loop that has no way of stopping its own execution. In other words, you either forgot to provide a means for terminating it or applied faulty logic allowing the loop to continue processing forever.

If, while testing a PowerShell script, you think something has gone wrong and that an endless loop may be executing, you can break out of the loop and terminate your script by pressing Ctrl + C.

Setting Up do until Loops

The `do until` loop executes until a test condition evaluates to true. To put it another way, the `do until` loop executes as long as a condition is false. Like the `do while` loop, the test performed by the `do until` loop is specified at the bottom of the loop, thus ensuring that the loop always executes at least once.

The syntax of the `do until` loop is shown here.

```
do {
    code block
} until (condition)
```

To see how to work with this type of loop, consider the following example.

```
$i = 1

do {
    Write-Host $i
    $i++
} until ($i -gt 10)
```

This example is very similar to the `do while` example, except that this time the loop has been set up to run until the value of `$i` is greater than 10. When executed, this example counts to 10 exactly like the `do while` loop did, demonstrating that each of these two loops can be used interchangeably. The `do until` loop can also be used to control the collection of user input as demonstrated in the following example.

```
$response = "Play"

do {
```

```
$response = Read-Host "Do you want to play again (Y/N)"
} until ($response -eq "N")
```

Here, a loop has been set up that prompts the user to respond with a value of Y or N. If the user enters Y, the loop repeats. If this were a real script, the loop would include additional logic required to perform a particular task, which would be performed again each time the user responded with an input of Y. As is, the loop continues to run and to prompt the user for input until the user finally enters a response of N. An example of the output generated by this example is shown here.

```
Do you want to play again (Y/N): y
Do you want to play again (Y/N): y
Do you want to play again (Y/N): y
Do you want to play again (Y/N): y
Do you want to play again (Y/N): n
PS C:\>
```

Creating for Loops

The for statement is used to create a loop that runs until a specified condition becomes true. The for loop supports a number of different variations but is generally used to execute a specific number of times, based on the value of a variable that is used as a counter to keep track of the number of iterations made by the loop. The value of the counter can be increased or decreased based on the logic being implemented.

The syntax of the for loop is shown here.

```
for (initialization; condition; step)
{code block}
```

All three parameters specified above are optional. *initialization* is a placeholder representing a variable that will be used to control the execution of the loop. *condition* represents an expression that is evaluated each time the loop iterates to determine whether the loop should run again. As along as the value of the *condition* remains true, the loop will run again. *step* specifies an incremental value that is added to the value specified by the *initialization* placeholder. If not specified, Windows PowerShell uses a default value of 1 for *step*.

As the following example demonstrates, all of the parameters that make up the for loop are optional.

```
for (;;) {
  Write-Host "Hi!."
}
```

When executed, this example begins looping forever as the following output demonstrates. To terminate the loop's executions, you must press Ctrl + C in order to force the termination of the script.

```
Hi!
Hi!
Hi!
 .

 .

 .
```

The for loop has limited value when used in this manner. Instead, it is more typical that the for loops be set up using all of their parameters as demonstrated here.

```
for ($i = 1; $i -le 10; $i++) {
   Write-Host $i
}
```

In this example, a for loop has been set up to iterate 10, displaying the value of $i upon each iteration. Before starting, the loop defines and initializes a variable named $i, setting it equal to 1. The loop is set up to iterate as long as the value of $i is less than 10. The value of $i is incremented by 1 at the end of each iteration of the loop. When executed, this example displays the following output.

```
1
2
3
4
5
6
7
8
9
10
```

As you can see, the for loop is very flexible. For example, the value assigned to the *step* parameter at the end of each iteration can be decremented instead of incremented, as demonstrated in the following example.

```
for ($i = 10; $i -ge 1; $i--) {
   Write-Host $i
}
```

Here, the value of $i is initially set equal to 10 and is decremented by one each time the loop iterates, resulting in the following output.

```
10
9
8
7
6
5
4
3
2
1
```

The for loop can also be used to process the contents of arrays as demonstrated in the following example.

```
$numbers = @( "a", "b", "c", "d", "e")

for ($i = 0; $i -le $numbers.Length - 1; $i++) {
  Write-Host $numbers[$i]
}
```

Here, an array named $numbers is created and populated with a list of 10 numbers. Next, a for loop is defined. The value of a variable named $i is defined and initialized with a value of 1. Next, the *condition* parameter is defined and consists of an expression that uses the array's Length property to determine the length of the array and then subtracts 1 from this value (since arrays are zero based). Lastly, the value of $i is incremented each time the loop iterates. The output produced when this loop executed is shown below.

```
a
b
c
d
e
```

The value assigned to the *step* parameter does not need to always be 1. As the following example demonstrates, you can increment (or decrement) this value by any value you want.

```
$numbers = @(1, 2, 3, 4, 5, 6, 7, 8, 9, 10)

for ($i = 0; $i -le $numbers.Length - 1; $i += 2) {
```

```
Write-Host $numbers[$i]
}
```

Here, the value of $i is incremented by two upon each iteration of the loop, resulting in the following output.

```
1
3
5
7
9
```

As you can see, by incrementing the value of $i by two each time the loop iterates, every other value in the $numbers array was processed.

 For more information on the for loop, enter Get-Help about_for at the Windows PowerShell command prompt.

Creating foreach Loops

The foreach loop is designed to facilitate the processing of collections of data. It is tailor-made to process lists, including arrays, in which you do not know in advance how many elements are stored. While you could certainly use other types of loops to do the same thing, the foreach loop offers a convenient way to process lists because it does not require you to set and increment an index number.

The syntax of the foreach loop is shown here.

```
foreach (element in collection)
{code block}
```

element is a placeholder representing an element stored in the collection. Upon each iteration of the loop, the value of element is updated with the next item stored in the collection. collection is the name of the array to be processed.

The following example demonstrates how to set up a foreach loop in order to process the contents of an array.

```
$numbers = @(1, 2, 3, 4, 5, 6, 7, 8, 9, 10)

foreach ($i in $numbers) {
   Write-Host $i
}
```

In this example, an array named $numbers has been defined and assigned a list of 10 num-bers. A foreach loop is then set up to process each element stored in the array. Upon the first iteration of the loop, the first element in the array is assigned to $i and the Write-Host cmdlet is then used to display its value. Upon the second iteration, the value of $i assigned the value of the second array element. Processing continues until all array elements have been processed. If executed, this example would display the output shown here.

```
1
2
3
4
5
6
7
8
9
10
```

The foreach loop can also be used to process data returned by cmdlets such as Get-Process and Get-ChildItem that return results in the form of a collection. For example, the following statements can be added to a Windows PowerShell script to generate a list of all services cur-rently running on the computer.

```
foreach ($x in Get-Service) {

  if ($x.Status -eq "Running") {Write-Host $x.Name}

}
```

As you can see, this example uses a foreach loop to iterate though the output generated by the Get-Service cmdlet. Each time the loop iterates the name of a service, it is assigned to $x. An if statement is then used to examine the Status property for each service to deter-mine whether it is equal to Running. The Write-Host cmdlet is then used to display the name of each running service by referencing each service's Name property. When executed, this example will produce output similar to the following.

```
ALG
AudioSrv
Browser
CryptSvc
DcomLaunch
```

```
Dhcp
Dnscache
ERSvc
Eventlog
EventSystem
FastUserSwitchingCompatibility
helpsvc
lanmanserver
lanmanworkstation
LmHosts
LxrSII1s
Netman
Nla
NVSvc
omniserv
PlugPlay
Pml Driver HPZ12
PolicyAgent
ProtectedStorage
RasMan
RpcSs
SamSs
Schedule
seclogon
SENS
SharedAccess
ShellHWDetection
Spooler
srservice
SSDPSRV
stisvc
TapiSrv
TermService
Themes
TrkWks
UMWdf
W32Time
WebClient
```

```
winmgmt
wscsvc
wuauserv
WUSB54Gv4SVC
```

As the preceding example demonstrates, `foreach` loops can be used to iterate through all of the command output generated by any cmdlet that generates its output in the form of a collection and does so without requiring that you define and maintain a counter or provide any other controlling logic.

 For more information on the `foreach` loop, enter `Get-Help about_foreach` at the Windows PowerShell command prompt.

Using while Loops

The `while` loop is designed to create a loop that runs as long as, or while, its conditional test remains true. The `while` loop has the following syntax.

```
while (condition)
{code block}
```

`condition` is an expression, which is evaluated each time the loop is run. If the value of `condition` evaluates to true, the loop is run. Otherwise, its execution terminates. Obviously, in order to prevent an endless loop, it is important that you include the programming logic required to terminate the loop.

The following example demonstrates how to set up a `while` loop.

```
$i = 1

while ($i -le 10) {
  Write-Host $i
  $i++
}
```

Here, a variable named `$i` is defined and assigned an initial value of 1. Next, a `while` loop is defined that executes as long as, or while, the value of `$i` remains less than 10.

```
1
2
3
4
```

```
5
6
7
8
9
10
```

You will see examples of the while loop in action later when you work on this chapter's game script.

For more information on the while loop, enter Get-Help about_while at the Windows PowerShell command prompt.

ALTERING LOOP EXECUTION

Sometimes certain conditions may occur in which you will want to prematurely terminate the execution of a loop. For example, if you wrote a foreach loop in order to search an array for a given element and you found that element somewhere in the middle of the array, rather than iterating through the rest of the array just for the fun of it, you'll probably want to break out of the loop and get on with the business at hand. Alternatively, you may want to prematurely stop the current iteration of a loop without actually terminating the loop itself. Windows PowerShell supports both of these actions through the break and continue commands.

Using the break Command

When the break command is executed, the innermost loop is terminated and processing control jumps to the next statement that follows the end of the loop.

Loops can be a little confusing to work with when you are just starting out as a new programmer. The reason I stated that the break command terminates the execution of the "innermost" loop in the preceding sentence is because loops can be embedded within one another. The break command will terminate the inner loop in which it is embedded but will have no impact on the outer loop.

The following example demonstrates how to use the break command to terminate the processing of a loop.

```
for ($i = 1; $i -le 10; $i++) {
  if ($i -eq 5) {
```

```
      break
   }
   Write-Host $i
}
```

Here, a for loop has been set up to execute 10 times. Within the loop, an if statement has been added that inspects the value of $i upon each iteration. Upon finding that $i equals 5, the if statement executes the break command, thus terminating the loop and resulting in the following output.

```
1
2
3
4
```

Using the continue Command

When the continue command is executed, the current iteration of the innermost loop is terminated. However, the loop keeps on executing, if appropriate. For example, if a PowerShell script executed the continue command while in the middle of processing an array, and the continue command was executed, any processing for the current array element would be skipped and the loop would continue on processing the rest of the elements stored in the array.

The following example demonstrates how to use the continue command to interrupt the processing of a loop and force it to resume execution back at the beginning of the loop.

```
$i = 1

while ($i -le 10) {

   if ($i -eq 5) {
     $i++
     continue
   }

   Write-Host $i
   $i++

}
```

Here, a while loop has been set up to execute 10 times. Within the while loop, an if statement has been defined that executes the continue command when the value of $i becomes equal to 5. When this occurs, the current iteration of the loop is terminated and the loop resumes executing back at the beginning of the loop. The end result is that the fifth iteration of the loop is never finished and the number 5 is not displayed in the output generated by the example, as shown here.

```
1
2
3
4
6
7
8
8
9
10
```

TRICK   Windows PowerShell also supports the exit command. When executed, this command terminates the execution of the entire script, not just the current iteration of a loop. An example of how to use the exit command is provided here.

```
if ($x -gt 100) {
  Write-Host "Error - Maximum value exceeded."
  exit
}
```

When included as part of a PowerShell script, the if statement shown above will terminate the script's execution if it gets executed and the value of $x exceeds 100. If run at the Windows PowerShell command line, the exit command will close the current PowerShell session and also close the Windows command console window.

BACK TO THE ROCK, PAPER, SCISSORS GAME

Okay, it is time to turn your attention back to the chapter's main game project, the Rock, Paper, Scissors game. The development of this game will demonstrate how to control script execution using loops to facilitate input collection as well as to control the termination of gameplay.

Designing the Game

The Rock, Paper, Scissors game challenges the player to outguess the computer by selecting superior moves each time a new round is played, based on the scoring rules outlined in Table 6.1.

Player Choice	Computer Choice	Results
Rock	Rock	Tie
Rock	Scissors	Player Wins
Rock	Paper	Player Loses
Paper	Paper	Tie
Paper	Rock	Player Wins
Paper	Scissors	Player Loses
Scissors	Scissors	Tie
Scissors	Paper	Player Wins
Scissors	Rock	Player Loses

TABLE 6.1 ROCK, PAPER, SCISSORS SCORING RULES

The player's move is specified by entering a letter corresponding to a valid move (R for Rock, P for Paper, or S for Scissors). The computer's move is generated based on a randomly selected number. In addition to guiding the player through each round of play, the game continuously collects a number of game statistics (total games played, wins, losses, and ties), which are displayed at the end of the game.

The overall logical flow of the Rock, Paper, Scissors game is fairly simple. To set it up, we will complete its development in twelve steps, as outlined here:

1. Create a new script file.
2. Define and initialize script variables.
3. Display the game's welcome screen.
4. Set up a loop to control gameplay.
5. Generate the computer's move.
6. Prompt the player to make a move.

7. Validate the player's move.

8. Translate the player's move.

9. Display the computer's and player's moves.

10. Analyze the results of gameplay.

11. Reset variable values for a new round of play.

12. Display game statistics.

Creating a New Script File

Let's begin the development of the Rock, Paper, Scissors game by creating a new PowerShell file named RockPaperScissors.ps1 and adding the following statements to it.

```
# ************************************************************************
#
# Script Name:    RockPaperScissors.ps1 (The Rock, Paper, Scissors Game)
# Version:        1.0
# Author:         Jerry Lee Ford, Jr.
# Date:           January 1, 2007
#
# Description:    This PowerShell script challenges the player to beat the
#                 computer in a game of Rock, Paper, Scissors
#
#
# ************************************************************************


#Clear the Windows command console screen
Clear-Host
```

Defining and Initializing Script Variables

Next, let's define and initialize variables used throughout the script by appending the following statements to the end of the script file.

```
#Define variables used in this script
$playGame = "True" #This variable controls game play
$randomNo = New-Object System.Random  #This variable stores a random object
$number = 0           #This variable stores the numeric version of the
                      #computer's move
$guess = 0            #This variable stores the numeric version of the
                      #player's move
```

```
$playerMove = ""        #This variable stores the string version of the
                        #player's move
$computerMove = ""      #This variable stores the string version of the
                        #computer's move
$noPlayed = 0           #This variable keeps track of the number of games
                        #played
$noWon = 0              #This variable keeps track of the number of games won
$noLost = 0             #This variable keeps track of the number of games lost
$noTied = 0             #This variable keeps track of the number of games tied
```

As you can see, comments were added to document the use and purpose of each variable.

Displaying the Game's Welcome Screen

The next step is to add the programming statements that are responsible for displaying the game's welcome screen. These statements, provided next, should be added to the end of the script file.

```
#Display the game's opening screen
Write-Host "`n`n`n`n`t`t`tW E L C O M E   T O   T H E"
Write-Host "`n`n`n`t      R O C K,   P A P E R,   S C I S S O R S   G A M E"
Write-Host "`n`n`n`t`t`t    By Jerry Lee Ford, Jr."
Write-Host "`n`n`n`n`n`n`n`n`n Press Enter to continue."

#Pause the game until the player presses the Enter key
Read-Host
```

Setting Up a Loop to Control Gameplay

The overall execution of the Rock, Paper, Scissors game is controlled by a while loop. To set it up, add the following statements to the end of the script file.

```
#Loop until the player guesses the secret number
while ($playGame -ne "False") {



}
```

As shown above, this loop is set up to execute until the value of $playGame is set equal to false. This variable is set to true at the beginning of the game and remains that way until the player later decides to stop playing by entering Q (for quit) when prompted to play another round. The rest of the statement that makes up the Rock, Paper, Scissors game will be added to this loop, with the exception of the statements that display game statistics at the very end of the game.

Generating the Computer's Move

As has been the case with previous game scripts, a random number must be generated. This time, the random number will be used to select the computer move each time a new round of play occurs. The statements responsible for generating this random number and for associating that number with a specific move are shown in the following code, and should be added to the beginning of the while loop (after the opening curly brace) that you created in the previous section.

```
#Generate the game's random number (between 1 - 3)
#Value assignment: 1 = Rock, 2 = Paper and 3 = Scissors
$number = $randomNo.Next(1, 4)

#Translate the computer's move to English
if ($number -eq 1) {$computerMove = "Rock"}
if ($number -eq 2) {$computerMove = "Paper"}
if ($number -eq 3) {$computerMove = "Scissors"}
```

As you can see, the game generated a number in the range of 1 to 3. A value of 1 will represent a move of Rock. A value of 2 will represent a move of Paper, and a value of 3 represents a move of Scissors.

Prompting the Player to Make a Move

Next, the game needs to prompt the player to make a move, which is accomplished by appending the following statements to the end of the game's main while loop, just before the closing curly brace.

```
#Prompt the player to guess a number
while ($guess -eq "") {

  Clear-Host  #Clear the Windows command console screen

  #Display instructions
  Write-Host "`n`n"
  Write-Host " Enter one of the following options:`n"
  Write-Host " --------------------`n"
```

```
Write-Host " R = Rock"
Write-Host " P = Paper"
Write-Host " S = Scissors"
Write-Host " Q = Quit`n"
Write-Host " ------------------------`n`n`n`n`n`n`n`n`n"

    #Collect the player's guess
    $guess = Read-Host " Make a move"


}
```

Here, another while loop has been set up that prompted the player to enter one of four menu options. The player's input is then stored in a variable named $guess.

Validating the Player's Move

After the player has responded to the prompt to make a move, the game needs to validate the player's input to ensure that it is valid. This is accomplished by appending the following statements to the end of the game's main while loop.

```
#validate the player move
if ($guess -eq "Q") {   #Player has decided to quit playing

    Clear-Host  #Clear the Windows command console screen

    Write-Host "`n`n"
    Write-Host " Game over. Thanks for playing Rock, Paper, Scissors."
    Write-Host "`n`n`n`n`n`n`n`n`n`n`n`n`n`n`n`n`n"
    Write-host " Press Enter to view game stats and quit the game."

    Read-Host  #Pause while the player reads the screen

    $playGame = "False"  #Set variable to false indicating the game is over

    continue  #Skip the remainder of the loop

}
elseif (($guess -ne "R") -and ($guess -ne "P") -and ($guess -ne "S")) {

    Clear-Host  #Clear the Windows command console screen
```

```
Write-Host "`n`n`n Invalid input. Please try again."

Read-Host  #Pause while the player reads the screen

$guess = ""  #Clear out the player's previous guess

continue  #Skip the remainder of the loop
```

}

Here, an if statement has been set up to determine if the player entered a value of Q or q. If this is the case, a message is displayed thanking the player for playing the game and then the value of $playGame is set equal to false. This signals the player's decision to halt gameplay. Next, a continue command is executed, halting the current execution of the loop.

If the player did not enter Q when prompted to make a move, an elseif statement is then executed in order to determine whether the player entered an R, a P, or an S (i.e., a valid move). If the player did not enter a valid move, an error message is displayed asking the player to try again and the value of $guess is set to an empty string to ready the game for another guess. Finally, the continue command is executed, forcing a new iteration of the loop.

Assuming that the player entered a valid move, the code in this if statement and its associated elseif statement is skipped and processing continues with the code statements outlined in the next section.

Translating the Player's Move

Next, add the following statements to the end of the game's main while loop. These statements will execute only if the statements defined in the previous section have validated the player's move.

```
#Translate the player's move to English
if ($guess -eq "R") {$playerMove = "Rock"}
if ($guess -eq "P") {$playerMove = "Paper"}
if ($guess -eq "S") {$playerMove = "Scissors"}
```

As you can see, these statements consist of three if statements that assign a value of Rock, Paper, or Scissors to the $playerMove variable based on the player's move (as specified by the value of $guess).

Displaying the Computer's and Player's Moves

The next set of statements, which should be added to the end of the script's main `while` loop, begin the process of displaying the results of the current round of play. Specifically, they use the `Write-Host` cmdlet to display the value of the `$computerMove` and `$playerMove` variables, thus displaying the moves attributed to the computer and player.

```
Clear-Host  #Clear the Windows command console screen

Write-Host " `n`n`n Results:`n"
Write-Host " -------------------------`n"
Write-Host " The computer picked: $computerMove`n"
Write-Host " You picked: $playerMove`n"
Write-Host " -------------------------`n`n"

$noPlayed += 1  #Increment count by 1
```

In addition to displaying the moves made during the current round of play, the last statement shown above incremented the value of `$noPlayed`. This variable is used to keep track of the total number of rounds played since the Rock, Paper, Scissors game was started.

Analyzing the Results of Gameplay

Next, the game needs to figure out whether the player has won, lost, or tied the game and then display the results of this analysis, which is accomplished by adding the following statements to the end of the script's main `while` loop.

```
switch ($computerMove)
{

  "Rock" {  #The computer picked rock

    if ($playerMove -eq "Rock") {
      $noTied += 1  #Increment count by 1
      Write-Host " You tie!"
    }

    if ($playerMove -eq "Paper") {
      $noWon += 1  #Increment count by 1
      Write-Host " You win!"
    }
```

```powershell
      if ($playerMove -eq "Scissors") {
        $noLost += 1   #Increment count by 1
        Write-Host " You lose!"
      }

    }

    "Paper" { #The computer picked paper

      if ($playerMove -eq "Rock") {
        $noLost += 1   #Increment count by 1
        Write-Host " You lose!"
      }

      if ($playerMove -eq "Paper") {
        $noTied += 1   #Increment count by 1
        Write-Host " You tie!"
      }

      if ($playerMove -eq "Scissors") {
        $noWon += 1   #Increment count by 1
        Write-Host " You win!"
      }

    }

    "Scissors" { #The computer picked scissors

      if ($playerMove -eq "Rock") {
        $noWon += 1   #Increment count by 1
        Write-Host " You win!"
      }

      if ($playerMove -eq "Paper") {
        $noLost += 1   #Increment count by 1
        Write-Host " You lose!"
      }

      if ($playerMove -eq "Scissors") {
```

```
      $noTied += 1  #Increment count by 1
      Write-Host " You tie!"
    }

  }

}


#Pause the game until the player presses the Enter key
Read-Host
```

As you can see, these statements have been organized into three tests by the switch statement. The first test checks to see if the computer's move, as indicated by $computerMove, is equal to Rock. Likewise, the next two tests examine whether the computer's move is Paper or Scissors. Within each of these three tests, three if statements are defined that are responsible for comparing the player's move, as indicated by $playerMove, to the computer's move to determine the results of the current round of play. Based on the results of this analysis, a message is displayed showing the results. Also, inside each if statement is a statement that increments the value of the $noTied, $noWon, and $noLost variables as appropriate, thus keeping track of game statistics.

Resetting Variable Values for a New Round of Play

The last set of statements to be added to the end of the game's main while loop are outlined below. These statements are responsible for resetting variable values to their default setting in order to ready the game for a new round of play.

```
#Reset variables to prepare for a new round of play
$number = 0          #Reset the computer's guess back to zero
$guess = 0           #Reset the numeric version of the player's guess
                     #back to zero
$playerMove = ""     #Reset the string version of the player's guess back
                     #to an empty string
$computerMove = ""   #Reset the string version of the player's guess
                     #back to an empty string
```

Displaying Game Statistics

The last task performed by the game before it stops running is the display of statistics collected during gameplay. The statements that display this information are outlined in the following code and should be added to the end of the script file below the main while loop.

```
#Clear the Windows command console screen
Clear-Host

#Display the game statistics
Write-Host "`n`n`n Game Statistics`n"
Write-Host " —————————————————--`n"
Write-Host "`n Number of games played: $noPlayed"
Write-Host "`n Number of games won:    $noWon"
Write-Host "`n Number of games lost:   $noLost"
Write-Host "`n Number of games tied:   $noTied`n"
Write-Host " ———————————————--"
Write-Host "`n`n`n`n`n`n Press Enter to continue."

#Pause the game until the player presses the Enter key
Read-Host

#Clear the Windows command console screen
Clear-Host
```

As you can see, these statements clear the screen and display game statistics, stored in variables embedded inside a series of strings.

The Final Result

Well, that's it. At this point your Rock, Paper, Scissors scripts should be ready to run. So, go ahead and see how it works. If you run into any errors, use the error messages that are displayed to locate the area within your script where errors are occurring and then double-check your typing in order to find out where you may have made a typo or two.

SUMMARY

In this chapter you learned how to set up the execution of do while, do until, for, foreach, and while loops. Using these loops, you can create and execute programming logic that repeatedly processes collections of statements in a centralized location in order to process large amounts of data. Loops also serve as an effective tool for repeatedly executing a series of commands over and over again—for example, when prompting for and validating user input. As you have seen, you can also use loops to process data passed through the object pipeline or stored in arrays. You also learned how to use the break and continue commands to exercise control over the execution of loops.

Now, before you move on to Chapter 7, "Organizing Scripts Using Functions," why don't you set aside a little extra time to improve the Rock, Paper, Scissors game by tackling the following list of challenges?

CHALLENGES

1. As currently written, the Rock, Paper, Scissors game is a little cryptic. Consider adding additional text throughout the game to provide the player with a more user-friendly experience.

2. In addition to the four options displayed at the beginning of each player turn, consider adding an option that provides the player with access to a help screen from which players unfamiliar with the Rock, Paper, Scissors game can learn the rules for playing the game.

3. At the end of the game, statistics are displayed that show the player the number of games won, lost, and tied. In addition to showing the player these raw numbers, consider doing a little arithmetic and providing the player with some percentages (e.g., the percentage of games won, lost, and tied).

4. Consider providing the user with the ability to display game statistics at any point during the game. For example, you might provide the player with the ability to enter S in order to display the game statistics.

ORGANIZING SCRIPTS USING FUNCTIONS

One missing tool in your Windows PowerShell programming arsenal is the ability to organize your PowerShell scripts into functions. Functions allow you to write code statements once in a named code block and then call upon them for execution as many times as necessary from anywhere in your PowerShell script. By helping to centralize programming logic, functions make your program code easier to maintain and understand. Functions also affect variable scope, allowing you to further localize variable access, thus helping you to write tighter code. This chapter will teach you how to work with functions. In addition, you will also learn how to work with filters, which, although similar to functions, provide you with a tool for handling large amounts of object pipeline data more efficiently. You will also learn how to create your next computer game, the PowerShell Hangman game.

Specifically, you will learn how to do the following:

- Set up functions to perform specific tasks
- Develop functions that accept arguments and return a result
- Use functions as a means of limiting scope
- Create filters in order to efficiently process object pipeline data

PROJECT PREVIEW: THE POWERSHELL HANGMAN GAME

This chapter's game project is the PowerShell Hangman game. Although a little different from the traditional children's hangman game, this PowerShell game still captures the spirit of the original. When first started, the game displays the screen shown in Figure 7.1, welcoming the player and prompting her for permission to start a round of play.

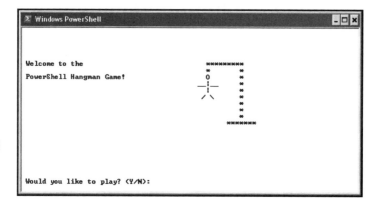

FIGURE 7.1

The PowerShell Hangman game's welcome screen.

After getting the player's permission to start a new round, the game prompts the player to make a guess, as demonstrated in Figure 7.2.

FIGURE 7.2

The player must enter a single character guess and press the Enter key.

After each guess, the game displays a screen similar to the one shown in Figure 7.3. The player is given a maximum of 12 guesses to guess the game's secret word, which is represented by a series of underscore characters. This screen also lists every valid guess made so far by the player (invalid guesses, such as numbers and most special characters are not accepted or counted against the player). This screen also keeps the player informed of how many guesses she has left.

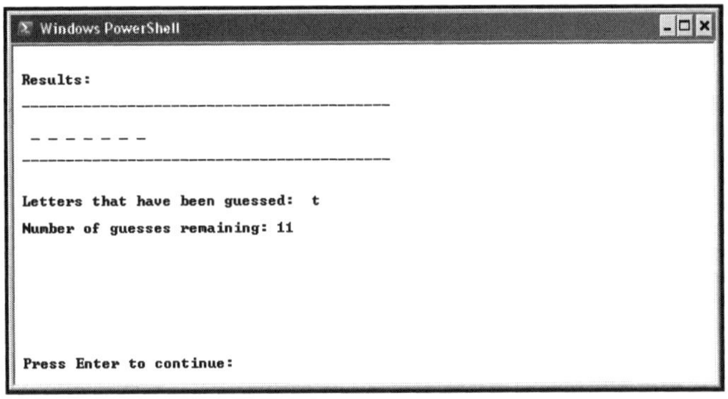

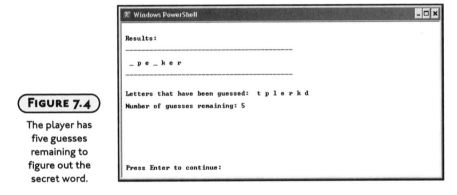

FIGURE 7.3

The player has missed her first guess.

Figure 7.4 shows how the game might look after the player has made a number of additional guesses.

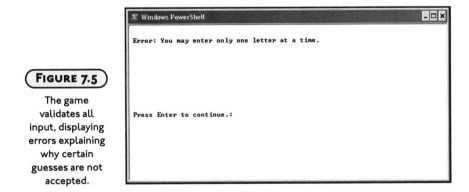

FIGURE 7.4

The player has five guesses remaining to figure out the secret word.

The game rejects guesses consisting of most special characters, numbers, or multiple letters. For example, Figure 7.5 shows the screen that is displayed in the event the player attempts to enter more than one letter at a time.

FIGURE 7.5

The game validates all input, displaying errors explaining why certain guesses are not accepted.

Gameplay ends when the player guesses the secret word, at which time the screen shown in Figure 7.6 is displayed, acknowledging the player's success and informing her how many guesses were necessary to win.

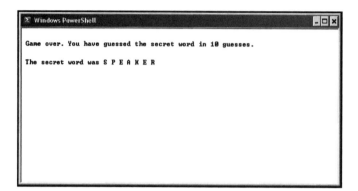

FIGURE 7.6

The player has won the game by guessing the secret number.

Gameplay also ends when the player runs out of guesses, as demonstrated in Figure 7.7.

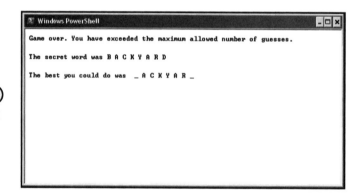

FIGURE 7.7

The player failed to guess the game's secret word before running out of guesses.

CHANGING SCRIPT DESIGN USING FUNCTIONS AND FILTERS

In the last couple chapters you were introduced to a number of different programming constructs that you can use to improve the overall organization of your Windows PowerShell scripts. Using the `if` and `switch` statements, you learned how to set up conditional tests and to group related sets of statements for execution when certain conditions evaluate as being true. Using the `do while`, `do until`, `for`, `foreach`, and `while` loops, you learned how to group related statements that perform a given task repeatedly, centralizing key programming logic and reducing the overall number of code statements required to create PowerShell scripts. Now it is time to learn about functions and filters.

A *function* is a named code block that can be executed by referencing its name. When called, all of the statements inside a code block are evaluated and executed. Functions can accept arguments and return a result. A *filter* is very similar to a function. There is nothing that you can do with a filter that you cannot do with a function. The difference between the two is that filters are designed to more efficiently process large amounts of object pipeline data.

HINT Predefined functions abound in Windows PowerShell. For example, when you type **C:** or **D:** to switch between drives at the Windows PowerShell command prompt, you are actually executing functions that in turn make calls to the Set-Location cmdlet.

Improving Script Organization

One of the primary benefits of functions is that they help to reduce the number of lines of code required to write a script. Functions also facilitate the modular development of scripts by providing you with the ability to organize code statements into named code blocks, which can then be executed over and over again from any location within the script file. Functions make your Windows PowerShell scripts more manageable, providing you with the building blocks required to create larger and more complex scripts without necessarily increasing complexity or ending up with tons of code. For example, suppose you were planning on writing a new PowerShell game that performs the following tasks.

- Prompts the player for permission to execute
- Displays a welcome screen
- Manages the collection of user input
- Displays a short story incorporating user input
- Prompts the player to play again

One way to develop this script would be to begin by defining any variables that are needed followed by a series of functions, each of which is responsible for managing one of the tasks outlined above. The rest of the script would then consist of programming logic that calls upon these functions when needed.

Creating Reusable Code

As has already been stated, functions provide you with a way of improving the organization of your PowerShell script files by letting you group related sets of code statements together and then making them callable from any location within the script.

HINT I strongly suggest that you use functions as the primary organizational tool within all your Windows PowerShell scripts. Using functions to organize script files, you can break things down into smaller and more easily manageable units. This will help you to separate your programming logic into discrete modules, which can be created and tested a unit at a time.

Perhaps the biggest benefit provided by functions is their ability to assist you in the development of reusable code. As a general rule, anytime you find that you need to perform a given task more than once, such as retrieving random numbers each time a new round of gameplay is started, it is probably a good candidate for inclusion in a function. Once created, you can call upon a given function as many time as necessary, using a single calling statement, thus facilitating code reuse and resulting in a leaner and meaner PowerShell script.

ENHANCING SCRIPT ORGANIZATION WITH FUNCTIONS

Using functions, you can break down your Windows PowerShell scripts into manageable blocks of code, calling on each block as appropriate. Functions provide you with the building blocks required to build modular code, thus facilitating code maintenance. Code testing is also simplified because, using functions, you can develop your PowerShell script in small chunks, each of which can be individually tested and verified. Functions also result in smaller scripts. Smaller scripts are easier to understand and maintain. After all, it is a lot easier to modify statements located in a single function than it would be to modify that same set of statements if they were instead used over and over again in different parts of a script file.

Function Structure

In its simplest form, a function consists of the keyword `function`, followed by the name assigned to the function and then a code block, as demonstrated here.

```
function Write-Greeting {
  Write-Host "Hello World!"
}
```

HINT Unlike variables, there are no hard and fast rules that you must follow when naming functions. However, it is a good idea to assign descriptive names to your functions that help identify a function's purpose. In this book, you see that I have elected to follow a function naming scheme that mimics the naming scheme used by cmdlets. Specifically, functions are assigned names that begin with a verb, followed by the - character and then a noun. I suggest that you develop your own naming scheme and then stick to it in all your Windows PowerShell scripts. This will help to make you code easier to read and manage.

Here, a function named `Write-Greeting` has been created. When called, this function uses the `Write-Host` cmdlet to display a text string. Of course, you can include as many statements as you want within a function's code block. You can execute this function from anywhere within the PowerShell script where it has been added by specifying its name, as demonstrated by the following.

```
function Write-Greeting {
  Write-Host "Hello World!"
}
```

```
Write-Greeting
```

Here, a function is defined and initialized and then executed by specifying its name.

I recommend that you define all your functions in a central location, at the beginning of your PowerShell script files. This will ensure that all your functions are defined and initialized before they are called upon. It will also help to make your program code easier to read and will make things a lot easier to find. As such, I suggest you modify your Windows PowerShell script template as shown here.

```
# ********************************************************************
#
# Script Name:
# Version:
# Author:
# Date:
#
# Description:
#
#
# ********************************************************************

# initialization section


# functions and filters section


# main processing section
```

As you can see, I have added three additional sections to the script template. The *initialization section* identifies the location within the script where script-level variables should be defined and initialized. The *functions and filters section* identifies the location where any functions and filters will be defined. The *main processing section* identifies the location where the script's controlling logic should be placed.

Going forward, this modified version of the template will be used in the development of the book's game scripts.

Processing Arguments

Although there is plenty of value in being able to organize groups of related statements into named code blocks in order to be able to repeatedly execute them as a unit, functions are even more useful when you set them up to process inputs passed to them as arguments. For example, in the next section you will learn how to set up a function that adds together any two numbers that are passed to it. Functions can also process output generated by cmdlets.

TRICK By developing functions that accept and process inputs, referred to as *arguments*, you make the functions independent of the PowerShell script in which they reside. Therefore, you can copy and paste a function into another PowerShell script and use it without modification, as long as it still gets called and passed the appropriate inputs in its new script. This facilitates code reuse and over time you should be able to develop a small library of functions, which you can use as building blocks in the development of your Windows PowerShell scripts. This should enable you to work smarter and faster by saving you the trouble of reinventing the wheel each time you start a new development project.

Passing Arguments

Windows PowerShell provides you with several different ways of passing arguments to PowerShell scripts. One way is to specify parameters representing each argument in a comma-separated list, enclosed in parentheses, immediately after the function name, as demonstrated by the following.

```
function Add-Numbers ($x, $y) {

  $z = $x + $y
  Write-Host "$x + $y = $z"


}
```

In this example, a function named Add-Numbers has been defined that accepts two arguments, $x and $y, which it then adds together. When this function is called for execution somewhere within a PowerShell script, you must pass two arguments that correspond to the two parameters required by the function. You pass these arguments in much the same way that you pass data to cmdlets, as demonstrated here.

```
Add-Numbers 3 4
```

When executed, this statement calls on the Add-Numbers function, passing it a value of 3 and 4. The function would then execute, displaying the results shown here.

```
3 + 4 = 7
```

Another option for setting up functions to accept arguments is to use the param keyword to define each argument. When used, the param keyword must be the first word specified inside the function's code block. Arguments accepted by the function must be specified as parameters, separated by commas, all of which are enclosed within parentheses, as demonstrated by the following.

```
function Add-Numbers {
  param ($x, $y)

  $z = $x + $y
  Write-Host "$x + $y = $z"


}
```

This function can be called from anywhere within the PowerShell file in which it is defined, as demonstrated here.

```
Add-Numbers 1 6
```

When executed, the Add-Numbers function generates the results shown below.

```
1 + 6 = 7
```

 TRICK Like many cmdlet parameters, function parameters are positional and named. This means that you can pass arguments to functions as comma-separated lists, provided that you arrange the arguments in the list to match up correctly with corresponding parameters defined in the function, or you can pass arguments by specifying the name of a parameter followed by the argument to be passed to that parameter. For example, the following statement demonstrates how to pass arguments to the Add-Number function by position.

```
Add-Numbers 2 2
```

Likewise, the following example demonstrates how to pass arguments to the Add-Numbers function by name.

```
Add-Numbers -x 2 -y 2
```

A function can also access arguments passed to it via the $args special variable. The $args variable is an array that is automatically populated with a list of all incoming arguments that have been passed to the function, as demonstrated in the following example.

```
function Add-Numbers {

  $z = $args[0] + $args[1]
  Write-Host "The total of all arguments passed is $z"

}
```

Here, the Add-Numbers function has been modified to reference two arguments that it expects to receive as $args[0] and $args[1]. For example, if called by this statement

```
Add-Numbers 2 5
```

this new version of the Add-Numbers function would generate the following output.

```
The total of all arguments passed is 7
```

Since $args is an array, you can process it using a foreach loop, as demonstrated here.

```
function Add-Numbers {

  foreach ($i in $args) {

    $z += $i

  }

  Write-Host "The total of all arguments passed is $z"

}
```

This version of the Add-Numbers function can be called and passed any number of arguments, as demonstrated by the following.

```
Add-Numbers 1 6 3 5 4
```

Using its `foreach` loop, the Add-Numbers function will total up each argument passed to it and display a result similar to that shown here.

```
The total of all arguments passed is 19
```

 While you can use either the `param` keyword or `$args` special variable to access argument data passed to functions, I suggest that you stick with the `param` keyword since it requires that you explicitly identify each incoming argument, making your code easier to read and understand.

Specifying Argument Data Type

Windows PowerShell also allows you to specify the data type of parameters in order to ensure that only values of a specific data type are accepted. This is accomplished by specifying the required data type as part of the parameter definition, as demonstrated here.

```
function Add-Numbers {
  Param ([int]$x, [int]$y)


  $z = $x + $y
  Write-Host "$x + $y = $z"


}
```

In this example, `[int]` was pre-appended to the beginning of each parameter definition in order to specify that both parameters accept only integer arguments. To see how this works, you could create this function and then call on it to execute using the following statement.

```
Add-Numbers -x 2 -y 2
```

Next, you might try calling on the function using the following statement.

```
Add-Numbers -x A -y 2
```

In response, the following error message will be displayed.

```
Add-Numbers : Cannot convert value "A" to type "System.Int32". Error: "Input st
ring was not in a correct format."
At C:\MyScripts\xxx.ps1:14 char:15
+ Add-Numbers -x  <<<< A -y 2
```

As you can see from the text of the error message, Windows PowerShell was not able to convert the argument of A to an integer as required by the function. Now, if you were to go back and remove the integer requirement for both of the function's parameters, you could call on the function as shown next and this time you won't see an error message. Instead, PowerShell appends both arguments together.

```
A + 2 = A2
```

Windows PowerShell supports a wide range of data types. Table 7.1 lists a number of these data types. You can specify any of these data types when defining function arguments.

TABLE 7.1 WINDOWS POWERSHELL DATA TYPES	
Data Type	**Data Type**
[array]	[hashtable]
[bool]	[int]
[byte]	[long]
[char]	[single]
[decimal]	[string]
[double]	[switch]
[float]	

Assigning Default Values to Arguments

Windows PowerShell also allows you to assign default values to function arguments, thus initializing a default value that will be used in place of an argument when that argument is not passed as expected to the function. For example, the Add-Numbers function, shown next, has been modified to assign a default value of zero to both of its parameters.

```
function Add-Numbers {
  Param ([int]$x = 0, [int]$y = 0)

  $z = $x + $y
  Write-Host "$x + $y = $z"


}
```

If you were to call on this version with the Add Numbers function as shown below, Windows PowerShell would assign 2 as the value of the $y parameter and 0 as the value of the $x parameter.

```
Add-Numbers -y 2
```

When called as shown, the `Add-Numbers` function generates the following output.

```
0 + 2 = 2
```

Processing Incoming Data

Functions get access to pipeline data through a special variable named `$input`. This variable is automatically populated with all incoming pipeline objects before the function begins to execute. If necessary, Windows PowerShell will delay the execution of a function until all incoming pipeline object data has been collected.

As an example of how to access incoming pipeline object data, consider the following example.

```
function Get-FileNames {

  $input | Where-Object {$_.Name -ne "WINDOWS" } | Sort-Object

}
```

Here, a function named `Get-FileNames` has been defined. The function uses the `$input` variable to collect any data passed to the function via the object pipeline. This data is then passed down the pipeline to the `Where-Object` cmdlet. The `Where-Object` cmdlet then filters out any object reference to a folder named Windows. Any remaining object data is then passed to the `Sort-Object` cmdlet.

Before running the preceding example, you need to change the current working directory to the root of your C: drive where the Windows folder resides using the `Set-Location` cmdlet, as demonstrated here.

```
Set-Location C:\
```

To run the function and insert it into the object pipeline, you could type the following statement. It executes the `Get-ChildItem` cmdlet and then pipes its output to the `Get-Filenames` function.

```
Get-ChildItem | Get-Filenames
```

When executed, the function will display output similar to the following.

```
    Directory: Microsoft.PowerShell.Core\FileSystem::C:\

Mode                LastWriteTime         Length    Name
----                -------------         ------    ----
d---                3/28/2006   1:56 PM             MyModules
```

```
-a---       4/10/2003    1:19 AM       0              AUTOEXEC.BAT
d---        4/20/2006   12:02 PM                      cgi-bin
-a---       4/10/2003    1:19 AM       0              CONFIG.SYS
d---        4/10/2003    1:22 AM                      Documents and Settings
-a---      10/11/2004    9:01 PM       1810432        ffastunT.ffl
d---        9/8/2006     8:16 PM                      hegames
-a---      10/15/2006    7:59 AM       119583         hpfr5100.log
d---        6/4/2003     8:58 PM                      I386
d---        9/5/2005    10:21 PM                      ICON Collection
-a---       9/18/2005    4:28 PM       1801287        MyApplication
d---        3/28/2006    1:56 PM                      MyModules
d---       10/15/2006   11:47 AM                      MyScripts
-a---       2/20/2006    1:52 PM       1323           net_save.dna
d---        9/15/2005    9:04 PM                      NVIDIA
d---       10/24/2005   11:48 PM                      Perl
-a---       6/24/2005    9:39 PM       584            Plugins
d-r--       9/9/2006     5:10 PM                      Program Files
-a---       3/25/2005    3:29 PM       108            PS.PS
d---        2/26/2006    3:25 PM                      REALbasic CR-ROM
d---       10/8/2006     2:49 PM                      temp
d---        9/18/2006    2:01 PM                      TextFiles
d---       10/6/2003    10:20 PM                      Westwood
-a---      10/15/2006   11:57 AM       0              yyyy.txt
```

Returning a Result

PowerShell functions are capable of returning data back to calling statements. This is accomplished by setting a variable to the value you want to return and then making a reference to that variable in the last statement executed by the function, as demonstrated in the following example.

```
function Add-Numbers {
  Param ([int]$x = 0, [int]$y = 0)

  $result = $x + $y
  $Result


}
```

In this example, the Add-Numbers function takes two integer values passed to it as arguments and adds them together. It then returns this result back to the statement that called it by assigning the value to be returned to the $result variable, which is then referenced against the last statement executed by the function. The following statements demonstrate how to execute this version of the Add-Numbers function and then retrieve and display the data that it returns.

```
$x = Add-Numbers 2 2
Write-Host   "2 + 2 = $x"
```

When called, the function is passed arguments of 2 and 2. Once executed, the function returns a value of 4, which is then assigned to the $x variable in the statement that executed it. The proof that everything worked as expected is provided when the second statement shown above executes and displays the following output.

```
2 + 2 = 4
```

Restricting Variable Scope

Up to this point in the book, all the examples that you have seen of variable usage have involved the use of script-level variables, meaning that once defined, the variables could be referenced from any location within your PowerShell scripts. However, now that functions have been introduced, things are going to change.

As was discussed in Chapter 4, access to variables is restricted by scope. Within a PowerShell script, any variable defined outside of a function is a script-level variable. Script-level variables are also local variables to all parts of the script file residing outside of functions. However, functions can still access script-level variables using a modified variable reference that includes the script label. Specifically, script-level variables can be accessed directly by name from any function defined within the script using the following syntax.

```
$localVariable = $script:variableName
```

HINT   Script-level scope is established each time a Windows PowerShell script is executed and ends when the script stops running.

Here, $localVariable is the name of a new variable that is local to the function in which it is defined. $script identifies the resource being referenced as a script-level variable and variableName specifies the name assigned to the variable. For example, in the following example, a script-level variable named $userName has been defined. Next, a call is made to a function named Get-UserName. Within the function, the $userName variable is referenced and assigned a value using the Read-Host cmdlet.

```
$userName = ""

function Get-UserName {
   $script:userName = Read-Host "What is your name?"
}


Get-UserName
Write-Host "Hello $userName"
```

Variables can also be defined within functions. In this case, any such variables are local in scope to the function. If you want, you can restrict access to these variables by declaring them as private. Variables with a private scope can only be accessed within their current scope. Therefore, a variable declared within a function that has a private scope can only be accessed within its function, as demonstrated below.

```
function Get-UserName {


   $private:x = Read-Host "What is your name?"
   Write-Host "Hello $x"
}



Get-UserName
```

In this example, a variable named $x is declared inside the Get-UserName function and assigned a value supplied by the user. The value of $x is then displayed by using the Write-Host cmdlet, which also resides inside the function. When executed, the name supplied by the user is displayed. For example, if the user entered William, the following output would be displayed.

```
Hello William
```

However, if you were to modify this example by moving the Write-Host statement outside of the function as shown below, the user's name would not be displayed since $x has a private scope and exists only within the function where it is defined.

```
function Get-UserName {


   $private:x = Read-Host "What is your name?"


}
```

```
Get-UserName
write-Host "Hello $x"
```

When executed, this example displays the following output, regardless of the name entered by the user:

```
Hello
```

TRAP Note that even though the value of $x does not exist outside of the script in which it was defined, the preceding example will not generate an error because Windows PowerShell does not force programmers to formally declare and initialize variable values prior to using them. While this may cause unexpected problems in most scripts, in the preceding example this behavior allowed the graceful transition.

REPLACING FUNCTIONS WITH FILTERS

A filter is very much like a function, except that instead of waiting for all incoming data to be received and stored in $input, filters have immediate access to incoming data as it becomes available via the $_ variable. Filters are structured exactly like functions, except that the filter keyword is specified in place of the function keyword, as demonstrated by the following.

```
filter Get-OddEven {

  $x = $_ % 2

  if ($x -eq 1) {
    $result = "Odd"
  }
  else {
    $result = "Even"
  }

  $result

}
```

In this example, a filter named Get-OddEven has been created that determines whether a number is odd or even. This filter takes any numeric value passed to it and divides it by two using the modulus operator (%). If the result of this operation yields a value of one, then the value passed to the function was an odd number; otherwise, it was an even number.

If called by the following statement

```
@(5, 4, 6) | Get-OddEven
```

the `Get-OddEven` function will display the following output.

```
Odd
Even
Even
```

In reality, filters and functions are pretty much equivalent. The difference is that filters are able to act upon pipeline object data as soon as it becomes available through the `$_` special variable, whereas functions have to wait for all incoming pipeline data to arrive and populate the `$input` variable before processing. To process a large list of data objects stored in the `$input` variable, you will usually have to set up a loop inside a function in order to iterate through each object. Filters also eliminate any need to use loops to process incoming data. As a result of these differences, filters can be more efficient and result in faster processing than functions when large amounts of data are being passed through the object pipeline.

Often, you can forego the creation of custom filters and instead used the `Foreach-Object` and the `Where-Object` cmdlets to filter data from the object pipeline. However, while these cmdlets are sufficient for simple operations, to perform complex logical operations on pipeline data you will need to set up a filter.

BACK TO THE POWERSHELL HANGMAN GAME

Okay, it is time to turn your attention back to the chapter's main game project, the Power-Shell Hangman game. The PowerShell Hangman game is a word-guessing game in which the player is challenged to guess a randomly selected secret word, a letter at a time. To win, the player must guess each letter in the word in 12 guesses or fewer.

The overall construction of the PowerShell Hangman game will be completed in 10 steps, as outlined here.

1. Create a new script file using the PowerShell script template.
2. Define and initialize game variables in the initialization section.
3. Define functions located in the functions and filters section.
4. Prompt the player for permission to play the game.
5. Create a loop to control overall gameplay.
6. Randomly select the game's secret word.

7. Create a loop to control the collection and analysis of player input.

8. Collect and validate player guesses.

9. Display the result of each guess.

10. Determine when the game is over.

11. Challenge the player to play again.

Creating a New Script

The first step in the creation of the PowerShell Hangman game is to create a new script file named Hangman.ps1 using the new version of the Windows PowerShell script template, as shown below.

```
# **********************************************************************
#
# Script Name:    Hangman.ps1 (The PowerShell Hangman Game)
# Version:        1.0
# Author:         Jerry Lee Ford, Jr.
# Date:           January 1, 2007
#
# Description:    This PowerShell script challenges the player to play
#                 a computer version of Hangman
#
# **********************************************************************


# initialization section

# functions and filters section

# main processing section
```

Defining and Initializing Script-Level Variables

The next step in the creation of the PowerShell Hangman game is to define and initialize script-level variables. This is accomplished by adding the following statements to the initialization section of the script file.

```
#Define variables used in this script
$playGame = "False"  #Controls gameplay and when to stop gameplay
$randomNo = New-Object System.Random  #This variable stores a random object
```

```
$response = ""   #Store the player's input when prompted to play a game
$number = 0   #Stores the game's randomly generated number
$secretWord = ""   #Stores the secret word for the current round of play
$attempts = 0   #Keeps track of the number of valid guesses made
$status = "True"   #Controls the current round of play
$guesses = ""   #A list of letters by the player during gameplay
$reply   #Stores player letter guesses
$tempstring   #Stores a display string with hidden characters that is used
               #to represent the secret word during gameplay
$validReply   #Stores the player's response when prompted to play a new game
$rejectList = '~!@#$%^&-_={}]|\:;",..?/<>'   #String listing unacceptable input
$GuessesRemaining   #Keeps track of the number of guesses the player has left

#Create an Associative array and load it with words
$words = @{}
$words[0] = @("", "", "", "", "", "", "", "", "", "", "", "", "", "", "")
$words[1] = @("C", "O", "M", "M", "A", "N", "D", "E", "R")
$words[2] = @("F", "L", "A", "G")
$words[3] = @("T", "O", "A", "S", "T", "E", "R")
$words[4] = @("M", "A", "R", "K", "E", "R")
$words[5] = @("P", "I", "C", "T", "U", "R", "E")
$words[6] = @("D", "E", "S", "K")
$words[7] = @("G", "L", "O", "B", "E")
$words[8] = @("S", "P", "E", "A", "K", "E", "R")
$words[9] = @("B", "A", "C", "K", "Y", "A", "R", "D")
$words[10] = @("P", "E", "N", "C", "I", "L")
```

Comments have been added that describe the use and purpose of each variable. Take note of the $words array, which is used to store 10 words from which the game will randomly select each time a new game is played. Each element in the $words array is actually an array itself whose elements consist of the letters that spell out a given word. Also note that $words[0] contains a list of 10 empty strings and not the letters of a game word. This array is used later in the script to keep track of correct player guesses.

Defining Custom Functions

The PowerShell Hangman game has one custom function, shown next, that you need to add to the functions and filters section of the script file. The function's name is Check-Answer and, as its name implies, its job is to determine whether the player's guess is correct.

```
#This function determines if the player's guess is correct or incorrect
function Check-Answer {
  param ($reply)  #Argument containing the player's guess

  #Access script-level variable representing valid users guesses and
  #add the current guess to it
  $script:guesses = $script:guesses + " " + $reply

  #Loop through each letter in the secret word (e.g., each element in the
  #array) and see if it matches the player's guess
  for ($i = 0; $i -le $secretWord.length - 1; $i++) {
    if ($secretWord[$i] -ne $reply) {  #The guess does not match
      #Place an underscore character into $word[0] in place of the letter
      if ($words[0][$i] -eq "") {$words[0][$i] = "_"}
    }
    else {    #The guess matches
      #Place the letter being guessed into $word[0]
      $words[0][$i] = $reply
    }
  }

}
```

This function begins by defining a parameter named $reply, which will be used to store the player's most recent guess. The first thing this function does after being called is append the letter being processed ($reply) to a script-level variable named $guesses. $guesses is used to store a string containing all of the guesses made by the player and is displayed later in the game to remind the player of the number of guesses that have already been made.

Next, a for loop is set up to iterate through the contents of an array named $secretWord. This array is populated later in the script file with a copy of all the letters that make up the game's randomly selected secret word. The loop iterates through each letter (array element) that makes up the secret word. If the loop finds a letter in the secret word that matches the player's guess, it writes that to the corresponding array element in the $word[0] array. Thus all of the letters that make up the game's secret word are represented by the _ characters and since letters are guesses, the appropriate _ character is replaced by letter guessed by the player.

Prompting the Player to Start the Game

Before starting a new round of play, the game requires that the player give it permission to do so. This is accomplished by adding the following statements to the beginning of the script file's main processing section.

```
#Prompt the player to guess a number
while ($playGame -ne "True") {

  Clear-Host  #Clear the Windows command console screen

  #Display the game's opening screen
  Write-Host "`n`n`n`n"
  write-Host " Welcome to the                    *********"
  Write-Host "                                   *       *"
  Write-host " PowerShell Hangman Game!        0       *"
  Write-host "                                  —|—     *"
  Write-host "                                   |      *"
  Write-host "                                  / \     *"
  Write-host "                                          *"
  Write-host "                                          *"
  Write-host "                                          *"
  Write-host "                                   *******"

  #Collect the player's guess
  $response = Read-Host "`n`n`n`n`n`n`n Would you like to play? (Y/N)"

  #validate the player's input
  if ($response -eq "Y"){
    $playGame = "True"
  }
  elseif ($response -eq "N") {
    Clear-Host
    Write-host " `n`n Please return and play again soon."
    Read-Host
    exit
  }
  else {
    Clear-Host
```

```
      Write-Host "`n`n Invalid input. Please press Enter try again."
      Read-Host
   }

}
```

As you can see, this part of the script is controlled by a while loop that iterates until the value of $playGame is set equal to true. Within the loop, a text-based graphic showing the hangman character is displayed and the player is prompted to enter a value of Y or N. If the player responds by entering Y, the value of $playGame is set to true, and as a result, the while loop ends and the rest of the script is executed.

If the player responds instead by entering N, the exit command is run, thus terminating the execution of the game. If the player responds by entering anything else, the loop runs again to prompt the player to enter a valid selection.

Setting Up a Loop to Control Gameplay

The rest of the script is controlled by a while loop that executes until the player decides to end the game. The statements that make up this loop are shown next and should be appended to the end of the script's main processing section. The rest of the statements that make up this script will be embedded within this loop.

```
#Prompt the player to guess a number
while ($status -eq "True") {


}
```

Selecting a Secret Word

The next step in the development of the PowerShell Hangman game is to embed the following statements in the script's main loop.

```
#Reset variables at the beginning of each new round of play
$tempString = ""
$words[0] = @("", "", "", "", "", "", "", "", "", "", "", "", "", "", "")
$attempts = 0
$guesses = ""
$reply = ""
```

```
#Generate a random number between 1 and 10
$number = $randomNo.Next(1, 11)

$secretWord = $words[$number]   #Populate an array with the letters that
                                #make up the game's secret word using the
                                #random number to specify the array index
```

A new round of gameplay begins each time this loop iterates. When this happens, numerous variables need to be reset to their default values to get the game ready. Also, a random number must be generated and used to select a new word for the player to guess.

Setting Up a Loop to Process User Guesses

Next, another loop needs to be set up to collect and process the player's guesses. The code statements that perform this task are shown next and should be embedded inside of the game's main loop, immediately after the last set of statements that you entered.

```
#Create a loop to collect and analyze player input
while ($reply -eq "") {



}
```

Collecting and Validating User Input

Next, you need to add the statements that are responsible for collecting and validating player input. These statements are shown next and should be embedded within the previous while loop.

```
Clear-Host  #Clear the Windows command console screen

$reply = Read-Host "`n`n Enter a guess"  #Collect the player answer

if ($reply -eq "") {  #If an empty string was submitted, repeat the
  continue            #loop
}

#It is time to Validate player input

if ($reply.Length -gt 1) {  #Limit input to one character at a time
```

```
Clear-Host  #Clear the Windows command console screen
Write-Host "`n`n Error: You may enter only one letter at a time."
Read-Host "`n`n`n`n`n`n`n`n`n`n Press Enter to continue."
$reply = ""  #Clear out the player's input
continue  #Repeat the loop

}


$reply = [int]$reply  #See if the user's guess can be converted to an
                      #integer

if ($reply.GetTypeCode() -ne "String") {  #Numeric input is not allowed

  Clear-Host  #Clear the Windows command console screen
  Write-Host "`n`n Error: Numeric guesses are not allowed."
  Read-Host "`n`n`n`n`n`n`n`n`n`n Press Enter to continue."
  $reply = ""  #Clear out the player's input
  continue  #Repeat the loop

}


if ($rejectList -match $reply) {

  Clear-Host  #Clear the Windows command console screen
  Write-Host "`n`n Error: Special characters are not permitted."
  Read-Host "`n`n`n`n`n`n`n`n`n`n Press Enter to continue."
  $reply = ""  #Clear out the player's input
  continue  #Repeat the loop

}


Clear-Host  #Clear the Windows command console screen

$attempts++  #Only increment for good guesses
```

The loop begins by prompting the player to enter a guess (i.e., a letter). The player's input is then assigned to a variable named $reply. A check is made to ensure that the player did not respond by simply pressing the Enter key. If this is the case the continue command is executed and the loop iterates and runs again.

Take note of the expression evaluated as the condition for the last two if state-ments. The first of these two if statements uses the GetTypeCode() method. This method retrieves the data type associated with a given resource. The second of these two if statements uses the -match comparison operator to determine whether the value of $reply can be found anywhere within the values stored in $rejectList. You will learn more about the -match operator in Chapter 8, "Working with Files and Folders."

Next, a series of if statements is executed. Each if statement is responsible for helping to validate a different aspect of the player's input. The first if statement executes the continue command if it finds that the player entered two or more characters as input. The second if statement checks to see if the player entered a number instead of a letter. Note that just before the second if statement executes, the value of $reply is converted to an integer ([int]$reply). If the conversion is successful, the if statement executes and the player is informed that numeric input is not allowed. Otherwise, the second if statement's code block is skipped. The third if statement checks to see if the player entered a special charac-ter instead of a letter. A list of special characters is stored in $rejectList. If a special char-acter is found, the continue command is executed.

If none of the three if statements finds a problem with the player's input, the player's guess is considered to be valid and the value of $attempts is incremented by 1. Note that since each if statement's code block executes the continue command when invalid input is found, the value of $attempts is not incremented for these guesses and thus the guesses do not count against the player.

Displaying the Results of Each Guess

Once a valid guess has been made, the game needs to process it and display the information showing the player the current status of the game. This is accomplished by adding the fol-lowing statements to the bottom of the previous while loop, immediately after the last set of statements that you just added.

```
#Now that player input has been validated, call on the Check-Answer
#function to process the input
Check-Answer $reply

$tempString = ""   #Clear out this variable used to display the
                   #current state of the word being guessed

#Loop through $words[0] and create a temporary display string that
#shows the state of the word being guessed
```

```
for ($i = 0; $i -le $words[0].length - 1; $i++) {
  $tempString = $tempString + " " + $words[0][$i]
}


#Display the current state of the secret word based on the input
#collected from the player
Write-Host "`n`n Results:`n"
Write-Host " ---------------------------`n"
Write-Host " $tempString`n"
Write-Host " ---------------------------`n`n"
Write-Host " Letters that have been guessed: $guesses`n"


#Calculate the number of guesses that the player has left
$GuessesRemaining = (12 - $attempts)


#Display the number of guesses remaining in the current round of play
Write-Host " Number of guesses remaining: $GuessesRemaining"
```

The first statement shown above calls on the script's Check-Answer function, passing it the player's guess as an argument. Next, a variable named $tempString is cleared out and then assigned the contents stored in the $words[0] array, thus creating a string representing the current state of the game's secret word, as guessed by the player. This string is then displayed. The value of $guesses is also displayed, showing the player how many letters have been guessed so far. Lastly, the value of $guessesRemaining is calculated and displayed, showing the player how many guesses are left.

Determining When the Game Is Over

Now it is time to see if the game is over. Gameplay ends when either the player guesses the game's secret word or the number of guesses has been exhausted. To accomplish these two checks, add the following statements to the bottom of the previous while loop, immediately after the last set of statements that you just added.

```
#Pause the game to allow the player to review the game's status
Read-Host "`n`n`n`n`n`n`n`n`n Press Enter to continue"


#The secret word has been guessed if there are no more underscore
#characters left in it - therefore the player has guessed it
if ($tempString -notmatch "_") {
```

```
Write-Host "`n Game over. You have guessed the secret word!" `
             "in $attempts guesses.`n`n"
Write-Host " The secret word was $secretWord `n`n"
Write-Host "`n`n`n`n`n`n`n`n" `
             "`n`n`n`n`n`n`n"
Read-Host   #Pause gameplay
$reply = "Done"   #signal the end of the current round of play
continue   #Repeat the loop

}


#The player is only allowed 12 guesses, after which the game ends
if ($attempts -eq 12) {

  Clear-Host
  Write-Host "`n Game over. You have exceeded the maximum allowed" `
               "number of guesses.`n`n"
  Write-Host " The secret word was $secretWord `n`n"
  Write-Host " The best you could do was $tempString`n`n`n`n`n`n`n`n" `
                 "`n`n`n`n`n`n`n"
  Read-Host   #Pause the game
  $reply = "Done"   #signal the end of the current round of play
  continue   #Repeat the loop

}


$reply = ""   #Clear out the player's input
```

As you can see, the statements shown above are organized into two if statements. The first if statement checks to see if the player has won the game. If this is the case, then every letter that makes up the secret word will have been guessed and the value stored in $tempString will not contain any underscore characters. The second if statement checks to see if the value of $attempts is equal to 12, indicating that the player has run out of guesses without discovering the game's secret word. If either of the two conditions tested by these two if statements provides true, the value of $reply is set equal to Done, terminating the execution of the while loop that is responsible for collecting and processing player input.

Challenging the Player to Play Another Game

Finally, to wrap up the PowerShell Hangman game, you need to add the following statements at the bottom of the game's main `while` loop. These statements are responsible for challenging the player to play another game.

```
$response = ""  #Reset value to allow the loop to continue iterating

#it is time to prompt the player to play another round
$validReply = "False"  #Set variable to ready its use in the while loop

#Loop until valid input is received
while ($validReply -ne "True") {

  Clear-Host  #Clear the Windows command console screen

  #Prompt the player to play a new game
  $response = Read-Host "`n`n Play again? (Y/N)"

  #Validate the player's input  #Keep playing
  if ($response -eq "Y"){

    $validReply = "True"
    $status = "True"

  }
  elseif ($response -eq "N") {  #Time to quit

    Clear-Host  #Clear the Windows command console screen
    Write-host " `n`n Please return and play again soon."
    Read-Host  #Pause gameplay
    $validReply = "True"
    $status = "False"

  }
  else {  #Invalid input received

    Clear-Host  #Clear the Windows command console screen
    Write-Host "`n`n Invalid input. Please press Enter to try again."
```

```
    #$validReply = "False"
    Read-Host   #Pause gameplay


  }


}
```

As you can see, the player is required to provide a response of Y or N. Entering Y starts a new round of play. Entering N results in $validReply being set to true, thus ending the execution of the script's main while loop, effectively terminating the script.

SUMMARY

This chapter showed you how to use functions and filters as a means of improving the overall organization and structure of your Windows PowerShell scripts. You learned how functions support the centralization of programming logic, reduce the overall size of scripts, and support code reuse. You learned how to define and execute functions. You learned how to pass arguments and return results. You also learned how to insert functions in the object pipeline. You learned how functions affect variable scope as well as how to access script-level variables within functions. On top of all this, you learned how to develop filters as an alternative to functions in order to more efficiently process large amounts of object pipeline data.

Now, before you move on and begin reading Chapter 8, I suggest you take a little extra time to improve the PowerShell Hangman game by tackling the following list of challenges.

CHALLENGES

1. As it is currently written, the PowerShell Hangman game gives the player 12 guesses to figure out the game's secret word. To make this game work more like the traditional children's game, change things so that the player is only allowed to make six incorrect guesses. This way, correct guesses will not be counted against the player. You may also want to associate each guess with a body part. For example, the first miss would represent a head, the second miss would represent the body, the third and fourth misses might represent arms, and the fifth and sixth misses would represent legs. You might even try displaying a text-based graphic, similar to that of the game's opening menu, at the end of each turn. You could use this graphic to represent the number of misses (e.g., after the first missed guess the graphic would show a head, after the second missed guess it would show the head and body, and so on).

2. Currently, the PowerShell Hangman game only has 10 words to randomly choose from. To make the game more challenging, consider modifying the game to support 20 or 30 different words.

3. As currently written, the game only has one custom function, which is responsible for determining if the player's guesses are correct. However, there are numerous opportunities for further modularizing the script by reorganizing different parts of it into functions. Review the code in the main processing section of the script and look for opportunities to enhance its organization with functions.

4. The way the PowerShell Hangman game is currently written, it is possible for the player to figure out what the game's secret word is too late in the game for the player to have enough guesses left to finish supplying each of the letters that make up the secret word. Address this situation by giving the player the option of typing in the entire word in place of her last guess.

5. As currently designed, the PowerShell Hangman game prevents the player from entering two characters at a time, entering numeric or special characters, or even just pressing the Enter key without keying in a guess. However, there is no logic in place to prevent the player from accidentally entering the same valid guess more than once. Consider modifying the script to prevent this from being allowed.

Part

III

Advanced Topics

WORKING WITH FILES AND FOLDERS

indows PowerShell provides you with access to cmdlets that provide you with the ability to work with files and folders in many ways. This chapter will teach you how to develop PowerShell scripts that can create, delete, rename, copy, move, and delete files and folders. You will learn how to determine if files and folders exist before you attempt to work with them. This chapter will also show you how to write to files and read data from them. You will learn how to work with different types of files, including plain text files, CSV files, and XML files. You will also learn how to use regular expressions to specify matching file and folder names and to use other cmdlets that allow you to control the format of cmdlet output and to print the output provided by cmdlets or stored in text files.

Specifically, you will learn how to:

- Administer files and folders
- Write to and read from different types of files
- Use regular expressions to perform complex pattern matching
- Control the display of cmdlet output using formatting cmdlets

PROJECT PREVIEW: THE POWERSHELL TIC-TAC-TOE GAME

This chapter's game project is an implementation of the classic children's Tic-Tac-Toe game. This game requires two players and begins by displaying the screen shown in Figure 8.1.

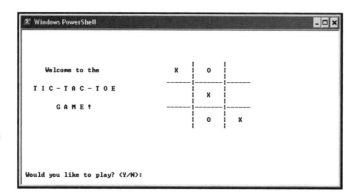

FIGURE 8.1

The welcome screen for the Tic-Tac-Toe game.

The welcome screen also prompts players for permission to start a new game. Once that permission is given, the screen shown in Figure 8.2 appears, prompting Player X to make a move.

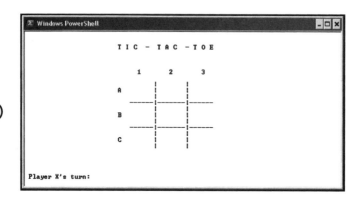

FIGURE 8.2

Players X is always the first player to make a move in each game.

Moves are made by entering the coordinates of an available game board square, as demonstrated in Figure 8.3

Valid moves are A1–C3. Any other moves are rejected by the game. In addition, the game rejects moves that have already been made, thus preventing one player from selecting a square that was already selected earlier in the game.

Gameplay ends when one player manages to line up three squares in a row, as demonstrated in Figure 8.4.

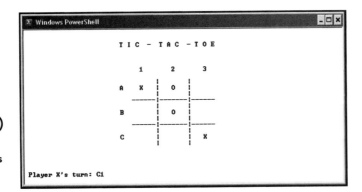

FIGURE 8.3

Square C1 is being specified as Player X's next move.

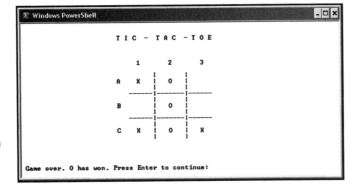

FIGURE 8.4

Player O has won the game.

The game also ends once every game board square has been selected without either player managing to win. In this case a tie is declared, as demonstrated in Figure 8.5.

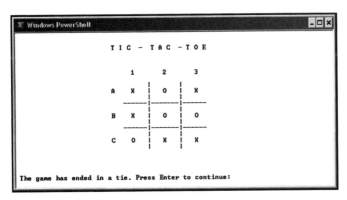

FIGURE 8.5

The game has ended in a tie.

Players are prompted to play again at the end of each game. If the players elect to start a new game, the game board is cleared and Player X is prompted to make a move. Otherwise, the players are invited to return and play again and the game closes.

USING THE POWER OF REGULAR EXPRESSIONS

Up to this point in the book, you have been validating data based on expected input, such as Y or N, when prompting the user for permission to perform a given action. However, there will be times when you are unable to strictly control the input provided to your PowerShell scripts. Instead, you must be prepared to accept any of a host of different inputs. To accommodate this type of situation, you need to learn how to work with regular expressions. A *regular expression* is a pattern used to describe matching data. Regular expressions have many uses and benefits. For example, regular expressions can be used to facilitate string searches within text documents. As this chapter's game project demonstrates, regular expressions are also an important tool that can be used to validate user input.

Matching Simple Patterns

Regular expressions are generally evaluated from left to right. Windows PowerShell implements regular expressions using the -match operator. Matches occur when a specified pattern is found in a specified source string. Perhaps the simplest regular expression pattern is one that defines a specific pattern made up of one or more characters, as demonstrated by the following.

```
if ("Once upon a time" -match "ONCE") {
  Write-Host "Match!"
}
```

Here, the source string "Once upon a time" is searched to see if it contains a matching pattern of "ONCE". When executed, this example results in a match. By default, matches are not case-sensitive. However, using the -cmatch operator, you can perform case-sensitive matches, as demonstrated here.

```
if ("Once upon a time" -cmatch "ONCE") {
  Write-Host "We have a match!"
}
```

In this example, a match does not occur. Windows PowerShell also makes it easy for you to perform negative pattern matching operations by supplying you with the -notmatch operator, which can be used as demonstrated by the following.

```
if ("Once upon a time" -notmatch "UPON") {
  Write-Host "We have a match!"
}
```

Here, a match occurs only if the pattern being searched for cannot be found in the specified search string. Windows PowerShell also allows you to perform case-sensitive pattern matching using the -cnotmatch operators, as demonstrated here:

```
if ("Once upon a time " -cnotmatch "time") {
  Write-Host "We have a match!"
}
```

When executed, this example results in a match.

Matching Alternative Patterns

Windows PowerShell's support for regular expressions also lets you set up pattern matches that can look for different sets of possible matches. To specify this type of pattern match, you use the | character in order to separate each possible matching string.

```
if ("mar" -match "war|mar|jar") {
  Write-Host "Match!"
}
```

In this example, a pattern has been defined that looks for any of three matching patterns. If any one of these patterns is found, the match is successful. To be more efficient, you could rewrite the previous example, as demonstrated next.

```
if ("mar" -match "(wa|ma|ja)r") {
  Write-Host "Match!"
}
```

In this more efficient pattern, the unique portions of each possible pattern match have been grouped together and enclosed within parentheses and the shared portion of the pattern match has been placed outside of the parentheses.

Working with Regular Expression Characters

Every character included as part of a regular expression will match itself. However, Windows PowerShell supports a collection of regular expression characters, also known as metacharacters, that are an exception to this rule. A *metacharacter* is a character that alters the manner in which a pattern match is evaluated. For example, consider the following example.

```
if ("The winner of this year's award is Mrs. Ford!" -match "Mr.") {
  Write-Host "Match!"
}
```

In this example, a regular expression has been set up to match against the characters Mr followed by an optional character, as represented by the . character. The . character is a metacharacter that is used to define a pattern that matches any one character. As a result, Mr., Mrs., and even Mrt will all match the "Mr." pattern. If you really wanted to match the period character as a period and not as a metacharacter, then you would need to precede it with a \, as demonstrated below.

```
if ("The winner of this year's award is Mrs. Ford!" -match "Mr\.") {
  Write-Host "Match!"
}
```

The . and \ characters used in the two previous examples are just two of a number of metacharacters supported by Windows PowerShell. Table 8.1 provides a list of additional regular expression characters.

TABLE 8.1 REGULAR EXPRESSION CHARACTERS (METACHARACTERS)

Character	Description	Example
.	Matches a single character	`"Molly" -match "M...y"`
[value]	Matches at least one character specified inside brackets	`"Molly" -match "M[io]lly"`
[range]	Matches at least one character specified within a range	`"Randy" -match "[R-T]andy"`
[^]	Matches any character except those specified within brackets	`"Randy" -match "[^RC]andy"`
^	Matches characters located at the beginning of a string	`"William" -match "^Wil"`
$	Matches characters located at the end of a string	`"William" -match "iam$"`
*	Matches zero or more occurrences of the preceding character	`"Daddy" -match "d*"`
?	Matches zero or one occurrence of the preceding character	`"Daddy" -match "d?"`
\	Matches the character following the escape (\) character	`"Big$" -match "Big\$"`

Working with Quantifiers

Using regular expressions, you can also set up pattern matches that match based on the number of repeating matches. This is accomplished using the regular expression quantifiers listed in Table 8.2.

Character	Description	Example
*	Must match zero or more times	"ss" -match "\w*"
+	Must match one or more times	"123123123" -match "123+"
?	Must match no more than one time	"ss" -match "\w?"
{n}	Must match n times	"ss" -match "\w{2}"
{n,}	Must match at least n matches	"ss" -match "\w{2,}"
{n,m}	Must match at least n, but not more than m times	"ss" -match "\w{2,3}"

TABLE 8.2 REGULAR EXPRESSION QUANTIFIERS

For example, the following statement demonstrates how to set up a regular expression that matches on one or more occurrences using the + regular expression quantifier character.

```
if ("The winner of this year's award is Mrs. Ford!" -match "win+er") {
  Write-Host "Match!"
}
```

Here, a match occurs if the string being searched contains a substring that matches the pattern of "win+er". This pattern looks for the letter wi followed by one or more instances of the letter n, followed by the letters er. Therefore, this pattern will match up against the word winner.

Matching Patterns Based on Ranges

Regular expressions also provide you with the ability to develop a pattern that looks for a specific type of data or that searches for a range of characters. This can be accomplished by using the character class patterns outlined in Table 8.3.

TABLE 8.3 CHARACTER CLASS PATTERNS

Pattern	Description
[abc]	Matches any of the specified lowercase characters
[abcdefghijklmnopqrstuvwxyz]	Matches any lowercase letter in the alphabet
[a - z]	Shorthand for specifying a match on any lowercase letter
[A - Z]	Shorthand for specifying a match on any uppercase letter
[0123456789]	Matches a number between 0–9.
[0 - 9]	Shorthand specifying a match between 0–9

Note that to work with character class patterns, you must enclose them inside a pair of matching brackets ([]), as demonstrated next.

```
if ("March 13th" -match "[0-9]") {
  Write-Host "Match!"
}
```

Here, a regular expression has been set up to look for the occurrence of a numeric match between 0 and 9. When executed, this example finds a match. However, the following example would not find a match.

```
if ("March Thirteenth" -match "[0-9]") {
  Write-Host "Match!"
}
```

Character classes are so commonly used in developing regular expressions that a series of shortcuts, listed in Table 8.4, have been developed to make them more convenient to work with.

TABLE 8.4 CHARACTER CLASS SHORTCUTS

Shortcut	Description
\d	Equivalent to [0 - 9]
\w	Equivalent to [0-9A-Za-z_]
\s	Equivalent to [\t\f\r\n\v]
\D	Matches any character besides [0 - 9]
\W	Matches any character besides [0-9A-Za-z_]
\S	matches any character besides [\t\f\r\n\v]

For example, the following `if` statement sets up a regular expression that results in a match as long as no numeric characters are found in the string being searched.

```
if ("I am forty two." -match "\D") {
  Write-Host "Match!"
}
```

Likewise, the following example sets up a regular expression to search a string to make sure that it contains numeric characters.

```
if ("I am 42." -match "\d") {
  Write-Host "Match!"
}
```

 This review of Windows PowerShell's support for regular expressions has been relatively brief. An in-depth discussion about regular expressions is beyond the scope of this book. To learn more, read *Mastering Regular Expressions, Second Edition* (ISBN: 0596002890). You can also enter the following command at the PowerShell command prompt.

```
Get-Help about_regular_expressions
```

Administering Files and Folders

Windows PowerShell provides you with many ways of administering files and folders on your computer. It provides you with the ability to create, delete, rename, copy, move, or delete files and folders.

 If you are going to follow along with the examples provided in the sections that follow, you will need to make sure that you have similarly named files and folders on your computer for things to work correctly.

Verifying File and Folder Existence

As was just stated, Windows PowerShell provides you with the tools needed to administer files and folders. However, before you attempt to administer a file or folder, it is a good idea to first check and make sure that the file or folder exists. After all, files and folders can disappear for any number of reasons. For example, someone else using the computer might delete them or rename them. To see if a file exists, you use the `Test-Path` cmdlet, as demonstrated by the following.

```
$fileFound = Test-Path C:\MyScripts\Hangman.ps1

if ($fileFound -eq "True") {
  Write-Host "File found."
}
```

In this example, a variable named $fileFound is set to True or False based on whether the Test-Path cmdlet is able to find a file named hangman.ps1 in the C:\MyScripts folder. The Test-Path cmdlet can also be used to determine whether a folder exists, as demonstrated here.

```
$fileFound = Test-Path C:\MyScripts

if ($fileFound -eq "True") {
  Write-Host "Folder found."
}
```

In this example, MyScripts is a folder residing at the root of the computer's C: drive. Once you have used the Test-Path cmdlet to ensure that the file or folder you want to work with exists, you can perform a host of administrative operations on the file or folder, as demonstrated in the sections that follow.

Retrieving File and Folder Information

As the following example shows, you can use the Get-Item cmdlet to retrieve information about a given file or folder. In this example, the Mode, LastWriteTime, Length, and Name properties of the hangmang.ps1 file are displayed.

```
PS C:\MyScripts> Get-Item Hangman.ps1


    Directory: Microsoft.PowerShell.Core\FileSystem::C:\MyScripts


Mode                LastWriteTime               Length Name
----                -------------               ------ ----
-a---               10/15/2006    2:32 PM         10176 Hangman.ps1
```

Using the Get-Item cmdlet, you can easily create a script that retrieves a specific property value for a file or folder, as demonstrated here.

```
$fileFound = Test-Path C:\MyScripts\Hangman.ps1

if ($fileFound -eq "True") {
  $lastWritten = $(Get-Item C:\MyScripts\hangman.ps1).LastWriteTime
}
```

Here, the `Test-Path` cmdlet is used to make sure that the `Hangman.ps1` file exists. If it does, the `Get-Item` cmdlet is then passed `C:\MyScripts\hangman.ps1` as an argument. Note that the `Get-Item` cmdlet and its argument are enclosed within parentheses and preceded by a `$` character in order to establish an object reference. Once the reference is set up, related object properties can then be accessed using standard dot notation. When executed, this example will generate output similar to that shown below, assuming that the specified file exists.

```
Sunday, January 21, 2007 2:32:14 PM
```

Copying and Moving Files and Folders

Windows PowerShell also provides you with the ability to copy and moves files and folders. This is accomplished using the `Copy-Item` and `Move-Item` cmdlets. For example, the following example demonstrates how to copy a file from one folder to another.

```
Copy-Item C:\System.log C:\Temp
```

In this example, a file named `System.log` is copied from the root of the `C:` drive to the `C:\Temp` folder. If necessary, you can use wildcard characters to copy multiple files from one folder to another, as demonstrated here.

```
Copy-Item C:\*.log C:\Temp
```

Here, any `.log` files found on the root of `C:` are copied to `C:\Temp`.

You can also use the `Copy-Item` cmdlet to copy one folder into another folder, as demonstrated here.

```
Copy-Item C:\MyScripts C:\Temp
```

When executed, this statement makes a copy of the `C:\MyScripts` folder and places it in the `C:\Temp` folder. However, none of the contents of `C:\MyScripts` are copied, just a copy of the folder itself. You can modify this example by passing the `-recurse` parameter to the `Copy-Item` cmdlet in order to instruct Windows PowerShell to recursively copy a folder and all its contents, including any subfolders, into another folder, as shown here.

```
Copy-Item C:\MyScripts C:\Temp -recurse
```

Using the `Move-Item` cmdlet, Windows PowerShell also lets you move files and folders. For example, the following demonstrates how to copy a file from one folder to another.

```
Move-Item C:\System.log C:\Temp
```

Use wildcard characters to move multiple files from one folder to another, as shown here.

```
Move-Item C:\*.log C:\Temp
```

By default, the Move-Item cmdlet will not override and replace any existing files in the destination folder. However, by adding the -force parameter, you can instruct the Move-Item cmdlet to overwrite and replace existing filenames.

```
Move-Item C:\*.log C:\Temp -force
```

Deleting Files and Folders

Windows PowerShell provides you with the ability to delete files and folders by using the Remove-Item cmdlet. For example, the following statement can be used to delete a file named Report.txt located in the C:\Temp folder.

```
Remove-Item C:\Temp\Report.txt
```

Using wildcard characters, you can remove groups of files from a folder, as demonstrated here.

```
Remove-Item C:\Temp\*.txt
```

You can use the Remove-Item cmdlet to delete both files and folders. For example, the following statement instructs PowerShell to delete all the files and folders stored in a folder named C:\Temp\HP_WebRelease.

```
Remove-Item C:\Temp\HP_WebRelease\*
```

In response to this statement, PowerShell will display output similar to that shown next, prompting you for permission to delete all of the folders found inside C:\Temp\HP_WebRelease.

```
The item at C:\Temp\HP_WebRelease\chs has children and the -recurse parameter
was not specified. If you continue, all children will be removed with the item.
 Are you sure you want to continue?
[Y] Yes  [A] Yes to All  [N] No  [L] No to All  [S] Suspend  [?] Help
(default is "Y"):
```

If you want, you can reformulate the previous command by passing any of the following parameters to the Remove-Item cmdlet.

- **-recurse.** Bypasses the display of the previous prompt message, instructing the Remove-Item cmdlet to recursively remove all contents.
- **-exclude.** Allows you to include a comma-separated list of files to exclude when the Remove-Item cmdlet executes.
- **-include.** Allows you to include a comma-separated list of files to include when the Remove-Item cmdlet executes.
- **-whatif.** Instructs the Remove-Item cmdlet to display a list showing the files and folder that it would have deleted had the -whatif parameter not been specified.

Renaming Files and Folders

Windows PowerShell provides you with the ability to programmatically rename files using the Rename-Item cmdlet as demonstrated here.

```
Rename-Item C:\MyScripts\Test.ps1 Test1.ps1
```

Here, two arguments are passed to the Rename-Item. The first argument is the name and path of the file to be renamed, and the second argument is the new name that is to be assigned. You may also use the Rename-Item cmdlet to rename a folder, as demonstrated here.

```
Rename-Item C:\MyFolder TestFolder
```

Searching Files

In addition to looking for, copying, moving, renaming, and deleting files and folders, Windows PowerShell also provides you with the ability to search inside text files and search their contents. This is accomplished using the Get-Content and the Select-String cmdlets. For example, let's say you had a log file named System.log that contained the following text.

```
01/27/2007 08:00:01 System backup started
01/27/2007 09:16:33 System backup completed
01/28/2007 08:00:01 System backup started
01/28/2007 09:13:13 System backup completed
01/29/2007 08:00:01 System backup started
01/29/2007 08:00:05 Error code 995 - Unable to locate backup media
01/30/2007 08:00:01 System backup started
01/30/2007 09:22:11 System backup completed
```

The Get-Content cmdlet provides you with the ability to read lines of text from a text file. The Select-String cmdlet gives you the ability to search a text string to see if it contains a substring. For example, you could search the log file shown above and look for any errors that may have occurred, as demonstrated here.

```
Get-Content C:\Temp\System.log | Select-String "Error"
```

Here, the Get-Content cmdlet is executed and passed C:\Temp\System.log as an argument. Next, each line in the log file is passed down the object pipeline and processed by the Select-String cmdlet, which has been told to look for the text Error inside each line. Any lines of text that include this text are then displayed. When executed, this command will generate the following output.

```
01/29/2007 08:00:05 Error code 995 - Unable to locate backup media
```

You can also use regular expressions to define a search pattern that you want to look for when searching text files and then display a text message indicating when a match occurs. For example, the following statements use the Get-Content cmdlet to assign the contents of a text file to an array variable named $records. Next, an if statement has been set up that uses the -match operator in order to define a regular expression that looks for occurrences of the words error, alert, and critical in any of the lines stored inside $records.

```
$records = Get-Content C:\Temp\System.log

if ($records -match "(error|alert|critical)") {
  Write-Host "Match!"
}
```

READING FROM AND WRITING TO FILES

In addition to providing you with the tools required to administer files and folders, Windows PowerShell also provides you with access to a number of cmdlets that you can use to create files and folders as well as read from and write to different types of files, including text, CVS, and XML files.

Creating Files and Folders

Windows PowerShell provides programmers with many ways to create new files. One way to create a new text file and to write data to it is to use the > redirection operator in order to write object pipeline data to text files.

```
Get-ChildItem > C:\Temp\DirectoryList.txt
```

When executed, this statement takes the output of the Get-ChildItem cmdlet and redirects it to C:\Temp\DirectoryList.txt. As a result, if you open the Directory.txt file, you'll see that it contains data similar to the following output.

```
Directory: Microsoft.PowerShell.Core\FileSystem::C:\MyScripts


Mode            LastWriteTime           Length Name
---             -------------           ------ ----
-a---           9/26/2006    9:14 PM      4661 FortuneTeller.ps1
-a---           10/9/2006   12:11 AM      4734 GuessMyNumber.ps1
-a---           10/15/2006   2:32 PM     10176 Hangman.ps1
```

TRICK If the file being written to already exists, its contents are replaced. To append to the end of a file, use the >> pipe operator as demonstrated below.

```
Get-ChildItem >> C:\Temp\DirectoryList.txt
```

Alternatively, you can create a new file using the New-Item cmdlet. For example, the following statement will create a new empty file named TextFile.txt in the C:\Temp folder.

```
New-Item C:\Temp\TestFile.txt -type file
```

As you can see, the first argument passed to the cmdlet is the name and path of the resources to be created. The second argument passed to the cmdlet is the type of resource to create (e.g., a file). You can use the New-Item cmdlet to create a new folder just as easily as a new file, as demonstrated below.

```
New-Item C:\Temp\MyNewFolder -type directory
```

In this example a new folder named MyNewFolder is created inside the C:\Temp folder. Also note that the second argument passed to the cmdlet specified the keyword directory and not folder. Both terms are, of course, synonymous but PowerShell requires you to specify directory when creating new folders.

If the file or folder you are attempting to create already exists, you will get an error message.

```
New-Item : The file 'C:\Temp\TestFile.txt' already exists.
At C:\MyScripts\xxx.ps1:3 char:9
+ New-item  <<<< C:\Temp\TestFile.txt -type file
```

If you want, you can add the -force parameter to replace the file or folder with an empty file or folder, as demonstrated here.

```
New-Item C:\Temp\TestFile.txt -type file -force
```

Writing to Text Files

Windows PowerShell provides you with a number of additional ways to create files and write output to them. For example, you have already seen how to create and write to new text files by redirecting object pipeline data with the > operator. Windows PowerShell also lets you write to text files using the Set-Content, Out-File, and Add-Content cmdlets.

Writing Text

Using the Set-Content cmdlet, you can write a string to a text file, as demonstrated here.

```
Set-Content C:\Temp\Temp.txt "Once upon a time..."
```

Here, the first argument passed to Set-Content is the name and path of the file to be created. The second argument is the string to be written to the text file. If a file of the same name already exists, the Set-Content cmdlet will automatically replace its content with the specified string.

You can also use the Out-File cmdlet to send data from the object pipeline directly to a file without seeing anything displayed in the Windows command console. For example, the following statement will redirect the output of the Get-ChildItem cmdlet to a file named Temp.txt in C:\Temp.

```
Get-Childitem | Out-File C:\Temp\Temp.txt
```

Like the Set-Content cmdlet, the Out-File cmdlet overwrites the contents of any like-named files.

Appending Text

If you want to add to an existing file when writing to it, as opposed to replacing its contents, you can use the Add-Content cmdlet to append data to the end of a file, as demonstrated by the following example.

```
Set-Content C:\Temp\Temp.txt "Once upon a time..."
Add-Content C:\Temp\Temp.txt "And they lived happily ever after."
Add-Content C:\Temp\Temp.txt ""
Add-Content C:\Temp\Temp.txt "`tThe end"
```

Here, a new file is created and written to using the Set-Content cmdlet. Next, the Add-Content cmdlet is used to write additional text to the file.

Reformatting Cmdlet Output

As you have just learned, Windows PowerShell provides you with many different ways of creating and writing data to text files. You have also seen examples of how to write pipeline object data directly into text files. In these examples, data was written using whatever format the last cmdlet applied to it. However, Windows PowerShell makes it easy to customize cmdlet output using the Format-List and Format-Table cmdlets.

The Format-List Cmdlet

The Format-List cmdlet processes object pipeline data and reformats it into a vertical list. Using the cmdlet's -property parameter, you can control which object properties are displayed in order to create custom reports and output.

For example, suppose you wanted to develop a PowerShell script that generated a report that showed a listing of all the files stored in the current working directory. This could be easily accomplished by adding the following statements to the script.

```
Get-ChildItem > C:\Temp.txt
```

When executed, this script would create a text file named Tempt.txt in the root folder on the computer's C: drive.

```
    Directory: Microsoft.PowerShell.Core\FileSystem::C:\MyScripts


Mode              LastWriteTime            Length Name
----              -------------            ------ ----
-a---          9/26/2006    9:14 PM          4661 FortuneTeller.ps1
-a---          10/9/2006   12:11 AM          4734 GuessMyNumber.ps1
-a---          10/15/2006   2:32 PM         10176 Hangman.ps1
-a---          9/10/2006    1:42 PM          1077 Workpaper.txt
-a---          9/26/2006   12:56 PM           831 Report.log
```

By passing the output of the Get-ChildItem cmdlet to the Select-String cmdlet, you can filter out all the files in the current working directory whose filenames do not include the string ps1. You might then pass the resulting output to the Format-List cmdlet, as shown here.

```
Get-ChildItem | Select-String PS1 | Format-List > C:\Temp.txt
```

When executed, this statement saves output similar to that shown here in a file named Temp.txt.

```
IgnoreCase : True
LineNumber : 3
Line       : # Script Name: FortuneTeller.ps1 (PowerShell Fortune Teller)
Filename   : FortuneTeller.ps1
Path       : C:\MyScripts\FortuneTeller.ps1
Pattern    : PS1

IgnoreCase : True
LineNumber : 3
Line       : # Script Name: GuessMyNumber.ps1 (The Guess My Number Game)
Filename   : GuessMyNumber.ps1
Path       : C:\MyScripts\GuessMyNumber.ps1
Pattern    : PS1
```

```
IgnoreCase : True
LineNumber : 3
Line       : # Script Name: Hangman.ps1 (The PowerShell Hangman Game)
Filename   : Hangman.ps1
Path       : C:\MyScripts\Hangman.ps1
Pattern    : PS1
```

The output shown here was generated using a default format generated by the `Format-List` cmdlet. It you prefer, you can exercise detailed control over the properties that are reported, as demonstrated here.

```
Get-ChildItem | Select-String PS1 | Format-List -Property Filename, Path >
C:\Temp.txt
```

Here, the `-property` parameter has been specified and two arguments included. When executed, this statement generates results similar to that shown here.

```
Filename : FortuneTeller.ps1
Path     : C:\MyScripts\FortuneTeller.ps1

Filename : GuessMyNumber.ps1
Path     : C:\MyScripts\GuessMyNumber.ps1

Filename : Hangman.ps1
Path     : C:\MyScripts\Hangman.ps1
```

The Format-Table Cmdlet

The `Format-Table` cmdlet is very similar to the `Format-List` cmdlet, except that it formats output in a horizontal table as opposed to a vertical list. For example, you might use the `Format-Table` cmdlet as shown next to formulate a statement that displays a tabular view of the contents of the current working directory, which is then saved as a report named `Temp.txt`.

```
Get-ChildItem | Select-String PS1 | Format-Table > C:\temp\Temp.txt
```

When executed, this statement will generate results similar to this:

IgnoreCase	LineNumber	Line	Filename	Path	Pattern
True	3	# Script ...	FortuneTe...	C:\MyScri...	PS1
True	3	# Script ...	GuessMyNu...	C:\MyScri...	PS1
True	3	# Script ...	Hangman.ps1	C:\MyScri...	PS1

Like the `Format-List` cmdlet, the `Format-Table` cmdlet lets you override its default format by specifying the data properties you want, as demonstrated here.

```
Get-ChildItem | Select-String PS1 | Format-Table Filename, Path >
C:\temp\Temp.txt
```

When executed, this statement will generate a report file containing output similar to that show here.

```
Filename                         Path
--------                         ----

FortuneTeller.ps1                C:\MyScripts\FortuneTeller.ps1
GuessMyNumber.ps1                C:\MyScripts\GuessMyNumber.ps1
Hangman.ps1                      C:\MyScripts\Hangman.ps1
```

As another example of how to work with the `Format-Table` cmdlet, let's write a statement that lists all of the processes running on the computer that currently have more than 600 open handles. To begin, let's format a statement that lists all the active processes, sorts them, and then displays only those with more than 600 open handles, as shown here.

```
Get-Process | Sort-Object | Where-Object {$_.Handles -gt 300} > C:\temp\Temp.txt
```

When executed, this statement will produce a report containing output similar to that shown here.

```
Handles     NPM(K)     PM(K)     WS(K)     VM(M)     CPU(s)       Id ProcessName
-------     ------     -----     -----     -----     ------       -- -----------
4393        6          6080      432       46        1,256.52     2844 CFD
657         20         13888     17500     115       817.45       2484 explorer
643         17         24664     1240      231       60.38        3388 mim
1675        60         20372     17552     153       174.52       900 svchost
```

Now that we have the set of results we are looking for, let's reformat the output using the `Format-Table` cmdlet's `-groupby` parameter to display a series of tables where processes are grouped by process names, as shown here.

```
Get-Process | Sort-Object | Where-Object {$_.Handles -gt 300} | Format-Table
-groupby Processname > C:\temp\Temp.txt
```

 Make sure that when you run this example and other examples like it at the Windows PowerShell command prompt, you do so by keying it in as a single statement.

When executed, this statement generates a report named `Temp.txt` that contains results similar to those shown here.

```
ProcessName: CFD

Handles     NPM(K)     PM(K)      WS(K)      VM(M)     CPU(s)      Id ProcessName
-----       ----       ----       ----       ----      ----        -- -----------
4440        6          6096       7628       47        1,257.27    2844 CFD


ProcessName: powershell

Handles     NPM(K)     PM(K)      WS(K)      VM(M)     CPU(s)      Id ProcessName
-----       ----       ----       ----       ----      ----        -- -----------
606         11         22568      31264      140       3.47        3548 powershell
638         12         50648      50676      168       20.33       3504 powershell


ProcessName: svchost

Handles     NPM(K)     PM(K)      WS(K)      VM(M)     CPU(s)      Id ProcessName
-----       ----       ----       ----       ----      ----        -- -----------
637         14         1924       1412       37        7.91        832 svchost
1673        60         20356      17540      152       174.52      900 svchost
```

Since multiple instances of some processes may be running at the same time, the `-groupby` parameter groups any like-named processes with more than 600 open handles together when formatting and displaying its output.

 The `Format-List` and `Format-Table` cmdlets provide detailed control over the display of cmdlet output. To learn more about these two cmdlets, type `Get-Help Format-List` and `Get-Help Format-Table` at the Windows PowerShell command prompt.

Reading from Text Files

Windows PowerShell can just as easily read from a text file as it can write to it. Windows PowerShell provides you with the ability to read from a text file using the `Get-Content`, cmdlet, as demonstrated here.

```
Get-Content C:\Temp\Temp.txt
```

As you can see, the only argument passed to the Get-Content cmdlet is the name and path of the text file to be read. When executed, this statement will display the contents of whatever has been stored in the specified text file. When executed, the Get-Content cmdlet automatically creates an array into which is stored each of the lines in the specified text file, making it possible, for example, for you to then process every line of text using a loop.

Erasing File Contents

If you want, you can programmatically erase the contents of a file without removing the file from the computer using the Clear-Content cmdlet. To use this cmdlet, you simply specify the name and path of the files to be erased as an argument as demonstrated here.

```
Clear-Content C:\Temp\Temp.txt
```

TRICK   You can use the Clear-Content cmdlet to erase more than just the content of text files. You can use it to clear out other types of files such as Microsoft Word documents.

Saving Data Output as HTML

Windows PowerShell is capable of saving output in many different file formats, including HTML. The advantage of HTML is that it can often be used to more effectively display information, especially when used on a web server to communicate with large groups of people. To save file output as an HTML file, you use the ConvertTo-Html cmdlet, as demonstrated below.

```
Get-Service | Where-Object { $_.status -eq "running" } |ConvertTo-HTML Name,
DisplayName, Status | Set-Content C:\Temp\Text.html
```

Here, the Get-Service cmdlet is used to generate a list of all processes running on the computer. Next, the Where-Object cmdlet is used to filter out all non-running services. The ConvertTo-Html cmdlet is then used to format the resulting output into an HTML file. Note that only the Name, DisplayName, and Status properties are outputted. Finally, the resulting HTML is written as a file named Text.html, as demonstrated in Figure 8.6.

Saving Data as an XML File

Windows PowerShell also provides you with the ability to save pipeline object data in the form of an XML file. XML stands for Extensible Markup Language. Its purpose is to facilitate the definition, storage, and transmission of data between applications. To generate an XML file, you use the Export-Clixml cmdlet, as demonstrated here:

```
Get-ChildItem | Export-Clixml C:\Temp\Test.xml
```

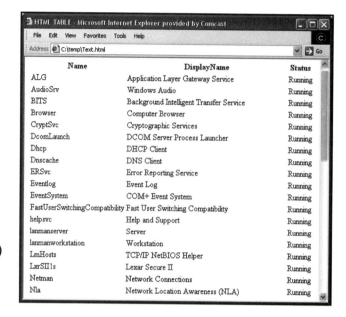

FIGURE 8.6

Displaying object pipeline data as an HTML file.

Here, the Get-ChildItem cmdlet is used to generate a list of files stored in the current working directory and then the Export-Clixml cmdlet is used to save the resulting output in an XML file. When executed, this statement will generate an XML file whose contents are similar to those shown in Figure 8.7.

FIGURE 8.7

An example of the output that is produced when an XML file is generated.

Reading Data from an XML File

Windows PowerShell also provides you with a cmdlet that lets you retrieve XML data, thus letting you use it again as input in another PowerShell script. To open and read an XML file, you need to use the `Import-Clixml` cmdlet, as demonstrated here.

```
$xmlFile = Import-Clixml C:\Temp\Test.xml
$xmlFile
```

In this example, the first statement uses the `Import-Clixml` cmdlet to retrieve the `Test.xml` file and store a copy of its content in `$xmlFile`. The second statement displays the contents stored in `$xmlFile`, which should look like this:

```
Directory: Microsoft.PowerShell.Core\FileSystem::C:\MyScripts


Mode            LastWriteTime           Length Name
----            -------------           ------ ----
                9/26/2006   9:14 PM       4661 FortuneTeller.ps1
                10/9/2006  12:11 AM       4734 GuessMyNumber.ps1
                10/15/2006  2:32 PM      10176 Hangman.ps1
```

Saving Data in a Comma-Separated Value File

One additional file format that Windows PowerShell can write to and read from is CSV. CSV stands for comma-separated values. CSV is a file format that is used to store comma-separated data as records separated by newlines and is commonly used by applications such as Microsoft Excel as a means of storing data in a format that can easily be moved between different applications.

To save pipeline object data in a CSV file, you use the `Export-Csv` cmdlet, as demonstrated here.

```
Get-ChildItem | Export-Csv C:\Temp\Test.csv
```

When executed, this statement will create a file containing output similar to that shown here, readying it for use by other applications, or for use as input into another PowerShell script.

```
#TYPE System.IO.FileInfo
PSPath,PSParentPath,PSChildName,PSDrive,PSProvider,PSIsContainer,Mode,Name,Length,Dir
ectoryName,Directory,IsReadOnly,Exists,FullName,Extension,CreationTime,CreationTimeUt
c,LastAccessTime,LastAccessTimeUtc,LastWriteTime,LastWriteTimeUtc,Attributes
Microsoft.PowerShell.Core\FileSystem::C:\MyScripts\FortuneTeller.ps1,Microsoft.PowerS
hell.Core\FileSystem::C:\MyScripts,FortuneTeller.ps1,C,Microsoft.PowerShell.Core\File
System,False,-a---
```

```
,FortuneTeller.ps1,4661,C:\MyScripts,C:\MyScripts,False,True,C:\MyScripts\FortuneTell
er.ps1,.ps1,"9/24/2006 3:12:14 PM","9/24/2006 7:12:14 PM","10/22/2006 8:42:36
PM","10/23/2006 12:42:36 AM","9/26/2006 9:14:10 PM","9/27/2006 1:14:10 AM",Archive
Microsoft.PowerShell.Core\FileSystem::C:\MyScripts\GuessMyNumber.ps1,Microsoft.PowerS
hell.Core\FileSystem::C:\MyScripts,GuessMyNumber.ps1,C,Microsoft.PowerShell.Core\File
System,False,-a---
,GuessMyNumber.ps1,4734,C:\MyScripts,C:\MyScripts,False,True,C:\MyScripts\GuessMyNumb
er.ps1,.ps1,"10/8/2006 5:37:04 PM","10/8/2006 9:37:04 PM","10/22/2006 8:42:36
PM","10/23/2006 12:42:36 AM","10/9/2006 12:11:47 AM","10/9/2006 4:11:47 AM",Archive
Microsoft.PowerShell.Core\FileSystem::C:\MyScripts\Hangman.ps1,Microsoft.PowerShell.C
ore\FileSystem::C:\MyScripts,Hangman.ps1,C,Microsoft.PowerShell.Core\FileSystem,False
,-a---
,Hangman.ps1,10176,C:\MyScripts,C:\MyScripts,False,True,C:\MyScripts\Hangman.ps1,.ps1
,"10/10/2006 1:30:50 PM","10/10/2006 5:30:50 PM","10/22/2006 8:42:36 PM","10/23/2006
12:42:36 AM","10/15/2006 2:32:14 PM","10/15/2006 6:32:14 PM",Archive
```

Reading Data from a Comma-Separated Value File

To read a CSV file into a PowerShell script, you need to use the Import-Csv cmdlet. As demonstrated next, this cmdlet takes one argument: the name and path of the CSV file to be imported.

```
$cvsFile = Import-Csv C:\Temp\Test.csv
$cvsFile
```

Here, the content of the previously saved CSV files has been imported back into a variable named $csvFile and then displayed, producing output similar to that shown here.

```
PSPath          : Microsoft.PowerShell.Core\FileSystem::C:\MyScripts\FortuneT
                  eller.ps1
PSParentPath    : Microsoft.PowerShell.Core\FileSystem::C:\MyScripts
PSChildName     : FortuneTeller.ps1
PSDrive         : C
PSProvider      : Microsoft.PowerShell.Core\FileSystem
PSIsContainer   : False
Mode            : -a---
Name            : FortuneTeller.ps1
Length          : 4661
DirectoryName   : C:\MyScripts
Directory       : C:\MyScripts
IsReadOnly      : False
```

```
Exists            : True
FullName          : C:\MyScripts\FortuneTeller.ps1
Extension         : .ps1
CreationTime      : 9/24/2006 3:12:14 PM
CreationTimeUtc   : 9/24/2006 7:12:14 PM
LastAccessTime    : 10/22/2006 8:42:36 PM
LastAccessTimeUtc : 10/23/2006 12:42:36 AM
LastWriteTime     : 9/26/2006 9:14:10 PM
LastWriteTimeUtc  : 9/27/2006 1:14:10 AM
Attributes        : Archive
```

.

.

.

SENDING OUTPUT TO THE PRINTER

Before we switch tracks and begin working on the chapter's game project, let's learn how to perform the last file operation: printing. Using the Out-Printer cmdlet, you can send data to a printer. When used without any arguments, the Out-Printer cmdlet submits print output to the computer's default printer, as demonstrated here.

```
"This is a printer test." | Out-Printer
```

Here, a text string has been piped to the Out-Printer cmdlet for printing. Similarly, you can send a text file to the default printer, as demonstrated here.

```
Get-Content C:\a.txt | Out-Printer
```

In fact, you can redirect any pipeline object data to the printer, as shown here.

```
get-location | Format-List | Out-Printer
```

When executed, this statement will print out a document containing the following output.

```
Drive        : C
Provider     : Microsoft.PowerShell.Core\FileSystem
ProviderPath : C:\
Path         : C:\
```

Finally, you can also direct the Out-Printer cmdlet to submit print output to a specific printer by passing the printer's name as an argument.

```
Get-Location | Format-List | Out-Printer "hp_deskjet"
```

Here, information about the current working directory is printed to a printer named hp_deskjet.

BACK TO THE POWERSHELL TIC-TAC-TOE GAME

Okay, it's time to turn your attention back to the chapter's main game project, the Power-Shell Tic-Tac-Toe game. The development of this game will demonstrate how to create a script that can interact with the player by displaying messages, retrieving command-line input, and applying programming logic to control the operation of the script.

Designing the Game

This game requires two players, Player X and Player O. Player X always starts off each game. The game validates player moves and keeps track of whose turn it is. The game displays a text-based graphic view of the Tic-Tac-Toe game board, which it updates after each player's turn. The game ends when one player lines up three board squares in a row (horizontally, vertically, or diagonally), or when all game board squares have been selected without either player being able to pull out a win.

The overall logical flow of the PowerShell script is fairly simple. To set it up, we will complete its development in 17 steps, as outlined here.

1. Create a new script file and add opening comment statements.
2. Define and initialize script variables.
3. Develop the Clear-Board function.
4. Develop the Get-Permission function.
5. Develop the Display-Board function.
6. Develop the Validate-Move function.
7. Develop the Check-Results function.
8. Develop the Display-Results function.
9. Ready the game for play.
10. Create a loop to control overall execution of the script.
11. Create a loop to control individual games.
12. Collect player moves.
13. Validate player moves.
14. Look for a winner.
15. Look for a tie.
16. Switch player turns.
17. Prompt players to start a new game.

Creating a New Script

The first step in the creation of the Tic-Tac-Toe game is to create a new PowerShell script file named TicTactoe.ps1 and apply your PowerShell template to it.

```
# **********************************************************************
#
# Script Name:    TicTacToe.ps1 (The Tic-Tac-Toe Game)
# Version:        1.0
# Author:         Jerry Lee Ford, Jr.
# Date:           January 1, 2007
#
# Description:    This PowerShell script is a two player implementation of the
#                 popular Tic-Tac-Toe game
#
# **********************************************************************


# Initialization Section

# Functions and Filters Section

# Main Processing Section
```

Defining and Initializing Script Variables

Next, you need to define and initialize variables used throughout the script. This is accomplished by adding the following statements to the initialization section of the script file. Note that the purpose of each variable is documented by comments that have been added to the script statements.

```
#Define variables used in this script
$startGame = "False"  #Controls when the game terminates
$playGame = "True"    #Controls the play of an individual round of play
$player = "X"         #Specifies the current player's turn
$winner = ""          #Specifies the winner
$moves = 0            #Counts the number of moves made
$move = ""            #Stores the current player's move
$tie = "False"        #Specifies when a tie occurs
```

```
#Variables representing game board squares
$A1 = "1"
$A2 = "1"
$A3 = "1"
$B1 = "1"
$B2 = " "
$B3 = " "
$C1 = " "
$C2 = " "
$C3 = " "
```

Preparing the Clear-Board Function

Now it is time to begin developing custom functions used by the script to perform specific tasks. The functions should be placed in the functions and filters section of the script file. The code of the first function, Clear-Board, is shown below.

```
#This function resets variables representing variable board squares
function Clear-Board {

    $script:A1 = " "
    $script:A2 = " "
    $script:A3 = " "
    $script:B1 = " "
    $script:B2 = " "
    $script:B3 = " "
    $script:C1 = " "
    $script:C2 = " "
    $script:C3 = " "

}
```

When executed, this function resets the variables representing game board squares to a string value made up of a single blank space, thus clearing out the game board and readying it for a new round of play.

Creating the Get-Permission Function

The Get-Permission function, shown next, is responsible for prompting the players for permission to start a new game.

```
#This function gets the player's permission to start a round of play
function Get-Permission {

   #Loop until a valid reply is collected
   while ($startGame -eq "False") {

      Clear-Host  #Clear the Windows command console screen

      #Display the game's opening screen
      Write-Host "`n`n`n`n"
      Write-Host "                                          |      |"
      Write-Host "        Welcome to the            X   |   0  |"
      write-Host "                                          |      |"
      Write-Host "                                   ————————|————"
      Write-Host "   T I C - T A C - T O E            |      |"
      Write-Host "                                          |   X  |"
      Write-Host "                                          |      |"
      Write-Host "           G A M E !               ————————|————"
      Write-Host "                                          |      |"
      Write-Host "                                          |   0  |   X"
      Write-Host "                                          |      |"

      #Collect the player's input
      $response = Read-Host "`n`n`n`n`n`n`n Would you like to play? (Y/N)"

      #Validate the player's input
      if ($response -eq "Y"){  #The player wants to play a new round
         $startGame = "True"
      }
      elseif ($response -eq "N") {  #The player wants to quit
         $startGame = "False"
         Clear-Host  #Clear the Windows command console screen
         exit        #Terminate script execution
      }

   }

}
```

As you can see, to liven things up a bit, this function displays a text-based graphic representing a Tic-Tac-Toe board and prompts the players to enter Y to start a new game. The function validates the player's input allowing only Y or N as valid commands. A response of N results in the termination of the script, which occurs when the exit command is executed.

Creating the Display-Board Function

The next function to be developed is the Display-Board function, whose code statements are shown below. This function is called in order to show the current status of gameplay and to prompt the player whose turn it is, as specified by the $player variable, to make a move. The player's move is then stored in $response.

```
#This function displays the game board, showing each player's moves
function Display-Board {

    Clear-Host  #Clear the Windows command console screen

    #Display the game board
    Write-Host "`n`n                         T I C  -  T A C  - T O E`n`n`n"
    Write-Host "                             1        2        3`n"
    Write-Host "                                     |        |"
    Write-Host "                      A     $A1     |  $A2   |  $A3"
    write-Host "                                     |        |"
    Write-Host "                              ---|---------|---"
    Write-Host "                                     |        |"
    Write-Host "                      B     $B1     |  $B2   |  $B3"
    Write-Host "                                     |        |"
    Write-Host "                              ---|---------|---"
    Write-Host "                                     |        |"
    Write-Host "                      C     $C1     |  $C2   |  $C3"
    Write-Host "                                     |        |"

    #Collect player move
    $move = Read-Host "`n`n`n`n Player $player's turn"
    $move  #Return the Player's input to the calling statement


}
```

Creating the Validate-Move Function

The Validate-Move function, shown here, is called after each player's turn. Its job is to ensure that only valid moves are accepted.

```
#This function determines if the player's input is valid
function Validate-Move {

  if ($move.length -eq 2) {  #Valid moves consist of 2 characters
    if ($move -match "[A-C][1-3]") {  #Regular expression test that looks
      $result = "Valid"                #for an instance of A, B, or C and an
    }                                  #instance of 1, 2, or 3.
    else {
      $result = "Invalid"  #The move is invalid if it is not A1, A2, A3,
    }                      # B1, B2, B3, C1, C2, or C3
  }
  else {
    $result = "Invalid"  #The move is invalid if it does not consists of 2
  }                      #characters

  #Move is invalid if it has already been assigned to a player during a
  # previous turn
  if (($move -eq "A1") -and ($A1 -ne " ")) {$result = "Invalid"}
  if (($move -eq "A2") -and ($A2 -ne " ")) {$result = "Invalid"}
  if (($move -eq "A3") -and ($A3 -ne " ")) {$result = "Invalid"}
  if (($move -eq "B1") -and ($B1 -ne " ")) {$result = "Invalid"}
  if (($move -eq "B2") -and ($B2 -ne " ")) {$result = "Invalid"}
  if (($move -eq "B3") -and ($B3 -ne " ")) {$result = "Invalid"}
  if (($move -eq "C1") -and ($C1 -ne " ")) {$result = "Invalid"}
  if (($move -eq "C2") -and ($C2 -ne " ")) {$result = "Invalid"}
  if (($move -eq "C3") -and ($C3 -ne " ")) {$result = "Invalid"}

  $result  #Return this value to the statement that called this function

}
```

This function begins by setting up an if statement to ensure that the player's move was specified as two characters. The first character represents a coordinate on the horizontal pane and the second character represents a coordinate on the vertical pane. An embedded if statement then executes a regular expression that determines whether the first character supplied by the player is a A, B, or C and whether the second character is a 1, 2, or 3. If the result of either of these two if statements evaluates as being false, the player's move is invalid. Next, a series of eight if statements is executed that checks to see if the move specified by the player was already made earlier in the game. The variable representing the selected game board square is then assigned a value of X or O as appropriate. Therefore, a variable whose value is a blank space is still available for selection and a variable assigned to a value of X or O is not.

Creating the Check-Results Function

At the end of each player's turn, the Check-Results function, shown here, is called. Its job is to see if the current player's last move has resulted in the player winning the game. This is accomplished by checking the values of the variable representing game-board squares. The variables representing each row and column in the game board are checked to see if they have all been assigned to the current player (i.e., if there are three Xs or Os in a row). In addition, the function also checks for a winner diagonally.

```
#This function checks the game board to see if there is a winner
function Check-Results {

    $winner = ""   #Always reset this value before checking

    #Look for a winner vertically
    if (($A1 -eq $player) -and ($A2 -eq $player) -and ($A3 -eq $player)) {
       $winner = $player
    }
    if (($B1 -eq $player) -and ($B2 -eq $player) -and ($B3 -eq $player)) {
       $winner = $player
    }
    if (($C1 -eq $player) -and ($C2 -eq $player) -and ($C3 -eq $player)) {
       $winner = $player
    }

    #Look for a winner horizontally
    if (($A1 -eq $player) -and ($B1 -eq $player) -and ($C1 -eq $player)) {
       $winner = $player
    }
    #Look for a winner horizontally
    if (($A2 -eq $player) -and ($B2 -eq $player) -and ($C2 -eq $player)) {
       $winner = $player
    }
```

```
#Look for a winner horizontally
if (($A3 -eq $player) -and ($B3 -eq $player) -and ($C3 -eq $player)) {
  $winner = $player
}

#Look for a winner diagonally
if (($A1 -eq $player) -and ($B2 -eq $player) -and ($C3 -eq $player)) {
  $winner = $player
}

if (($A1 -eq $player) -and ($B2 -eq $player) -and ($C1 -eq $player)) {
  $winner = $player
}

$winner  #Return this value to the statement that called this function

}
```

Creating the Display-Results Function

The last function that you will need to create is the Display-Results function. This function, shown below, is called at the end of each game in order to display the final status of the game and to identify who, if anyone, has won.

```
#This function displays the game board and the final results of a round
#of play
function Display-Results {

  Clear-Host  #Clear the Windows command console screen

  #Display the game board
  Write-Host "`n`n                    T I C  -  T A C  - T O E`n`n`n"
  Write-Host "                      1       2       3`n"
  Write-Host "                          |       |"
  Write-Host "                  A   $A1  |  $A2  |  $A3"
  write-Host "                          |       |"
  Write-Host "                     ----|-------|----"
  Write-Host "                          |       |"
  Write-Host "                  B   $B1  |  $B2  |  $B3"
  Write-Host "                          |       |"
  Write-Host "                     ----|-------|----"
  Write-Host "                          |       |"
  Write-Host "                  C   $C1  |  $C2  |  $C3"
  Write-Host "                          |       |"
```

```
if ($tie -eq "True") {  #Check to see if the game resulted in a tie
Read-Host "`n`n`n`n The game has ended in a tie. Press Enter to continue"
}
else {  #If a tie did not occur, identify the winner
 Read-Host "`n`n`n`n Game over. $player has won. Press Enter to continue"
}


}
```

In addition to displaying the game board, this function examines the value of $tie to deter-mine whether the game has ended in a tie. If this is not the case, the appropriate player is identified as the winner.

Clearing the Game Board and Prompting for User Permission

Now that all variables and functions have been defined, it is time to work on putting together the programming logic that will drive the overall execution of the script. This code goes in the script file's main processing section. To begin, add the following statements.

```
Clear-Board  #Call function that resets the game board

Get-Permission  #Call function that asks the players for permission to
                # start a new round of play
```

The first statement calls on the Clear-Board function to clear out any variable assignment that may be left over from a previous game. The second statement calls on the Get-Permission function, which prompts the players for permission to start a new game.

Creating a Loop to Control Script Execution

The rest of the logic in the main processing section is enclosed in the following loop, which should be added to the bottom of the main processing section. This loop executes until the value of $Terminate is set equal to True, which occurs only after the players tell the game to close.

```
while ($Terminate -ne "True") {  #Loop until the player decides to quit


}
```

Creating a Loop to Control Individual Gameplay

Within the while loop that you just added to the script file, you need to create a second inner loop. This loop, shown below, will control the execution of individual games.

```
while ($playGame -eq "True") {  #This loop controls the logic required to
                                #play a round of Tic-Tac-Toe



}
```

As you can see, this loop has been set up to run while the value of $playGame is set equal to True. Once this occurs, the inner loop stops executing, returning control to the outer loop, which will then prompt the players to play another game. If the players elect to play a new game, the inner loop will be executed again. Otherwise, the game will be closed.

Collecting Player Moves

Next, add the following statements inside the inner loop. The first statement calls on the Display-Board function, which displays the game board and prompts the current player to make a move. The player's move is then returned and assigned to $move. The second statement executes the Validate-Move function. This function ensures that the move inputted by the player was valid and returns a value indicating the results of that analysis which is then stored in $validMove.

```
$move = Display-Board    #Call function that displays the game board and
                         #collects player moves


$validMove = Validate-Move  #Call the function that validates player moves
```

Validating Player Moves

Now that the player's move has been validated, it is time to take action based on the results of that analysis. This is accomplished by adding the following statement to the end of the inner loop.

```
if ($validMove -eq "Valid") {  #Process valid moves

  $moves++ #Increment variable that keeps track of the number of valid moves

  #Assign the appropriate game board square to the player that selected it
  if ($move -eq "A1") {$A1 = $player}
```

```
    if ($move -eq "A2") {$A2 = $player}
    if ($move -eq "A3") {$A3 = $player}
    if ($move -eq "B1") {$B1 = $player}
    if ($move -eq "B2") {$B2 = $player}
    if ($move -eq "B3") {$B3 = $player}
    if ($move -eq "C1") {$C1 = $player}
    if ($move -eq "C2") {$C2 = $player}
    if ($move -eq "C3") {$C3 = $player}

}
else {   #Process invalid moves

    Clear-Host   #Clear the Windows command console screen
    Read-Host "`n`n`n`n`n`n`n`n`nInvalid Move. Press Enter to try again"
    continue   #Repeat this loop

}
```

As you can see, an if statement has been set up that either increments the value of $moves and then assigns the appropriate game board square to the player or displays an error message instruction to try again.

Determining if Either Player Has Won the Game

The next set of statements to be added to the inner loop are shown below. The first statement executes the Check-Results function, which is responsible for determining if one of the players has won the game. The Check-Results function returns the results of its analysis, which is then assigned to $winner. The rest of the statements shown below are organized into two if statements. The first if statement checks to see if Player X has won the game. The second if statement does the same thing for Player 0.

```
$winner = Check-Results   #Call function that determines if the game is over
                          #and who, if anyone, has won

if ($winner -eq "X") {   #Perform the following actions when Player X wins

    Write-Host `a   #Make a beep sound
    Display-Results   #Call function that displays game results
    $playGame = "False"
    continue   #Repeat this loop

}
```

```
if ($winner -eq "O") {   #Perform the following actions when Player O wins

   Write-Host `a   #Make a beep sound
   Display-Results #Call function that displays game results
   $playGame = "False"
   continue   #Repeat this loop

}
```

In the event that one of the players has won the game, the following actions occur. First, a beeping sound is played by passing the `a escape character to the Write-Host cmdlet to notify the player that the game is over. The Display-Results function is then called. This function displays the final results of the game, informing the players who won. The value of $playGame is then set equal to False, which will terminate the execution of the inner loop when the following continue command is executed.

TRICK Up to this point in the book, all of the Windows PowerShell game scripts that you have developed have had one feature in common: They have been mute. However, if you want you can liven up your scripts a bit by adding a little touch of sound. Specifically, by inserting the `a escape character into a Write-Host statement as demonstrated below, you can play a beep sound at predefined points during the execution of your PowerShell scripts.

```
Write-Host `a   #Make a beep sound
```

The Tic-Tac-Toe game uses this feature to help notify players when a game has been won, lost, or tied.

Determining if a Tie Has Occurred

In the event that neither player has won the game, a check should be made to see if a tie has occurred. This is accomplished by adding the following statements to the end of the inner loop.

```
if ($moves -eq 9) {   #Perform the following actions when a tie occurs

   Write-Host `a   #Make a beep sound
   $tie = "True"
   Display-Results #Call function that displays game results
   $playGame = "False"
   continue   #Repeat this loop

}
```

As you can see, an if statement is used to examine the value of $moves and if it is set equal to 9, then every square on the game board has been selected and a tie is declared by setting $tie equal to True.

Switching Between Player Turns

If a tie has not occurred and neither player has been found to have won the game, the inner loop executes and prompts the next player to make a move. Before doing so, the following statements need to be executed and should therefore be added to the end of the inner loop.

```
#The game is not over yet so switch player turn
if ($playGame -eq "True") {
  if ($player -eq "X") {
    $player = "O"
  }
  else {
    $player = "X"
  }
}
```

As you can see, these statements toggle the value of $player between X and O each time they are executed, thus controlling whose turn it is.

Prompting Players to Play a New Game

The last set of code statements to be added to the script, shown below, should be added to the end of the outer loop. These statements set up a while loop that prompts the players to play a new game.

```
#This next set of statements only runs when the current round of play
#has ended

$response = "False" #Set default value in order to ensure the loop executes

#Loop until valid input is received
while ($response -ne "True") {

  Clear-Host  #Clear the Windows command console screen

  #Prompt the player to play a new game
  $response = Read-Host "`n`n Play again? (Y/N)"

  #Validate the player's input  #Keep playing
```

```
if ($response -eq "Y") {

    #Reset default variable settings to get ready for a new round of play
    $response = "True"
    $terminate = "False"
    $playGame = "True"
    Clear-Board
    $player = "X"
    $moves = 0
    $tie = "False"

}
elseif ($response -eq "N") {  #Time to quit

    Clear-Host  #Clear the Windows command console screen
    Write-host " `n`n Please return and play again soon."
    Read-Host  #Pause gameplay
    $response = "True"
    $terminate = "True"

}
else {  #Invalid input received

    Clear-Host  #Clear the Windows command console screen
    Write-Host "`n`n Invalid input. Please press Enter to try again."
    Read-Host  #Pause gameplay

}

}
```

Only user input of Y or N is accepted. A value of Y starts a new round of play by resetting the script variables back to their initial starting values. A reply of N terminates the game and the execution of the script.

The Final Result

Okay, that's it. Assuming you have not made any typos in keying in the script statements that make up the Tic-Tac-Toe game, everything should work as advertised. I suggest you take a little time to test the game and make sure it works as expected and then find a friend to play against and show off your programming skills to.

SUMMARY

In this chapter you learned the ins and outs of programmatically administering files and folders. This included learning how to create, delete, rename, copy, and move files and folders. You also learned how to read from and write to different types of files, including text files, CSV files, and XML files. You also learned how to use regular expressions to perform string pattern matching. On top of all this, you learned how to take control of cmdlet output using the Format-List and Format-Table cmdlets. Now, before you move on to Chapter 9, "Basic System Administration," I suggest you set aside a few additional minutes to improve the Tic-Tac-Toe game by tackling the following list of challenges.

CHALLENGES

1. Provide players with the ability to view a Help screen that explains the rules of the Tic-Tac-Toe game. In addition, revisit the text messages displayed by the game with an eye to making them more user friendly.

2. Keep track of the number of games played as well as the number of games won, lost, and tied by each player and make the display of this information available at the end of each game.

3. Consider modifying the game so that when it first starts it collects both player's names and then uses this information to inform each player, by name, whose turn it is and who has won the game.

BASIC SYSTEM ADMINISTRATION

T he purpose of this chapter is to provide you with working examples of the kinds of system tasks that you can perform with Windows PowerShell scripts, as well as to give you an appreciation for the types of information that Windows PowerShell puts at your fingertips. You will learn how to programmatically interact with the Windows registry and use it as a repository for script-configuration settings. You will learn how to automate the management and reporting of different Windows resources, including Windows processes and services. This chapter will also teach you how to create and instantiate new objects using .NET classes and COM objects, which will open up a whole new world of programming capabilities. On top of all this, you will learn how to create a new PowerShell game, PowerShell Blackjack.

Specifically, you will learn how to:

- Create registry keys and values and retrieve data stores in registry values
- Instantiate new objects based on .NET classes and COM objects
- Retrieve information about local and remote computers using WMI
- Administer Windows services, processes, and logs

PROJECT PREVIEW: THE POWERSHELL BLACKJACK GAME

In this chapter you will learn how to create a PowerShell version of the Blackjack card game. In this version of the game, the player will go head to head against the computer in an effort to get a better hand without busting by going over 21. When first started, the game's welcome screen is displayed, as shown in Figure 9.1.

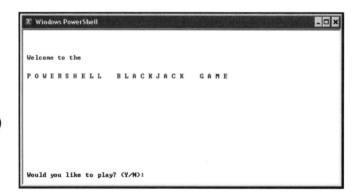

FIGURE 9.1

The welcome screen for the PowerShell Blackjack game.

The welcome screen is also responsible for prompting the player for permission to start a new round of play. This game interfaces with the Windows registry by accessing a key and value that you will set up as you work your way through this chapter. If the required key and value are not found in the registry and the player responds to the welcome screen by entering an N, the game will display an error message before terminating. If, however, the registry key and value are in place, the game will instead display the screen shown in Figure 9.2, should the player decide not to play the game after starting the script.

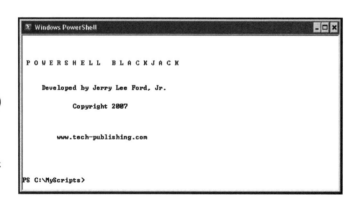

FIGURE 9.2

By default, the game ends by displaying information about itself and its developer.

If, instead of quitting, the player elects to play a hand, a screen similar to the one shown in Figure 9.3 is displayed, showing the player both her and the computer's opening card.

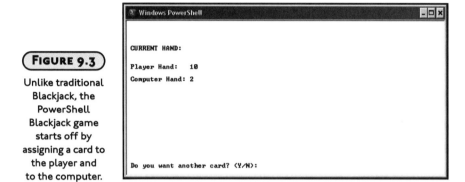

FIGURE 9.3

Unlike traditional Blackjack, the PowerShell Blackjack game starts off by assigning a card to the player and to the computer.

At the bottom of the screen, the player is prompted to take another card. In order to take a new card, the player must type Y. To pass on the new card and to stick with her hand, the player must enter an N. Any other input is ignored by the game. The player, at her discretion, may continue to take new cards, as demonstrated in Figure 9.4, until the value of her hand exceeds 21, in which case she busts.

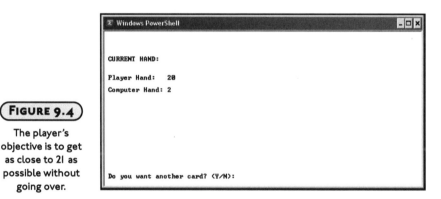

FIGURE 9.4

The player's objective is to get as close to 21 as possible without going over.

If the player busts, the computer wins without ever having to take its own turn. Assuming that the player does not bust, the computer goes next. The computer will continue to take new cards as long as the total value of its hand it less than 17. Once its hand exceeds a value of 17, the computer's turn ends (e.g., with a value over 17 but less than or equal to 21, or with a bust).

Figure 9.5 shows the results of a typical round of play. In this example, the player has beaten the computer.

FIGURE 9.5

The player has
won this hand.

At the end of each hand, the player is prompted to either press Enter to start a new hand or to type Q and press Enter to quit the game.

ACCESSING AND ADMINISTERING SYSTEM RESOURCES

Windows PowerShell provides system administrators, power users, and computer hobbyists with access to a host of system, application, and network resources. The number of possibilities is too great to cover them all in this book. Instead, this chapter will attempt to provide you with a sampling of examples that demonstrate some of the many avenues of system administration that windows PowerShell can assist you in automating.

Listing and Stopping Processes

Windows operating systems run various processes behind the scenes that work together to help keep your computer running smoothly. As you have already seen, you can use the Get-Process cmdlet to get a listing of all the processes running on a computer, as demonstrated here:

Get-Process

When executed, this statement will generate output similar to the following:

Handles	NPM(K)	PM(K)	WS(K)	VM(M)	CPU(s)	Id	ProcessName
17	2	540	180	25	0.09	3088	AcroTray
78	3	1948	184	33	0.20	2972	ALCXMNTR
102	5	1128	580	32	0.09	144	alg
334	9	4552	1360	63	6.92	3156	BackWeb-137903
2590	6	4296	5208	41	700.09	2424	CFD

549	6	1808	2380	28	244.97	540 csrss
612	18	16852	17948	103	798.88	1996 explorer
141	3	1036	2016	35	1.39	3164 FINDFAST

.

.

.

The amount of information returned by the Get-Process cmdlet can be a bit overwhelming. To help streamline output, you can pass a specified process name to the cmdlet as an argument, as demonstrated next.

```
Get-Process PowerShell
```

When executed, this statement displays process information for just the PowerShell process. Assuming that the specified process is currently running, this statement will generate output similar to that shown here.

Handles	NPM(K)	PM(K)	WS(K)	VM(M)	CPU(s)	Id ProcessName
----	----	----	----	----	----	-- ------
356	11	31636	31228	150	3.75	4000 powershel

You can also use a comma-separated list to display more than one process at a time, as demonstrated next. You may also use wildcards to match any number of processes.

```
Get-Process notepad, powershell
```

From time to time, things go awry on Windows. As a result, processes get hung up, misbehave, or fail to respond. When these types of circumstances occur, you can use the Stop-Process cmdlet to terminate these processes. For example, the following statement terminates a process by specifying its process ID.

```
Stop-Process 2932
```

You can just as easily terminate a process by specifying its process name, as demonstrated here.

```
Stop-Process -processname notepad
```

Administering Windows Services

Another key component of the Windows operating system is the software services that it runs under the covers in order to provide specific services. For example, the spooler service is responsible for managing print operations. Windows PowerShell lets you interact with and administer Windows services via a number of different cmdlets, as listed here.

- **Get-Service.** Retrieves a list of installed services.
- **Set-Service.** Changes a service's description, startup mode, or the display name of a service.
- **Suspend-Service.** Pauses the execution of a service. However, the service will continue to serve existing connections.
- **Resume-Service.** Resumes a paused service.
- **Stop-Service.** Stops a service.
- **Start-Service.** Starts a service.
- **Restart-Service.** Stops and then restarts a service.

To give you an idea of how you might use these cmdlets, take a look at the following PowerShell script. This script is a text-based Print Wizard that is designed to help the user self-diagnose and correct common printer problems before calling on the company's IT Help Desk for support. Admittedly, this script is rather simplistic, offering only a limited amount of instruction, and it lacks input validity checking, relying instead on the user to carefully follow instructions. Still, it provides a basis upon which a more sophisticated and robust script might be developed.

```
# *************************************************************************
#
# Script Name:    PrintWizard.ps1
# Version:        1.0
# Author:         Jerry Lee Ford, Jr.
# Date:           January 1, 2007
#
# Description:    This PowerShell script is designed to assist the user in
#                 resolving common printing problems.
#
# *************************************************************************


# Initialization Section

$response = ""   #Stores user input


# Functions and Filters Section
```

```
function Display-ServiceStatus {
  Get-Service | Where-Object {$_.Name -eq "Spooler"}
}

function Display-Thanks {
  Clear-Host
  Write-Host "`nThank you for using the Print Wizard."
  exit
}

function Contact-HelpDesk {
  Clear-Host
  Write-Host "`nContact the Help Desk for additional assistance."
  exit
}


# Main Processing Section

#Step 1 - Display the status of the Spooler service

Clear-Host

Write-Host "`nPRINT WIZARD`n"
Write-Host "The current status of the printer spooler service, which is"
Write-Host "responsible for managing the printing process, is: `n"

Display-ServiceStatus

Write-Host "`n`nA status of `"Running`" generally indicates that the"
Write-Host "spooler is operating correctly and the problem lies elsewhere."

$response = Read-Host "`n`nDoes this solve your problem? (Y/N)"

if ($response -eq "Y") {
  Display-Thanks
}
else {  #Step 2 - Check the paper supply
  Clear-Host
```

```
Write-Host "`nDoes your printer have paper in it? If not, add new paper"
Write-Host "and see if this fixes the problem."

$response = Read-Host "`n`nDoes this solve your problem? (Y/N)"

if ($response -eq "Y") {
  Display-Thanks
}
else {   #Step 3 - Restart the Spooler service
  Clear-Host
  Write-Host "`nSometimes stopping and starting the `"spooler`" service"
  Write-Host "will fix printing problems."
  $response = Read-Host "`nRestart the service? (Y/N)"
  if ($response -eq "Y") {
    Restart-service "Spooler"
    Clear-Host
    Write-Host "`nThe current status of the printer spooler service is:"`
                "`n`n"
    Display-ServiceStatus
  }
  else {
    Contact-HelpDesk
  }
  $response = Read-Host "`n`nDoes this solve your problem? (Y/N)"
  if ($response -eq "N") {
    Contact-HelpDesk
  }
  else {
    Display-Thanks
  }
}
}
```

As you can see, the script begins by defining a variable in which user input is stored, as well as three functions, which are used to display information about the status of the spooler server and to display text messages that are displayed as the script executes. When first started, the script executes the Get-Service cmdlet to generate a list of active services and then uses the Where-Object cmdlet to filter out all services except for the spooler service. The output of this command is then displayed, as shown in Figure 9.6.

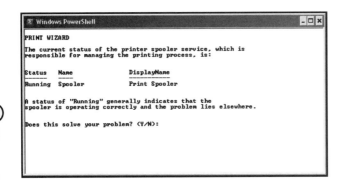

FIGURE 9.6

The Print Wizard displays the status of the spooler service.

The user is then asked to respond with a value of Y or N, depending on whether the printing problem is still occurring. Assuming that nothing has changed and that the user enters N, the screen shown in Figure 9.7 is displayed.

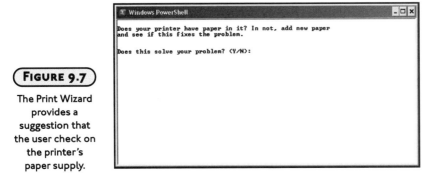

FIGURE 9.7

The Print Wizard provides a suggestion that the user check on the printer's paper supply.

At this point, the user is given new instructions to follow; in this case, checking the printer's paper supply. The script again asks the user if the printing problem has been resolved. If the user responds by again entering N, the screen shown in Figure 9.8 is displayed. This time, the script suggests that it may be helpful to restart the spooler service.

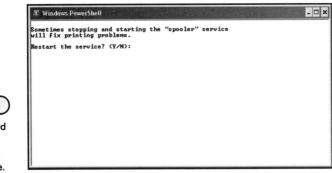

FIGURE 9.8

The Print Wizard suggests restarting the spooler service.

Assuming that the user responds in the affirmative, the script executes the Restart-Service cmdlet, passing it an argument of Spooler. The script then waits for the cmdlet to finish executing and displays the status of the service again, as demonstrated in Figure 9.9.

FIGURE 9.9

The Print Wizard redisplays the status of the spooler service after restarting it.

If the user's problem has not been corrected at this point, the script displays a message advising the user to contact the Help Desk.

Accessing Event Logs

Windows PowerShell also provides you with the ability to work with and view event logs stored on the computer using the Get-EventLog cmdlet. The Windows operating system and its applications write different types of messages to these event logs providing status and error information that can be used to track down and analyze problems. By passing an argument of -list to the Get-EventLog, you can instruct the cmdlet to generate a list of all the event logs on your computer, as demonstrated here.

```
Get-EventLog -list
```

When executed, this statement will display output similar to this:

Max(K)	Retain	OverflowAction	Entries	Name
512	0	OverwriteAsNeeded	225	Application
15,360	0	OverwriteAsNeeded	1,485	PowerShell
512	0	OverwriteAsNeeded	2,103	Security
512	0	OverwriteAsNeeded	2,297	System

Once you know what event logs are stored on your computer, you can view their contents. For example, the following statement displays a list of all the messages that have been written to the Application event log.

```
Get-EventLog Application
```

When executed, this statement will generate output similar to that shown below.

```
Index Time          Type Source              EventID Message
----- ----          ---- ----                ------- -------
225 Nov 05 00:13     Erro Application Error   1001 Fault bucket 02724608.
224 Nov 05 00:13     Erro Application Error   1000 Faulting application ...
223 Nov 04 13:24     Info crypt32             7 Successful auto update..
222 Nov 03 18:27     Erro Application Hang    1002 Hanging application R...
221 Nov 03 13:12     Info ITSS                1 The description for E...
220 Nov 03 13:12     Info ITSS                1 The description for E...
219 Nov 03 13:12     Info ITSS                1 The description for E...
218 Nov 02 21:52     Erro Application Hang    1002 Hanging application i...
217 Oct 30 13:57     Info LoadPerf            1000 Performance counters ...
216 Oct 30 13:57     Info LoadPerf            1001 Performance counters ...
215 Oct 30 13:57     Info SecurityCenter      1800 The Windows Security ...
214 Oct 29 20:46     Erro Application Error   1000 Faulting application ...
213 Oct 28 01:24     Erro Application Error   1001 Fault bucket 02724608.
```

Event logs can hold many thousands of messages. If you are looking for something that may have recently occurred, you can limit the amount of data that is returned by the Get-EventLog cmdlet by passing it the -newest parameter, which specifies how many of the most recently recorded messages you want to view, as demonstrated here.

```
Get-Eventlog Application -newest 4
```

When executed, this statement will generate output similar to this:

```
Index Time          Type Source              EventID Message
----- ----          ---- ----                ------- -------
224 Nov 05 00:13     Erro Application Error   1000 Faulting application ...
223 Nov 04 13:24     Info crypt32             7 Successful auto update..
222 Nov 03 18:27     Erro Application Hang    1002 Hanging application R...
221 Nov 03 13:12     Info ITSS                1 The description for E...
```

You may have noticed that the data returned by the Get-EventLog is truncated, making it pretty unusable. You can fix this using the Format-List cmdlet to generate a readable report.

```
Get-Eventlog application -newest 1 | Format-List > C:\Temp\Sample.txt
```

In this example, the last message recorded in the Application event log is retrieved and stored as a report in a text file named Sample.txt. When opened, this file will contain information similar to that shown here.

```
Index               : 224
EntryType           : Error
EventID             : 1000
Message             : Faulting application game.exe, version 1.0.0.1, faulting
                        module game.exe, version 1.0.0.1, fault address 0x00375ac6.
Category            : (0)
CategoryNumber      : 0
ReplacementStrings  : {game.exe, 1.0.0.1, game.exe, 1.0.0.1...}
Source              : Application Error
TimeGenerated       : 11/5/2006 12:13:29 AM
TimeWritten         : 11/5/2006 12:13:29 AM
UserName            :
```

It may be helpful to generate a report that contains only certain types of event messages. For example, you might only want to see messages that have a certain EventID value or that are generated by a particular source. This can be accomplished by piping the output of the Get-EventLog cmdlet to the Where-Object cmdlet, as demonstrated here.

```
Get-Eventlog application | Where-Object {$_.Source -eq "Userenv"}
```

When executed, this statement generates the following list of event messages, which you might then decide to format and save as a report.

```
Index Time         Type Source           EventID Message
----- ----         ---- ------           ------- -------
203 Oct 12 03:10    Warn Userenv            1517 Windows saved user HP...
167 Oct 09 21:21    Warn Userenv            1517 Windows saved user HP...
138 Sep 15 03:07    Warn Userenv            1517 Windows saved user HP...
102 Sep 06 13:28    Warn Userenv            1517 Windows saved user HP...
 90 Aug 30 20:57    Warn Userenv            1517 Windows saved user HP...
 75 Aug 15 03:07    Warn Userenv            1517 Windows saved user HP...
 71 Aug 10 21:21    Warn Userenv            1517 Windows saved user HP...
 65 Aug 01 20:23    Warn Userenv            1517 Windows saved user HP...
 38 Jul 17 03:08    Warn Userenv            1517 Windows saved user HP...
```

Retrieving System Information Using WMI

As you have just seen, Windows PowerShell provides you with access to cmdlets that collect information about different aspects of the computer. However, there is only a limited number of these cmdlets available. Windows PowerShell makes up for this by allowing you to use Microsoft's Windows Management Instrumentation (WMI) in order to tap into and access system information from a variety of different sources, including the operating system, services, application, and hardware.

WMI is a system-management interface designed to facilitate access to system information. Windows PowerShell encapsulates its support for WMI through the Get-WmiObject cmdlet. The amount of information that can be accessed through WMI is staggering. A complete discussion of WMI is well beyond the scope of this book. However, to give you an appreciation of WMI and the kinds of data that you can get from it, the next several sections will provide you with a series of examples that show how to access BIOS, processor, network, and application information.

Retrieving BIOS Information

Using the Get-WmiObject cmdlet, you can retrieve system BIOS information from any Windows computer. Computer administrators might use this information in order to determine on which computers to apply a BIOS update in the event a BIOS-related problem is discovered on certain models of computers.

All that you have to do to retrieve BIOS information is pass Win32-BIOS as an argument to the cmdlet.

```
$x = Get-WmiObject Win32_BIOS
$x
```

When executed, BIOS information is collected and stored in a variable named $x. In the preceding example, this data is then displayed. When executed, this example will display output similar to that shown here.

```
SMBIOSBIOSVersion : 3.10
Manufacturer      : American Megatrends Inc.
Name              : BIOS Date: 06/27/03 20:48:31 Ver: 08.00.08
SerialNumber      : MXM33409GZ NA200
Version           : A M I  - 6000327
```

Retrieving System Information

You can also use the Get-WmiObject cmdlet to retrieve processor information by passing it an argument of Win32_Processor as shown next. This information might prove useful in situations in which an administrator needs to determine if a computer's processor meets the minimum requirements to run a particular application. The information that is returned will include processor name, description, manufacturer, and other processor related data.

```
Get-WmiObject Win32_Processor
```

When executed, this statement will display output similar to this:

```
AddressWidth              : 32
Architecture              : 0
Availability              : 3
Caption                   : x86 Family 15 Model 2 Stepping 9
ConfigManagerErrorCode    :
ConfigManagerUserConfig   :
CpuStatus                 : 1
CreationClassName         : Win32_Processor
CurrentClockSpeed         : 2599
CurrentVoltage            :
DataWidth                 : 32
Description               : x86 Family 15 Model 2 Stepping 9
DeviceID                  : CPU0
ErrorCleared              :
ErrorDescription          :
ExtClock                  : 200
Family                    : 2
InstallDate               :
L2CacheSize               : 0
L2CacheSpeed              :
LastErrorCode             :
Level                     : 15
LoadPercentage            : 0
Manufacturer              : GenuineIntel
MaxClockSpeed             : 2599
Name                      :                    Intel(R) Pentium(R) 4 CPU 2.60GHz
.
.
.
```

Due to the volume of information that this statement generates, I've shortened the list of output a bit. Typically, to prevent information overload, you will want to use the `Format-List` cmdlet to limit the display of processor data to just the information that you are interested in.

```
Get-WmiObject Win32_Processor | Format-List Name, Caption, Manufacturer
```

When executed, this statement displays a far more manageable list of processor information.

```
Name             : Intel(R) Pentium(R) 4 CPU 2.60GHz
Caption          : x86 Family 15 Model 2 Stepping 9
Manufacturer     : GenuineIntel
```

Retrieving Networking Data

WMI also provides access to network information. Computer administrators might use this information to verify a computer network configuration or to troubleshoot network connectivity problems. For example, to retrieve a list of all active network protocols, you would pass `Win32_NetworkProtocol` as an argument to the `Get-WmiObject` cmdlet as shown here.

```
Get-WmiObject Win32_NetworkProtocol
```

When executed, this statement will display a list of information about all of the networking protocols installed on your computer, as demonstrated by the following output:

```
Caption               : Tcpip
GuaranteesDelivery    : True
GuaranteesSequencing  : True
ConnectionlessService : False
Status                : OK
Name                  : MSAFD Tcpip [TCP/IP]
.
.
.
```

Retrieving Application Data

WMI also provides you with access to information about the applications stored on your computer. A computer administrator might, for example, create a PowerShell script that retrieves a listing of all the applications installed on a computer. For example, the following statements will retrieve information about applications that have been installed using the Windows Installer service.

```
Get-WmiObject Win32_Product
```

When executed, this statement will display data similar to this:

```
IdentifyingNumber    : {2DFDD440-A33C-42E4-A366-71E6CB4246A0}
Name                 : Windows PowerShell
Vendor               : Microsoft Corporation
Version              : 1.0.9567.1
Caption              : Windows PowerShell
```

```
IdentifyingNumber      : {AC76BA86-7AD7-1033-7B44-A70800000002}
Name                   : Adobe Reader 7.0.8
Vendor                 : Adobe Systems Incorporated
Version                : 7.0.8
Caption                : Adobe Reader 7.0.8


IdentifyingNumber      : {7131646D-CD3C-40F4-97B9-CD9E4E6262EF}
Name                   : Microsoft .NET Framework 2.0
Vendor                 : Microsoft Corporation
Version                : 2.0.50727
<SPACE> next page; <CR> next line; Q quit
Caption                : Microsoft .NET Framework 2.0
```

Pulling WMI Data from Remote Computers

Assuming that you have the security permissions required to do so, the Get-WmiObject cmdlet can also be used to retrieve information from remote network computers. To do so, just append the -computername parameter to the end of your statements, as demonstrated here.

```
Get-WmiObject Win32_ComputerSystem -computername HP
```

In this example, the Get-WmiObject is executed and instructed to retrieve computer system data from a network computer named HP.

```
Domain               : MSHOME
Manufacturer         : HP Pavilion 061
Model                : DF253A-ABA a250n
Name                 : HP
PrimaryOwnerName     :
TotalPhysicalMemory  : 536195072
```

Consider as a practical example of this capability a scenario in which a computer administrator has been asked to install a new application on 20 computers residing on a company's local area network. Some of the computers might be behind locked doors or in rooms occupied by high-level executives and thus not readily accessible during the normal course of the day. In addition, the new application might require 500 MB of memory in order to run. Rather than physically visiting each computer to determine the amount of memory installed on it, the computer administrator could instead create a PowerShell script that remotely retrieves each computer's total physical memory. For example, the following statement could be used to display a list of computers on the LAN and their available physical memory.

```
Get-WmiObject Win32_ComputerSystem -computername HP1, HP2, HP3 | Format-List
Name, TotalPhysicalMemory
```

In this example, data is retrieved from the three network computers. As you can see, the names of each remote computer are provided to the -computername parameter as a comma-separated list. The resulting output is then piped to the Format-List cmdlet, which displays the name of each computer and its available physical memory, as demonstrated here.

```
Name                : HP1
TotalPhysicalmemory : 536195072

Name                : HP2
TotalPhysicalmemory : 1072390144

Name                : HP3
TotalPhysicalmemory : 536195072
```

Taking Advantage of .NET Classes

Windows PowerShell depends upon the .NET Framework for much of its capabilities. Numerous cmdlets have been designed to manipulate .NET resources or to retrieve data provided by .NET. However, you are not limited to just the .NET resources exposed by PowerShell cmdlets. Thanks to the New-Object cmdlet, you can create and instantiate an instance of other .NET classes. For example, you have already seen examples in this book of how to use the New-Object cmdlet to instantiate an instance of the Random class, as demonstrated here.

```
$randomNo = New-Object System.Random
```

When executed, this statement creates an instance of a Random object. Once instantiated, you have access to the properties and methods associated with this object. In the case of the Random object, you have access to its Next method, which generates a random number within a specified range.

```
$number = $randomNo.Next(1, 11)
```

Here, a random number (integer) is created in the range of 1 to 10 and assigned to a variable named $number.

Taking Advantage of COM Objects

The New-Object cmdlet just discussed in the previous section, can also be used to instantiate and control COM objects. *COM* stands for *Component Object Model* and is a Microsoft technology that allows Windows PowerShell to programmatically interact with and control objects, which includes Active X controls and various Windows applications (those that support COM).

As an example, the following statements demonstrate how to create a small PowerShell script that can use COM to instantiate an instance of Microsoft Word, create a new Word document, set a font type and font size, write output to the file, and then save it. Once the document is saved, the new document is closed and Word is then terminated.

```
$processList = Get-Process   #Retrieve a listing of active processes
$currentDate = Get-Date      #Retrieve the current date and time

$MSWord = New-Object -ComObject "Word.Application" #Instantiate Word

$MSWord.Documents.Add()   #Use the Document object's Add method to create
                          #a new document

$MSWord.Selection.Font.Name = "Arial" #Set the Font object's Name property
$MSWord.Selection.Font.Size = 12      #Set the Font object's Size property

#Use the Selection Object's TypeText method to write output to the document
$MSWord.Selection.Typetext($ProcessList)

#Use the ActiveDocument object's SaveAs method to save the document and
#then its Close method to close the document
$MSWord.ActiveDocument.SaveAs("C:\Temp\WordReport.doc")
$MSWord.ActiveDocument.Close()

#Use the application object's Quit method to terminate Microsoft Word
$MSWord.Quit()
```

When executed, this example displays the output shown in Figure 9.10.

In this example, I used the object model belonging to Word 97. Different applications have different object models. Different versions of the same application may also use slightly different versions of the same object model. Therefore, it may take a little research (using the application developer's documentation) before you can learn enough about an application's object model to be able to programmatically interact with it.

The application object resides at the top of the Word object model. Once used to instantiate an instance of Word, you can use other lower-level objects and their methods and properties to automate Word tasks. To learn more about the Word object model, visit http://msdn.microsoft.com/office.

FIGURE 9.10

A Microsoft Word document containing the output generated by the Get-Process cmdlet.

As another example of how to work with COM objects, consider the following statements.

```
$InternetExplorer = New-Object -ComObject "InternetExplorer.Application"
$InternetExplorer.Navigate("http://www.tech-publishing.com")
$InternetExplorer.Visible = "True"
```

When executed, this example uses the New-Object cmdlet to create an instance of Internet Explorer. Next, Internet Explorer's Navigate method is used to load the www.tech-publishing.com web page. Lastly, Internet Explorer's Visible property is set equal to True, making the browser and the specified web page visible. Figure 9.11 shows an example of the output that you will see if you create and run this example,

FIGURE 9.11

Using COM to automate the execution of Internet Explorer.

PROGRAMMATICALLY INTERACTING WITH THE WINDOWS REGISTRY

Another powerful capability of Windows PowerShell is its ability to interact with the Windows registry. This means that not only can you write PowerShell scripts that can access data stored in the Windows registry, but you can also store data in the registry.

The Windows registry is organized into five high-level keys, also referred to as *hives*. Registry keys are somewhat analogous to folders on the Windows file system. *Keys* are used to store other keys (or subkeys) and values. *Values* are analogous to files on the Windows file system. Actual data stored in the registry is stored inside values. Of the five high-level root keys, Windows PowerShell gives you access to the values stored in two of them, as outlined in Table 9.1.

TABLE 9.1 REGISTRY KEYS ACCESSIBLE BY THE WINDOWS POWERSHELL

Hive	Shortcut	Description
HKEY_CURRENT_USER	hkcu	Stores information about the currently logged on user
HKEY_LOCAL_MACHINE	hklm	Stores global computer settings

Windows PowerShell treats registry values as properties. This lets you use the Get-ItemProperty cmdlet to view information about a key and to list all its values, as demonstrated here.

```
Set-Location hklm:\SOFTWARE\Microsoft\PowerShell\1\PowerShellEngine
Get-ItemProperty .
```

The first statement shown here switches from the current provider, typically the Windows file system, to a subkey located on the HKEY_LOCAL_MACHINE hive. The second statement uses the Get-ItemProperty cmdlet to retrieve information about the current subkey. When executed, these statements will generate output similar to that shown next.

TRAP Windows operating systems use the registry to store data about the operating system as well as data about the computer's hardware, software, and user-configuration settings. The integrity of the registry is critical to the proper operation of the computer. Therefore, it is important that you take great care when working with it. Otherwise, if you accidentally change or delete the wrong key or value, it can have an unpredictable impact on the operation of your computer.

```
PSPath                     : Microsoft.PowerShell.Core\Registry::HKEY_LOCAL_MACHIN
                             E\SOFTWARE\Microsoft\PowerShell\1\PowerShellEngine
PSParentPath               : Microsoft.PowerShell.Core\Registry::HKEY_LOCAL_MACHIN
                             E\SOFTWARE\Microsoft\PowerShell\1
PSChildName                : PowerShellEngine
PSDrive                    : HKLM
PSProvider                 : Microsoft.PowerShell.Core\Registry
ApplicationBase            : C:\Program Files\Windows PowerShell\v1.0\
ConsoleHostAssemblyName    : Microsoft.PowerShell.ConsoleHost, Version=1.0.9567.1,
                             Culture=neutral, PublicKeyToken=31bf3856ad364e35,
                             ProcessorArchitecture=msil
ConsoleHostModuleName      : C:\Program Files\Windows PowerShell\v1.0\Microsoft.
                             PowerShell.ConsoleHost.dll
PowerShellVersion          : 1.0
RuntimeVersion             : v2.0.50727
```

Using the Get-ItemProperty cmdlet, you can also retrieve the data stored in a specific value, as demonstrated here.

```
$PSVer = $(get-ItemProperty
hklm:\SOFTWARE\Microsoft\PowerShell\1\PowerShellEngine).PowerShellVersion


$PSVer
```

Here, the data stored in the PowerShellVersion value is retrieved and displayed as shown below.

```
1.0
```

Note the syntax involved in setting up this operation. Specifically, in order to facilitate an object reference, you had to create a variable object reference by keying in a $ followed by parentheses, inside which you identified the logical path to the key that contains the value. With the object reference set up, you were then able to use familiar dot notation to identify the specific object property that you wanted to retrieve. Remember, Windows PowerShell treats registry values as object properties.

If you want, you can use the Regedit utility to visually verify the PowerShellVersion value and its associated data by clicking on Start > Run and then typing **Regedit** and pressing the Enter key. The Regedit utility lets you navigate the Windows registry in a manner similar to the way that Windows Explorer lets you navigate the Windows file system, as demonstrated in Figure 9.12.

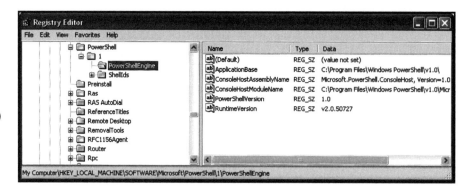

FIGURE 9.12

Using Regedit to view registry keys and values stored in the hklm hive.

To further demonstrate PowerShell's ability to interact with the Windows registry, let's develop a new PowerShell script that adds a new subkey and value to the hkcu hive. The key that will be created is named PSBlackjack and the value will be named Credits. Credits will be used to store a string value of true. Later, when you create this chapter's game project, the PowerShell Blackjack game, the game will look for the data stored in the Credits value to determine whether to display additional information about the game and its author at the conclusion of the game.

The code for this new PowerShell script, which you should name BJSetup.ps1, is provided here.

```
# ***********************************************************************
#
# Script Name:   BJSetup.ps1 (Setup script for the PowerShell Blackjack Game)
# Version:       1.0
# Author:        Jerry Lee Ford, Jr.
# Date:          January 1, 2007
#
# Description:   This PowerShell script creates a registry key for the
#                PowerShell Blackjack game under the HKEY_CURRENT_USER hive
#
# ***********************************************************************


# Initialization Section

$key = "PSBlackjack"   #Name of the registry key to be created
$value = "Credits"     #Name of the registry value to be created
$type = "string"       #Type of data stored in the new registry value
$data = "true"         #Data to be stored in the new registry value
```

```
# Functions and Filters Section

function Create-KeyAndValue {

  New-Item -name $key   #Create a new registry key

  New-ItemProperty $key -name $value -Type $type -value $data

}


# Main Processing Section

Set-Location hkcu:\

Create-KeyAndValue
```

As you can see, this is a relatively small and straightforward script. It begins by defining variables representing the key and value to be created as well as the type of data being stored (string) and its text. Next, a function named Create-KeyAndValue is defined that, when called, uses the New-Item cmdlet to create the new registry key and the New-ItemProperty cmdlet to create and store the Credits value inside the key.

Lastly, the statements in the main processing section change the focus from the file system to the hkcu hive and then create the new key and its value by executing the Create-KeyAndValue function. Once executed, this script generates the key and value required by the PowerShell Blackjack game, as shown in Figure 9.13.

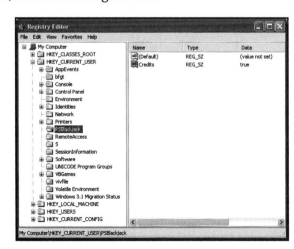

FIGURE 9.13

Viewing the PowerShell Blackjack game's newly created subkey and value using the Regedit utility.

BACK TO THE POWERSHELL BLACKJACK GAME

Okay, now it is time to return your attention back to the chapter's main game project, the PowerShell Blackjack game. This PowerShell script will interact with the Windows registry, accessing the PSBlackjack key and Credits value that were created earlier in the chapter when you created and executed the BJSetup.ps1 script. Based on the value assigned to Credits, the game will display or suppress the display of a screen that provides players with information about the game and its author. The overall logical flow of the PowerShell Blackjack game is straightforward. Its development will be completed in 12 steps, as outlined here:

1. Create a new script file using the Windows PowerShell template file.

2. Define and initialize script variables.

3. Create the Get-Permission function.

4. Create the Check-Registry function.

5. Create the Get-PlayerHand function.

6. Create the Deal-Hand function.

7. Create the Get-Card function.

8. Create the Get-ComputerHand function.

9. Create the Analyze-Results function.

10. Create the Get-PlayerHand function.

11. Create the Get-NewCard function.

12. Develop code for the main processing section.

Creating a New Script File

To start, use your PowerShell script template to create a new script file named Blackjack.ps1 and modify its contents, as demonstrated here.

```
# ***********************************************************************
#
# Script Name:   Blackjack.ps1 (The Blackjack Game)
# Version:       1.0
# Author:        Jerry Lee Ford, Jr.
# Date:          January 1, 2007
#
# Description:   This PowerShell script is a single player implementation of
#                the popular casino blackjack game
#
```

```
# ***********************************************************************


# Initialization Section

# Functions and Filters Section

# Main Processing Section
```

Defining and Creating New Variables

Now that you have created your new script file, let's add the following variable definitions to the script's initialization section.

```
$startGame = "False" #Variable used to determine if the game is played
$playerBusted = "False" #Variable used to track when the player busts
$randomNo = New-Object System.Random  #This variable stores a random object
$playerHand = 0       #Stores the current value of the player's hand
$computerHand = 0     #Stores the current value of the computer's hand
$playAgain = "True"   #controls the execution of the loop that controls the
                      #execution of logic in the main processing section
```

As you can see, these statements define a number of script variables and assign their initial values. Also, as you have seen in previous game scripts, the New-Object cmdlet is used to create a new instance of the Random object, which will be used later in the script to generate randomly selected numbers representing game cards.

Creating the Get-Permission Function

The Blackjack game consists of a number of custom functions, each of which is designed to perform a particular task. The first of these functions is the Get-Permission function, shown next. Add this function, as well as the functions that will follow, to the script's function and filters section.

```
#This function gets the player's permission to begin the game
function Get-Permission {

  #Loop until a valid reply is collected
  while ($startGame -eq "False") {

    Clear-Host  #Clear the Windows command console screen
```

```
#Display the game's opening screen
Write-Host "`n`n`n"
Write-Host " Welcome to the" -foregroundColor Blue
write-Host ""
Write-Host ""
Write-Host " P O W E R S H E L L    B L A C K J A C K     G A M E"`
   -foregroundColor Blue
Write-Host ""
Write-Host ""
Write-Host ""
Write-Host ""
Write-Host ""
Write-Host ""
Write-Host ""
Write-Host ""

#Collect the player's input
$response = Read-Host "`n`n`n`n`n`n`n Would you like to play? (Y/N)"

#Validate the player's input
if ($response -eq "Y"){  #The player wants to play
  $startGame = "True"
}
elseif ($response -eq "N") {  #The player wants to quit

   Check-Registry

   exit  #Terminate script execution

}


}


}
```

As you can see, this function uses a `while` loop to control the display of the script's welcome screen and to collect and validate the player's response when prompted to play the game. If the player enters Y when prompted to play the game, the value of `$startGame` is set equal to "True", terminating the execution of the loop and allowing the script to continue running.

If, on the other hand, the player enters N, the Check-Registry function is called and then the exit command is executed, thus terminating the script's execution.

> **TRICK** Note the addition of the -ForegroundColor parameter to the Write-Host cmdlet. This parameter provides you with the ability to specify the font color to be used when displaying text in the Windows command console. The Write-Host cmdlet also accepts a -BackgroudColor parameter that lets you specify the background color when displaying text in the Windows command console.

Creating the Check-Registry Function

The Check-Registry function is responsible for determining whether or not to display a screen at the end of the game. This screen provides a little information about the game and its author. It accomplishes this task by checking the value of the hkcu\PSBlackjack\Credits value stored in the Windows registry. If Credits is equal to "True", the additional screen is displayed. Otherwise, it is not displayed.

```
#This function retrieves a registry value that specifies whether or not
#the script should display a splash screen if the player chooses not to
#play a game after starting the script
function Check-Registry {

  Clear-Host    #Clear the Windows command console screen

  $currentLocation = Get-Location #Keep track of the current directory

  Set-Location hkcu:\  #Change to the HKEY_CURRENT_USER hive

  #Retrieve the data stored in the Credits value under the PSBlackjack
  #subkey

  $regKey = $(Get-ItemProperty hkcu:\PSBlackjack).Credits

  if ($regKey -eq "True") {  #If the registry value is set to true
                             #display the closing splash screen
    Write-Host " `n`n`n"
    Write-Host " P O W E R S H E L L   B L A C K J A C K`n`n`n"`
      -foregroundColor Blue
    write-Host "       Developed by Jerry Lee Ford, Jr.`n`n"
    Write-Host "            Copyright 2007`n`n`n`n"
    Write-Host "          www.tech-publishing.com`n`n`n`n`n`n"
```

```
}

Set-Location $currentLocation  #Restore the current working directory

}
```

Note that before using the Set-Location cmdlet to change the focus from the file system to the registry, the function sets the value of $currentLocation equal to the current working directory. Next, the Get-ItemProperty cmdlet is used to retrieve the value stored in Credits, which is then stored in $regKey. An if statement then analyzes the value of $regKey to determine whether to display the additional screen. Finally, the Set-Location cmdlet is executed again, restoring the focus back to the file system.

Creating the Play-Game Function

The next function to be developed is the Play-Game function, shown below. This function's job is to execute other functions, as appropriate, in order to manage both the player's and the computer's hand, as well as to analyze game results.

```
#This function controls the execution of an individual round of play
function Play-Game {

  Deal-Hand  #Call the function that deals the opening hands

  Get-PlayerHand  #Call the function that manages the player's hand

  #If the player has busted the game is over, otherwise it is the
  #computer's turn
  if ($script:playerBusted -eq "False") {
    Get-ComputerHand #Call the function that manages the computer's hand
  }

  Analyze-Results  #Call the function that analyzes game results and
                   #declares a winner
}
```

Creating the Deal-Hand Function

The Deal-Hand function, shown next, is called by the Play-Game function each time a new round of play is initiated. Its job is to see to it that an initial card is retrieved for both the player and the computer.

```
#This function deals the player and computer's initial hands
function Deal-Hand {

    $script:playerHand = Get-Card  #Assign a card to the player's hand
    $script:computerHand = Get-Card  #Assign a card to the computer's hand

}
```

As you can see, this function makes two calls to the Get-Card function, storing the results (i.e., cards) that are returned in script variables.

Creating the Get-Card Function

The code for the Get-Card function is shown next. When called, this function uses the Random object's Next method to generate a random number in the range of 1 to 13. If the random number turns out to be a 1, it is considered to be an ace. If the number is greater than 10, it is considered to be a face card (Jack, Queen, or King). The value of the randomly generated number is returned to the calling statement. However, if an ace is generated (e.g., 1) a value of 11 is returned and if a face card is generated (e.g., 11, 12, 13), a value of 10 is returned.

```
#This function retrieves a random number representing a card and returns
#the value of that card back to the calling statement
function Get-Card {

    $number = 0

    #Generate the game's random number (between 1 - 13)
    $number = $randomNo.Next(1, 14)

    if ($number -eq 1 ) {$number = 11} #Represents an ace
    if ($number -gt 10) {$number = 10} #Represents a jack, queen, or king

    $number  #Return the number back to the calling statements

}
```

Creating the Get-ComputerHand Function

The Get-ComputerHand function, shown next, is responsible for playing the computer's hand. It does so by setting up a while loop that executes as long as the value of the computer's hand is less than 17.

```
#This function is responsible for managing the computer's hand
function Get-ComputerHand {

  $tempCard = 0  #Stores the value of the computer's new card

  #The computer continues to take hits as long as its hand's value is less
  #than seventeen
  while ($computerHand -lt 17) {

    $tempCard = Get-Card  #Get a new card for the computer

    #Add the value of the new card to the computer's hand
    $script:computerHand = $script:computerHand + $tempCard

  }

}
```

As you can see, each time the loop executes, the Get-Card function is called and the value returned by this function is added to the $computerHand variable. This loop stops executing as soon as the value of this variable becomes 17 or greater.

Creating the Analyze-Results Function

The Analyze-Results function, shown below, is called by the Game-Play function and is responsible for determining whether the player or the computer won the game, or if they tied.

```
#This function analyzes and displays the results of each game
function Analyze-Results {

  Clear-Host  #Clear the Windows command console screen

  #Display the player and computer's final hand
  Write-Host "`n`n`n`n RESULTS:`n`n"
  Write-host " Player Hand:   $playerHand`n"
  Write-Host " Computer Hand: $computerHand`n`n"

  #See if the player busted
  if ($playerBusted -eq "True") {
    Write-Host "`a You have gone bust." -ForegroundColor Blue
  }
```

```
else {   #See if the computer busted
  if ($computerHand -gt 21) {
    Write-host "`a The computer has gone bust." -ForegroundColor Blue
  }
  else { #Neither the player nor the computer busted so look for a winner
    if ($playerHand -gt $computerHand) {
      Write-Host "`a You Win!" -ForegroundColor Blue
    }
    if ($playerHand -eq $computerHand) {
      Write-Host "`a Tie!" -ForegroundColor Blue
    }
    if ($playerHand -lt $computerHand) {
      Write-host "`a You lose." -ForegroundColor Blue
    }
  }
}


}
```

As you can see, if $playerBusted equals "True", the player has lost the game (i.e., the value of the player's hand has exceeded 21). If the player did not go bust, the function next looks to see if the computer went bust. If neither the player nor the computer went bust, the value of the player's hand is compared to the value of the computer's hand to determine who won (i.e., whose hand has the higher value).

Creating the Get-PlayerHand Function

The Get-PlayerHand function, shown below, is responsible for assisting players in managing their hands and is called by the Play-Game function.

```
#This function displays the value of both the player and computer's
#current hands and prompts the player to take another card
function Get-PlayerHand {

  $keepGoing = "True"   #Control the execution of the loop that manages
                        #the player's hand
  $response = ""        #Stores the players input

  #Loop until a valid reply is collected
```

```powershell
while ($keepGoing -eq "True") {

   Clear-Host  #Clear the Windows command console screen

   #Display the player and computer's current hands
   Write-Host "`n`n"
   Write-Host ""
   write-Host " CURRENT HAND:"
   Write-Host "`n"
   Write-Host " Player Hand:   $playerHand"
   Write-Host ""
   Write-Host " Computer Hand: $computerHand"
   Write-Host ""
   Write-Host ""
   Write-Host ""
   Write-Host ""
   Write-Host ""
   Write-Host ""

   #Prompt the player to take another card
   $response = Read-Host "`n`n`n`n`n`n`n Do you want another card? (Y/N)"

   #Validate the player's input
   if ($response -eq "Y"){
     Get-NewCard  #Get another card for the player
   }
   elseif ($response -eq "N") {   #The player wants to quit
     $keepGoing = "False"
     Clear-Host   #Clear the Windows command console screen
   }

   if ($playerHand -gt 21) {   #The player has gone bust
     $script:playerBusted = "True"
     $keepGoing = "False"
   }

}


}
```

This function uses a `while` loop to display the current value of both the player's and the computer's hand and to ask the player if she would like a new card. If the player responds in the affirmative, the `Get-NewCard` function is called. The loop stops executing when either the player decides to stop asking for new cards or when her hand busts by exceeding a value of 21.

Creating the Get-NewCard Function

The `Get-NewCard` function, shown below, is called whenever the player elects to add another card to her hand. It accomplishes this by calling the `Get-Card` function and then adding the value returned by that function to the `$playerHand` variable.

```
#This function is called whenever the player elects to get a new card
#and is responsible for updating the value of the player's hand
function Get-NewCard {

  $tempCard = 0  #Stores the value of the player's new card

  $tempCard = Get-Card  #Get a new card for the player

  #Add the value of the new card to the player's hand
  $script:playerHand = $script:playerHand + $tempCard

}
```

Adding Controlling Logic to the Main Processing Section

At this point, all of the script functions have been defined. All that remains is to add a little controlling logic to the script's main processing section. The statements that provide this logic are outlined here.

```
Get-Permission  #Call function that asks the players for permission to
                #start the game

#Continue playing new games until the player decides to quit the game
while ($playAgain -eq "True") {

  Play-Game  #Call function that controls the play of individual games

  #Prompt the player to play a new game
```

```
$response = Read-Host "`n`n`n`n`n`n`n`n`n`n Press Enter to play"`
    "again or Q to quit"

if ($response -eq "Q") {   #The player wants to quit
   $playAgain = "False"
   Clear-Host   #Clear the Windows command console screen
}
else { #The player did not enter Q so let's keep playing
   $playAgain = "True"
   $playerBusted = "False"
}

}
```

The first statement calls on the Get-Permission function, which prompts the player for per-mission to start a new game. The rest of the statements in the main processing section are embedded within a while loop that is responsible for prompting the player to play another game.

That's everything. Assuming that you did not make any typing mistakes when you keyed in the code statements that make up the PowerShell Blackjack game, everything should work as expected. Go ahead and give the game a run through. Once you have verified that every-thing works like it is supposed to, try feeding the game invalid input to ensure that the game handles it correctly. Once you are confident that all is well, share a copy with a friend and ask for feedback.

SUMMARY

In this chapter you were introduced to a number of different ways that you can use Windows PowerShell to access and automate Windows resources. In addition, you learned how to use WMI to collect system information and to programmatically interact with the Windows reg-istry. You also learned how to work with Windows processes, services, and event logs as well as how to instantiate new objects using .NET classes and the common object model. You even learned how to alter the presentation of text color in order to enhance the output gen-erated by cmdlets and script commands.

Now, before you move on to Chapter 10, "Debugging PowerShell Scripts," consider setting aside a little extra time to enhance the PowerShell Blackjack game by addressing the fol-lowing list of challenges.

CHALLENGES

1. Using the Tic-Tac-Toe game for inspiration, consider creating text-based graphic representations of each card assigned to the player and the computer, thus allowing the player to view her hand as if she was handling real cards.

2. Consider experimenting with the `Write-Host` cmdlet's `-ForegroundColor` and `-BackgroundColor` parameters to make the game more visually appealing.

3. In this implementation of Blackjack, the player and the computer both start with a single card. However, in most blackjack games, players start out with two cards. Modify the game to correct this deficiency. Also, in addition to reporting the total value of the player's hand, consider displaying the value of each card that is assigned.

4. Modify the opening welcome screen by adding a text-based graphic that displays an ace of spades and a 10 of hearts, thus immediately identifying the game and its purpose to players when it first starts up.

5. As currently written, the PowerShell Blackjack game is a little short on descriptive text. Consider adding instructions where you think it will be beneficial. Also, consider creating a help screen that players unfamiliar with the game can view to learn how the game is played.

6. Consider adding logic to the game that tracks the total number of games won, lost, or tied and display this information either at the end of the game or upon demand.

7. Currently, the game is hard-coded to treat a randomly generated value of 1 as an ace, automatically assigning it a value of 11. Considering giving the player the option of electing to treat aces as having a value of either 1 or 11.

DEBUGGING
POWERSHELL SCRIPTS

I f there is one inevitability in programming, it is that errors can and will occur. No matter how long you have been programming or how good you may be, errors are going to happen. Windows PowerShell scripting is no exception. Fortunately, as you will learn in this chapter, there are many tools at your disposal that you can use to track down, identify, and fix errors. In this chapter you will learn how to create error handlers that respond to errors and take appropriate action. In addition to showing you how to debug your PowerShell scripts, this chapter will also teach you how to develop your final PowerShell script, the PowerShell Game Console.

Specifically, you will learn how to:

- Read and analyze syntax, runtime, and logical errors
- Alter the logical execution of a script when cmdlet errors occur
- Create error handlers that trap and respond to errors
- Trace the logical flow of your PowerShell scripts and track variable values

PROJECT PREVIEW: THE POWERSHELL GAME CONSOLE

In this final chapter of the book, you will learn how to develop your final Windows Power-Shell computer game, the PowerShell Game Console. This script will provide you with a console view of all your Windows PowerShell games, allowing you to view and access them as a list of menu items. When started, the PowerShell Game Console will display a list of all the PowerShell scripts that it finds in the folder that you have used to store your Windows PowerShell games, as demonstrated in Figure 10.1.

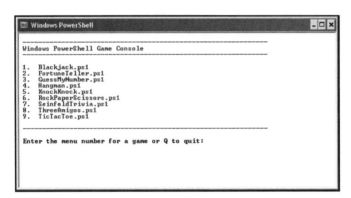

FIGURE 10.1

The PowerShell Game Console lets you start games by entering their menu number.

Once started, the selected PowerShell game runs within the same window as the game console, as demonstrated in Figure 10.2.

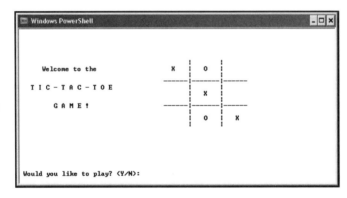

FIGURE 10.2

The player has used the game console to start the Tic-Tac-Toe game.

Each time the player finishes playing a selected PowerShell game, the game ends and the PowerShell Game Console reappears, prompting the player to select another game to play. When done playing games, the player closes the PowerShell Game Console by pressing the **Q** key and pressing the Enter key. In response, the screen shown in Figure 10.3 is displayed.

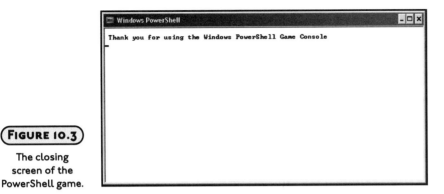

Thank you for using the Windows PowerShell Game Console

FIGURE 10.3

The closing
screen of the
PowerShell game.

UNDERSTANDING POWERSHELL ERRORS

As you have doubtless seen many times, Windows PowerShell scripts are subject to many different types of errors. For example, errors can occur if a script attempts to access a network resource that is not available, or if you make a typo when keying in a script statement, or if you make a mistake in the logic used to make your script run. Each of these three types of errors fall into a distinct category of errors, as outlined in the following list.

- **Syntactical Error.** An error occurring as a result of not following the syntax requirements of the PowerShell scripting language.

- **Runtime Error.** An error that occurs when a script attempts to perform an illegal action such as the division of a number by zero.

- **Logical Error.** An error that occurs when a script produces an unexpected result as the results of faulty programming logic and not as the result of a syntax or runtime error.

Each of these types of errors is explored further in the sections that follow.

Syntax Errors

Syntax errors occur when a script is initially loaded for execution. These types of errors occur when you make typos or if you fail to follow the syntax requirements of a command or cmdlet. For example, a syntax error will occur if you forget to provide the required closing double quotation marks at the end of a Write-Host statement, as demonstrated here.

```
Write-Host "once upon a time there were three little pigs.
```

When executed, this statement will generate the following error, preventing the script from executing.

```
Encountered end of line while processing a string token.
At C:\MyScripts\xxx.ps1:11 char:12
+ Write-Host " <<<< once upon a time there were three little pigs.
```

Syntax errors prevent PowerShell scripts from compiling and running. As such, they are easy to identify and fix. For example, if you examine the error message that was generated by the previous statement, you will see that it explicitly identifies the location and the text of the statement that caused the error, making it easy to locate and fix.

Runtime Errors

Unlike syntax errors, runtime errors are not caught and flagged when your PowerShell scripts are first started. Instead, they occur only when the statements that generate them are executed. As a result, unless you carefully test out of all the functionality of your PowerShell scripts, it is easy to let runtime errors sneak by. As a result, you run the risk that other people with whom you share your scripts will find your errors.

Some runtime errors are difficult if not impossible to avoid. For example, a computer's network connection may go down or one of its hard drives may crash. Still, most runtime errors can be eliminated by carefully testing every aspect of your PowerShell scripts, including seldom-used functionality. Runtime errors can also be handled by taking care to incorporate logic within your scripts to prevent errors from occurring. For example, if your script accepts user input, you should add extra programming logic to validate the user's input, rejecting any input that is not valid. Likewise, if you are developing a PowerShell script that is supposed to copy or move files, take the time to add the logic required to first ensure that the files to be manipulated do, in fact, exist.

Another way to locate and track down runtime errors is to test your PowerShell scripts under various conditions. For example, try to input invalid data to see if your script handles it correctly. If your script needs to access network resources, try disconnecting your computer's network connection in the middle of your script's execution. Proper testing is the key to the elimination of most runtime errors.

As an example of a typical runtime error, take a look at this.

```
$x = 10
$y = 0
$z = $x / $y
```

In this example, two variables have been declared and assigned values. Next, an attempt is made to divide one number by the other. The problem with this example is that it is illegal to divide any number by zero. As a result, when executed, this example will generate the following error.

```
Attempted to divide by zero.
At C:\MyScripts\xxx.ps1:13 char:10
+ $z = $x /  <<<< $y
```

Had the values of $x and $y been provided by the user, instead of hard-coded, this problem would have been avoided by validating the user's input and rejecting a value of 0 for the denominator.

Logical Errors

Unlike syntax and runtime errors, logical errors do not result in the display of error messages and are therefore often difficult to track down. Because logical errors represent a breakdown of the programming logic used to develop some part of a PowerShell script, the best way to deal with them is to prevent them from happening in the first place by carefully planning out your script's logic before you start writing it.

An example of a logical error is an endless loop, where a loop is started without providing a way to break out of it. Another example of a logical error is when you enter in the wrong logic when trying to perform a task. For example, suppose you wanted to write a script that added two numbers together. In doing so, suppose you inadvertently keyed in the following statement.

```
#The total number of units sold is calculated by adding $x and $y
$z = $x - $y
```

Obviously, the intention here was to add the values of $x and $y together. However, instead, the value of $y will be subtracted from $x. As a result, if the following statement was executed later in the script, unexpected results would be displayed.

```
Write-Host "Total number of units sold = $z"
```

In this example, instead of $z equaling 15, it has been set equal to 5, as shown below.

```
Total number of units sold = 5
```

In this example, the problem did not lie in the logic that was applied to the development of the script. Instead, the problem most likely occurred by accident, when the programmer entered in the - operator in place of the + operator. Thus, to catch logical errors, it is also important that you take the time to carefully analyze the results generated by your scripts to ensure that they are working as expected. Otherwise, your PowerShell scripts will do exactly what you tell them to do, even if it is not what you really wanted them to do. Logical errors can also be prevented by writing PowerShell scripts in a modular fashion, using functions to organize and store related statements. This allows you to test your scripts a module at a time as you are building them.

TERMINATING VERSUS NON-TERMINATING ERRORS

In addition to syntax, runtime, or logical errors, Windows PowerShell errors can also be classified as terminating and non-terminating. A *non-terminating error* is an error that does not prevent the script from continuing its execution. For example, the following script shows a non-terminating error. When executed, an error message is displayed when the third statement is executed. However, the script continues executing, allowing the remaining statements to execute.

```
$x = 10
$y = 0
$z = $x / $y

Write-host "I got here anyway!"
```

A *terminating error*, as you would expect, is an error that halts the execution of the Power-Shell script. As you will see later in this chapter, Windows PowerShell provides you with the ability to override the default termination behavior for cmdlet errors.

DISSECTING THE STRUCTURE OF ERROR MESSAGES

Anytime an error occurs, PowerShell stores information about the error in an object called ErrorRecord. This object provides you with access to a number of properties, each of which stores information about the error. These properties include:

- **Exception**. This property doubles as an object with its own properties. One of its properties is Message. By referencing Exception.Message, you can display a description of an error message

- **CategoryInfo**. This is a high-level category that classifies the type of error that has occurred.

- **ErrorDetails**. When available, this property provides additional detailed information about an error.

- **TargetObject**. When available, this property identifies the object that was active when the error was generated.

PowerShell stores information about the last error to occur (i.e., the most recent ErrorRecord object) in a special variable named $error. $error is an array. The last error is found in $error[0]; the second to last error in $error[1]; and so on. For example, using the properties belonging to the ErrorRecord object, you can easily display a test message containing the error message or the most recent error using the following statement.

```
Write-Host " Error: " + $error[0].exception.message
```

Telling Windows PowerShell How to React to Errors

By default, Windows PowerShell will continue to run your PowerShell scripts in the event a non-terminating error occurs. You can change this behavior by modifying the value assigned to the special $ErrorActionPreference variable. For example, you could instruct Windows PowerShell to stop executing a PowerShell script in the event a non-terminating error occurs by adding the following statement at the beginning of the script.

```
$ErrorActionPreference = "Inquire"
```

Windows PowerShell allows you to assign any of the values shown in Table 10.1 to the $ErrorActionPreference special variable.

TABLE 10.1 PowerShell ErrorAction Arguments

Value	Description
Continue	Generates an error but allows the script to continue executing
Stop	Generates an error and terminates the script
SilentlyContinue	Suppresses the display of the error and allows the script to continue executing
Inquire	Generates an error and asks the user how to proceed

If you want, you can specify an optional -ErrorAction argument at the end of the cmdlet statements in order to temporarily override the default global ErrorAction setting. For example, by default a script containing the following statement will continue executing in the event the cmdlet is unable to connect to the specified network computer.

```
Get-WmiObject Win32_ComputerSystem -computername HP1
```

The script continues executing because the default value of the $ErrorActionPreference variable is Continue. Thus, the previous statement will result in an error message being displayed, as demonstrated here, but the script will continue running.

```
Get-WmiObject : The RPC server is unavailable. (Exception from HRESULT: 0x80070
6BA)
At C:\MyScripts\xxx.ps1:12 char:14
+ Get-WmiObject  <<<< Win32_ComputerSystem -computername HP1
```

By specifying an -ErrorAction value of Stop at the end of the cmdlet statement, you can instruct the script to instead cease execution.

```
Get-WmiObject Win32_ComputerSystem -computername HP1 -ErrorAction Stop
```

When executed, the previous statement generates the following error message and the script stops running.

```
Get-WmiObject : Command execution stopped because the shell variable
"ErrorActionPreference" is set to Stop: The RPC server is unavailable. (Exception
from HRESULT: 0x800706BA)
At C:\MyScripts\xxx.ps1:12 char:14
+ Get-WmiObject  <<<< Win32_ComputerSystem -computername HP1 -ErrorAction stop
```

By specifying `SilentlyContinue` when executing the `-ErrorAction` argument, you can prevent errors from being displayed, thus keeping them from view by the user, as demonstrated here.

```
Get-WmiObject Win32_ComputerSystem -computername HP1 -ErrorAction
SilentlyContinue
```

If desired, you can specify `Inquire` as the value of `-ErrorAction`, as demonstrated below.

```
Get-WmiObject Win32_ComputerSystem -computername HP1 -ErrorAction inquire
```

If an error occurs when this statement executes, the Windows PowerShell will display the following prompt.

```
The RPC server is unavailable. (Exception from HRESULT: 0x800706BA)
[Y] Yes  [A] Yes to All  [H] Halt Command  [S] Suspend  [?] Help
(default is "Y"):
```

When you assign a value of `Inquire` to `-ErrorAction`, Windows PowerShell responds by displaying the list of choices defined in Table 10.2.

TABLE 10.2 POWERSHELL ERRORACTION INQUIRY OPTIONS

Option	Value	Description
Y	Yes	Allows the script to continue and process the error as appropriate
A	Yes to All	Automatically assumes a value of yes for any further inquiries
H	Halt Command	Stops the execution of the cmdlet
S	Suspend	Pauses the current pipeline and opens a new sub-shell. Allows you to troubleshoot before typing exit to close the sub-shell and then returns to decide which option you want to select once pipeline processing is resumed.
?	Help	Displays an explanation of the effects of each of the available options.

Whenever an error occurs, Windows PowerShell generates an exception. This exception can be trapped by an *exception handler* or *trap handler*, thus giving programmers the ability to add logic to their PowerShell scripts that can respond to errors. An error trap can even override the ErrorPolicy setting. Trap handlers also have access to the ErrorRecord object through the $_ special variable.

A trap handler is a mechanism that catches errors raised during script execution, giving you the opportunity to analyze and hopefully recover from errors. The syntax required to set up a trap handler is outlined here.

```
Trap [Exception] {
  Script statements
    .
    .
    .
  Return [Value] | Continue | Break
}
```

Here, *Exception* is an optional placeholder for an argument representing a specific type of error to be trapped. When specified, the trap handler will ignore any errors that occur and do not match the specified exception type. If omitted, the trap handler will fire for any exception that occurs within its scope. You can include any number of script statements within a trap handler. Typically, you would use $_ to access information about the exception and determine what action, if any, is appropriate to take as well as to change the value of ErrorPolicy when appropriate. Lastly, trap handlers can specify any of three optional termination options.

Return[*Value*] will exit the current scope and return the specified value. Continue tells PowerShell to continue script execution beginning with the statement that comes immediately after the statement that generated the error. Break terminates the execution of the current scope. If none of these options is returned, PowerShell returns the value of $_.

It is important to remember that Windows PowerShell provides for different scopes. When a script begins executing, it creates its own scope. Within the script, any functions that are defined generate their own sub-scopes. If you place a trap handler within a function and an error occurs within the function, the function's trap handler will be executed. If the function does not have its own trap handler, the error will be passed back to the parent scope and will be processed by a trap handler, if present, within this scope.

If you place a trap handler within a function and an error occurs, specifying an option of Continue will tell PowerShell to continue executing the next statement within the function.

Break instructs PowerShell to terminate the current scope, allowing the parent scope to handle the error (it the parent scope has a trap handler defined). Return [*Value*] instructs PowerShell to terminate the current scope and to return whatever value you specify to the parent scope.

TRICK If you want, you can define multiple trap handlers within each scope. In this case, each trap handler is executed in the order that it was defined, but only the optional Return[*Value*]/Continue/Break statement in the last trap handler is executed.

To get a better understanding of how to set up trap handlers, take a look at the following example.

```
trap {

  Clear-Host
  write-Host "`nAn unexpected error has occurred. Please record the following"
  write-host "message and notify the Help Desk.`n`n"

}


#The following statement generates a runtime error
$x = 10
$y = 0


$z = $x / $y
```

In this example, a trap has been set up to trap any error that occurs within the current scope. When executed, the trap handler displays a user-friendly error message, instructing the user to contact the Help Desk and report the error. The statements that follow generate a runtime error, resulting in the execution of the trap. When executed the following error is generated.

```
An unexpected error has occurred. Please record the following
message and notify the Help Desk.

Attempted to divide by zero.
At C:\MyScripts\xxx.ps1:13 char:10
+ $z = $x /  <<<< $y
```

This trap handler will execute for any error that occurs within the current scope. If you want, you could modify the trap handler so that it only executes when a specific type of error occurs, as demonstrated below.

```
trap [DivideByZeroException] {

  Clear-Host
  write-Host "`nAn unexpected error has occurred. Please record the following"
  write-host "message and notify the Help Desk.`n`n"

  Break

}
```

Here, the trap handler has been modified so that it will execute only in the event a DivideByZeroException error occurs. In addition, the Break option has been added to the end of the trap handler in order to instruct PowerShell to terminate the current scope and allow the parent scope's trap handler, if present, to handle the error.

TRACING SCRIPT EXECUTION

Often, all that you will need to track down and fix an error is the text of the error message that PowerShell generates. However, sometimes error messages alone do not provide enough information, especially when you are trying to track down a logical error. To track down and eliminate some problems, it often helps to know the order in which things are executing within your PowerShell scripts as well as the value of variables as they are accessed and changed.

Displaying Output Status Information and Tracking Variable Values

One way of keeping an eye on the inner working of your Windows PowerShell scripts is to place Write-Host statements at strategic points within your scripts. For example, you might display a statement at the beginning and end of each function that notifies you when the function is started and when it ends. You might also want to use the Write-Host statement to display the value of key variables so that you can keep an eye on their values as they are modified and referenced.

Because of the speed with which PowerShell processes script statements, it is also often helpful to place Read-Host statements after your Write-Host statements in order to pause script execution and give you time to examine the data that is displayed. For example, you might want to add Write-Host statements following function calls in order to be able to visually validate that the data returned by the function is what you anticipated.

To see an example of how you might make use of the Write-Host and Read-Host cmdlets to track the execution flow of a PowerShell script and keep an eye on variable values, take a look at the following example.

```
function Display-Message {
    param($x)
    Write-Host $x
    Write-Host "Function Display-Host now terminating"
}

Write-Host "Starting Script execution"
ForEach ($i in 1..5) {
    Write-Host "Calling the Display-Message function"
    Write-Host "and passed a value of $i"
    Read-Host
    Display-Message $i
}
```

When executed, this script displays the following messages and then pauses.

```
Starting Script execution
Calling the Display-Message function
and passed a value of 1
```

At this point you know that the script is about to call on the Display-Message function and that the value of $i is equal to 1. As soon as the Enter key is pressed, the following output is displayed.

```
Function Display-Host now terminating
Calling the Display-Message function
and passed a value of 2
```

Again, you can see that the Display-Host function is about to be called and the value of $i is now 2. As this simple example shows, you can effectively track the execution of small scripts or parts of larger scripts using the Write-Host and Read-Host cmdlets in order to keep an eye on variable values. This will allow you to verify that things are executing in the order you expect and to ensure that variables are being assigned the proper values.

If you do not want to see text messages, you might instead take advantage of the Write-Host cmdlet's ability to make beep sounds to let you know when something of interest has occurred. Once you have managed to track down and fix any errors, you can either remove the extra debugging statements that you added to the script or you can comment them out, leaving them in place should you need to debug the script again at a later date.

Using PowerShell's Debug Mode

While adding strategically placed `Write-Host` and `Read-Host` cmdlets throughout a script can be helpful in tracking down problems, this debugging technique is only suitable for small scripts or for limited use within larger scripts. For larger scripts, you will want to use the `Set-PSDebug` cmdlet to enable Windows PowerShell's debug mode.

The `Set-PSDebug` cmdlet accepts a number of optional parameters, which allow you to specify the level of detail and control you want during the debug session. One parameter is `-Trace`, which tells the cmdlet how much debug information you want to see. The following choices are available.

- **-Trace 0.** Turn tracing off.
- **-Trace 1.** Display each script statement that is executed.
- **-Trace 2.** Display information on variable values and function calls and display each script statement that is executed.

Another optional `Set-PSDebug` parameter is `-Step`, which, when specified, tells the cmdlet to pause and display the following list of options before executing each line in the script.

- **Yes.** Execute the next statement.
- **Yes to All.** Execute all remaining statement with additional prompting.
- **No.** Exits the script.
- **No to All.** Exits the script.
- **Suspend.** Pauses script execution.

To better learn how to work with the `Set-PSDebug` cmdlet in order to debug your PowerShell scripts, let's take a look at a few examples. For starters, create and save the following PowerShell script as PSTest.ps1.

```
function Display-Message {
  param($x)
  Write-Host $x
}

ForEach ($i in 1..5) {
  Display-Message $i
}
```

Next, run the script to make sure that it correctly displays a sequence of numbers from 1 to 5, as shown on the next page.

```
1
2
3
4
5
```

Next, let's enable PowerShell debug mode by typing the following statement at the Windows PowerShell command prompt.

```
Set-PSDebug -Trace 1
```

Here, debug mode is enabled and a trace level of 1 is established. Now, with the debug mode established, re-run your PowerShell script. This time, you should see the following output.

```
DEBUG:      1+ PSTest
DEBUG:      2+ function Display-Message {
DEBUG:     11+ ForEach ($i in 1..5) {
DEBUG:     13+    Display-Message $i
DEBUG:      6+    Write-Host $x
1
DEBUG:     13+    Display-Message $i
DEBUG:      6+    Write-Host $x
2
DEBUG:     13+    Display-Message $i
DEBUG:      6+    Write-Host $x
3
DEBUG:     13+    Display-Message $i
DEBUG:      6+    Write-Host $x
4
DEBUG:     13+    Display-Message $i
DEBUG:      6+    Write-Host $x
5
```

As you can see, setting the trace level to 1 results in the display of each statement that was executed in addition to the output normally displayed by the script. Obviously, this level of debugging is helpful in letting you keep an eye on the exact order in which the script statement and functions are executing, allowing you to determine if events are occurring in an order that you anticipated.

If setting the trace level to 1 does not give you enough information, you can always increase tracing to level 2 by executing the following statement directly at the Windows PowerShell command prompt.

```
Set-PSDebug -Trace 2
```

With the new debug mode setting now in place, execute the script again. This time the following output is displayed.

```
DEBUG:     1+ PSTest
DEBUG:      ! CALL script 'PSTest.ps1'
DEBUG:     2+ function Display-Message {
DEBUG:    11+ ForEach ($i in 1..5) {
DEBUG:    13+    Display-Message $i
DEBUG:      ! CALL function 'Display-Message'  (defined in file
'C:\MyScripts\PSTest.ps1')
DEBUG:     6+    Write-Host $x
1
DEBUG:    13+    Display-Message $i
DEBUG:      ! CALL function 'Display-Message'  (defined in file
'C:\MyScripts\PSTest.ps1')
DEBUG:     6+    Write-Host $x
2
DEBUG:    13+    Display-Message $i
DEBUG:      ! CALL function 'Display-Message'  (defined in file
'C:\MyScripts\PSTest.ps1')
DEBUG:     6+    Write-Host $x
3
DEBUG:    13+    Display-Message $i
DEBUG:      ! CALL function 'Display-Message'  (defined in file
'C:\MyScripts\PSTest.ps1')
DEBUG:     6+    Write-Host $x
4
DEBUG:    13+    Display-Message $i
DEBUG:      ! CALL function 'Display-Message'  (defined in file
'C:\MyScripts\PSTest.ps1')
DEBUG:     6+    Write-Host $x
5
```

As you can see, you now not only see each statement as it is executed, but you are also able to identify by name functions as they are called as well as variable values each time they are modified or referenced.

If you want, you can specify the -Step parameter when setting up debug mode, as demonstrated here.

```
Set-PSDebug -Step
```

When specified, -Step automatically sets a trace level of 1. To test this debugging option out, enter the previous statement at the Windows PowerShell command prompt and press Enter and then run your script again. This time, PowerShell pauses the execution of your script before each statement is executed, as demonstrated here.

```
Continue with this operation?
    1+ xxx
[Y] Yes   [A] Yes to All   [N] No   [L] No to All   [S] Suspend   [?] Help
(default is "Y"):
```

You can now specify the appropriate response to continue debugging your PowerShell script.

 To learn more about the Set-PSDebug cmdlet, type Get-Help Set-PSDebug at the PowerShell command prompt.

BACK TO THE POWERSHELL GAME CONSOLE

Okay, it is time to turn your attention back to the chapter's main project, the PowerShell Game Console. In this project, you will create a text-based game console that displays a menu of PowerShell game scripts, allowing players to start and play PowerShell games by entering their menu number. Once players finish playing a selected game, the game ends and the game console reappears, prompting the player to select another game to play.

Designing the Game

The PowerShell Game Console builds its menu on the fly based on the contents stored in the folder where your PowerShell scripts are stored. Although the script automatically filters out the display of any non-PowerShell script files, it is up to you to ensure that the folder contains only game scripts. Other PowerShell scripts, including the PowerShell game console itself and your standard PowerShell template script, should not reside in the folder.

When executed, the PowerShell Game Console displays a numbered list of all the game scripts in the PowerShell game folder and displays a prompt that allows players to start scripts based on their assigned menu number. As you can see, the overall logical flow of the PowerShell script is fairly simple. To set it up, you will complete its development in six steps, as outlined here:

1. Create a new script using the PowerShell script template.
2. Define and initialize script variables.

3. Create the `Get-GameListing` function.

4. Create the `Write-MenuList` function.

5. Create the `End-ScriptExecution` function.

6. Develop the script's primary controlling logic.

Creating a New Script File

The first step in the creation of the PowerShell Game Console script is the creation of a new script file named GameConsole.ps1. Create this script file using your PowerShell script template file and then modify the new script file as shown here.

```
# ************************************************************************
#
# Script Name:    GameConsole.ps1 (The PowerShell Game Console)
# Version:        1.0
# Author:         Jerry Lee Ford, Jr.
# Date:           January 1, 2007
#
# Description:    This PowerShell script provides a listing of PowerShell
#                 game scripts and allows the player to play any game by
#                 entering its menu number.
#
# ************************************************************************


# Initialization Section

# Functions and Filters Section

# Main Processing Section
```

Defining and Initializing Script Variables

This script will use an array named `$menuList` to store a list of all the PowerShell scripts located in the C:\MyScripts folder. In addition, the controlling logic outlined in the script's main processing section will be controlled by a `while` loop that monitors the value of `$playAgain` in order to determine when to halt the execution of the PowerShell Game Console. Add the following statements to the script file's initialization section in order to define and initialize these two variables.

```
$menuList = @()  #Stores an array containing information about script games
$playAgain = "True"  #Controls the execution of a loop that controls game
                        #execution
```

Creating the Get-GameListing Function

The PowerShell Game Console script has a number of custom functions, each of which is responsible for performing a particular task. The code for the first function is shown below. This function, named Get-GameListing, is responsible for retrieving a list of files stored in the C:\MyScripts folder and then storing the list in the $gameList array. Note that the ForEach-Object cmdlet is used to filter out any non-PowerShell script before the resulting list is stored in the $gameList array. Once populated, the contents of the array are then returned to the statement that called upon the function.

```
#This function gets the player's permission to begin the game
function Get-GameListing {

   $gameList = @() #Stores an array containing a list of PowerShell scripts
   $i = 0  #Used to set the index value of the array when adding elements
             #to it

   Clear-Host  #Clear the screen
   Write-Host  #Display a game console header
   Write-Host " ----------------------------------- "
   Write-Host " Windows PowerShell Game Console" -foregroundColor darkred
   Write-Host " ----------------------------------- "

   Set-Location C:\MyScripts  #Specify the location of the game scripts

   #Load an array with a list of all the PowerShell scripts in the
   #specified folder
   $gameList = Get-ChildItem . *.ps1  # | ForEach-Object -process {$i++;
      $gameList[$i] = $_.Name }
   $gameList = Get-ChildItem . *.ps1  # | ForEach-Object -process `
      {$i++; $gameList[$i] = $_.Name}

   $gameList  #Return the contents of the array to the calling statement

}
```

HINT

You will need to customize your version of this script by substituting the path and name of the folder where you have chosen to store your Windows PowerShell games. You will also want to make sure that this folder only contains game scripts and not other PowerShell scripts that you may have developed. You will also need to add this folder to your default path as described back in Chapter 1, "Introducing Windows PowerShell."

TRICK

Take note of the use of the ; (semicolon) character to separate $i++ from $gameList[$i] = $_.Name in the statement that loads the $gameList array. Here, the ; character servers as an end-of-line marker, allowing you to place two separate statements on a single line.

Creating the Write-MenuList Function

The next function to be added to the script is the Write-MenuList function, which is outlined below. This function is responsible for taking the list of filenames passed to it and using them to build a numbered list of menu items.

```
#This function displays a menu listing of PowerShell games
function Write-MenuList {

  param($list)  #The list of games to be displayed is passed as an array
  $Counter = 0  #Used to number each menu item

  Write-Host ""

  ForEach ($i in $list) {  #Iterate for each script stored in the array

    $counter++  #Increment the counter by 1

    if ($counter -lt 10) {  #Format the display of the first 9 scripts
      Write-Host " $counter.  $i" -foregroundColor blue
    }
    else {  #Format the display of all remaining scripts
      Write-Host " $counter. $i" -foregroundColor blue
    }

  }

  Write-Host "`n ------------------------------- "

}
```

As you can see, the list of filenames passed to this function is temporarily stored in an array named $list, which is then processed using a ForEach loop. Upon each iteration of the loop, a filename is displayed, preceded by a number that uniquely identifies the file (i.e., as specified by the value of $i).

Writing the End-ScriptExecution Function

The last function to be added to the script is the End-ScriptExecution function, shown below. This function is responsible for displaying a message that thanks the player for using the PowerShell Game Console and then, after a three-second pause, clears the screen.

```
function End-ScriptExecution {

  Clear-Host #Clear the screen

  Write-Host "`n Thank you for using the Windows PowerShell Game Console"

  Start-Sleep 3  #Pause the execution of the script for 3 seconds

  Clear-Host  #Clear the screen

}
```

Developing the Programming Logic for the Main Processing Section

Now it is time to wrap things up by adding the programming logic in the main processing section that will manage the overall execution of the PowerShell Game Console. The script statements that make up this logic are outlined here.

```
$response = 0  #Stores player input

#Continue playing new games until the player decides to close the
#game console
while ($playAgain -eq "True") {

  #Call the function that generates an array containing a list of
  #game scripts
  $menuList = Get-GameListing

  #Call the function that converts the contents of the array into a list
  #of menu items
  Write-MenuList $menuList
```

```
#Prompt the player to pick a game to play
$response = Read-Host "`n Enter the menu number for a game or Q to quit"

#Prepare to close the game console when the user decides to quit
if ($response -eq "Q") {
  $playAgain = "False"  #Modify variable value in order to halt the loop
  continue  #Repeat the loop
}

#Convert the player's input to an integer and then validate the
#player's input
if ([int]$response -lt 1) {  Anything below 1 is not a valid menu number
  Clear-Host  #Clear the screen
  Write-Host "`n `a`aInvalid selection."
  Read-Host    #Pause the script until the player presses the Enter key
  continue     #Repeat the loop
}

if ([int]$response -gt $menuList.length) {
  Clear-Host  #Clear the screen
  Write-Host "`n `a`aInvalid selection."
  Read-Host    #Pause the script until the player presses the Enter key
  continue     #Repeat the loop
}

Invoke-Expression $menuList[$response -1]  #Execute the selected script

Clear-Host  #Clear the screen

}

End-ScriptExecution
```

As you can see, a while loop has been defined to control the overall execution of the script. This loop executes until the player enters a menu command of Q, signaling that it is time to close the console. Upon each iteration of the loop, the Get-GameListing function is executed in order to generate a list of games to be displayed. Next, the Write-MenuList function is executed in order to display the list of PowerShell scripts that has been assembled. Next the player is prompted to select a game. The player's input is then evaluated. Once a valid menu selection has been specified, the Invoke-Expression cmdlet is used to start the specified PowerShell game by specifying the array index number of the selected menu item.

HINT   The `Invoke-Expression` cmdlet provides you with the ability to execute other PowerShell scripts by passing the cmdlet the name and path of the script.

The Final Result

Well, that is it. If all has gone according to plan, your version of the PowerShell Game Console should be ready to run. If you have made a few typos and are getting errors, use the debugging information presented in this chapter to track down the errors.

SUMMARY

Congratulations on completing the final chapter of this book. This chapter has helped to round out your understanding of Windows PowerShell programming by teaching you how to track down and fix problems that inevitably occur as part of the script-development process. You learned how to override the manner in which PowerShell responds to cmdlet errors. You learned how to develop error handlers that trap and respond to errors. You also learned how to trace the logical execution flow of your PowerShell scripts as well as how to keep an eye on the values stored in variables at various stages of script execution.

Before you put down this book and move on to tackle other opportunities, why not spend a few final minutes tackling the following list of challenges?

CHALLENGES

1. Modify the PowerShell Game Console to give the player the ability to start new games by entering the name of a PowerShell script in addition to specifying its menu number.

2. Currently, the name and path of the folder where PowerShell game scripts are stored is hard-coded in the script itself. Consider enhancing the Windows Power-Shell Game Console to use the registry to store the name and path of the game. In addition, considering giving the player the option of specifying the name and path of a different folder where PowerShell script games might be stored.

3. If you have a website, you might consider adding an option to the PowerShell Game Console that allows the player to automatically visit your website in order to check on the availability of new PowerShell script games. This can be accomplished using the `New-Object` cmdlet and COM to load your website using Internet Explorer.

Part
IV

Appendices

APPENDIX

WHAT'S ON THE COMPANION WEBSITE?

T o become proficient with any programming language, you must spend time working with the language, developing new scripts, and experimenting with different programming techniques. Obviously, this means dedicating yourself to the development of new PowerShell scripts in an effort to push you into tackling more and more challenging tasks. It also helps to have a collection of source code that you can use as the basis for your new scripts.

Assuming that you have created each of the sample game scripts presented in this book as you've gone along, you now have a good starter set of scripts from which you can learn and expand. However, if you did not get the chance somewhere along the way to create one or more of the sample game scripts outlined in this book, you are in luck. Copies of every game script covered in this book have been uploaded to the book's companion website and are ready for you to download. The website address is www.courseptr.com/downloads. From there, enter the title of this book to locate the files.

I wrote this book with the intention that you would read it from cover to cover. If you read this book in this manner, then you should already have a good idea of what each game script does. However, just in case you found yourself skipping around a bit and did not review each chapter's game script, I have provided a summary of what each script does in Table A.1.

TABLE A.1 POWERSHELL SCRIPT FILES LOCATED ON THE COMPANION WEBSITE

Chapter	Application	Description
Chapter 1	Knock Knock Joke	This script provides a gentle introduction to PowerShell scripting by demonstrating the steps involved in creating and executing a scripts that tells knock-knock jokes.
Chapter 2	The Story of the Three Amigos	This script demonstrates how to collect user input and use it in the creation of a mad-lib style story.
Chapter 3	PowerShell Fortune Teller	This script provides random answers to questions asked by a player, providing different answers based on the time of day.
Chapter 4	The Seinfield Trivia Quiz	This script demonstrates how to store and retrieve data in variables in order to build a trivia game that tests the player's knowledge of Seinfield trivia.
Chapter 5	Guess My Number	This script demonstrates the implementation of conditional logic through the development of a number guessing game in which the player is challenged to guess a secret number in the lowest number of guesses.
Chapter 6	Rock, Paper, Scissors	This script re-creates a command-line version of the classic children's game, demonstrating how to control script execution with a loop.
Chapter 7	PowerShell Hangman	This script demonstrates how to organize scripts using functions through the development of a hangman-style word-guessing game.
Chapter 8	PowerShell Tic-Tac-Toe	This script re-creates the classic children's Tic-Tac-Toe game through the development of a two-player PowerShell game.
Chapter 9	PowerShell Blackjack	This script demonstrates how to create a Blackjack-styled card game that pits the player against the computer.
Chapter 10	PowerShell Game Console	This script brings together all of the programming concepts covered in this book through the creation of a game console that provides the player with easy access to the book's PowerShell games.

WHAT NEXT?

s you no doubt have concluded after reading this book, Microsoft Power-Shell provides a robust, powerful scripting environment that goes well beyond traditional shell scripting. Windows PowerShell provides an entirely new programming language designed from the ground up to integrate with and leverage the capabilities provided by the .NET Framework. As this book has demonstrated, Microsoft PowerShell is a great programming language for first-time programmers and computer hobbyists. Yet, it is also powerful enough to satisfy the needs of professional programmers.

While you have already learned a great deal about how to program using Windows PowerShell scripting, there is still a lot more to be learned. Therefore, rather than viewing this book as the end of your Windows PowerShell scripting education, you should view it as the beginning. To become a truly effective Microsoft PowerShell programmer, you must continue to read and learn as much as possible. To help get you started, I have provided this appendix, where you will find an assortment of useful Windows PowerShell information. It includes information about a PowerShell IDE, assorted PowerShell reading materials, websites, mailing lists, and blogs.

WINDOWS POWERSHELL IDEs

As I was writing this book, there were two Windows PowerShell IDEs under development. These PowerShell IDEs provide a much better script-editing and testing environment than simply working with Notepad and the command prompt and can significantly improve your code-development experience.

DEFINITION

An IDE, or *integrated development environment*, is a graphical software-development tool that integrates a source-code editor with other application-development tools to aid in the creation of scripts or applications.

The first PowerShell IDE is PowerShellIDE, available as a free download at www.power-shell.com/. PowerShell IDE provides a long list of features, including:

- Statement color coding
- Direct command-line access
- Debugging features including support for breakpoints
- Context aware code completion
- Variable and property views

Figure B.1 shows an example of PowerShellIDE in action.

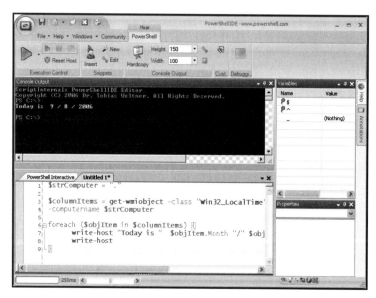

FIGURE B.1

The PowerShellIDE manages the display of script code, output, and variable and property values.

The other PowerShell IDE is PowerShell Analyzer, which is also available as a free download at www.powershellanalyzer.com. Like PowerShellIDE, PowerShell Analyzer comes with lots of bells and whistles that are designed to help you work faster and smarter when interacting with Windows PowerShell and developing scripts. A sampling of PowerShell Analyzer features includes:

- Statement color coding
- Direct command-line access
- Automatic display of keyword syntax
- Variable and property views

Figure B.2 shows an example of PowerShell Analyzer in action.

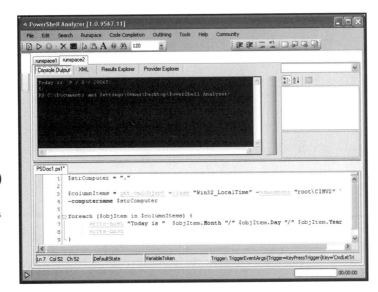

FIGURE B.2

The PowerShell Analyzer provides easy access to tools that help simplify and speed up script development.

RECOMMENDED READING

Because PowerShell is a brand-new technology, there were no other books on the subject published at the time that I was writing this book. However, Microsoft provides its own PowerShell documentation in the form of a quick start and a user guide. While first-time programmers and individuals new to PowerShell scripting may find these guides challenging, they will serve as an excellent next step for you once you have finished reading this book. Information on both of these guides is provided on the following page.

Getting Started Guide for the Windows PowerShell

by Microsoft Corporation

Available as a PDF file in the Windows PowerShell Documentation Pack that can be downloaded for free at:

www.microsoft.com/downloads/details.aspx?familyid=B4720B00-9A66-430F-BD56-EC48BFCA154F&displaylang=en

Windows PowerShell (PS) User Guide

by Microsoft Corporation

Available as a PDF file in the Windows PowerShell Documentation Pack that can be downloaded for free at:

www.microsoft.com/downloads/details.aspx?familyid=B4720B00-9A66-430F-BD56-EC48BFCA154F&displaylang=en

LOCATING MICROSOFT POWERSHELL RESOURCES ONLINE

Despite its relatively new arrival, PowerShell already has a significant presence on the Internet. A great deal of information is available at the websites described in the sections that follow. You will want to visit them regularly in order to stay on top of the latest developments. You will also find that many of these websites provide access to free sample code, which you can download and learn from.

The first place to start when you are ready to go online is Windows PowerShell's official website, which is located at www.microsoft.com/windowsserver2003/technologies/management/powershell/default.mspx, as shown in Figure B.3.

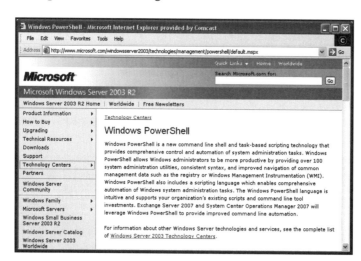

FIGURE B.3

Microsoft's official PowerShell website.

PowerShell Websites

Microsoft also provides online access to a collection of PowerShell sample scripts as part of its Microsoft TechNet Script Center website. These scripts demonstrate how to automate Active Directory, the desktop, Windows applications, and many other areas. You can learn more about and download these sample scripts at www.microsoft.com/technet/scriptcenter/scripts/msh. The site is shown in Figure B.4.

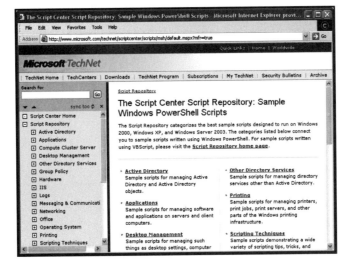

FIGURE B.4

Sample PowerShell scripts are grouped by category in the Microsoft Script Center Script repository.

There are plenty of other quality websites that provide information on PowerShell. For example, you may want to check out the PowerShell Information Centre at www.reskit.net/monad/, as shown in Figure B.5.

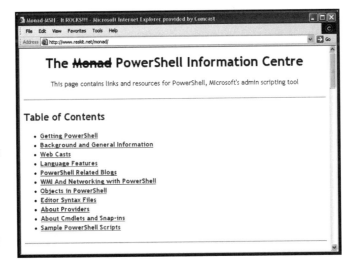

FIGURE B.5

The PowerShell Information Centre provides links to PowerShell resources located on the Internet.

Another helpful site for you to check out is channel9.msdn.com/wiki/default.aspx/Channel9. WindowsPowerShellQuickStart. This site provides access to an online PowerShell Quick Start guide, as shown in Figure B.6. This time-saving web page provides easy access to an online command reference.

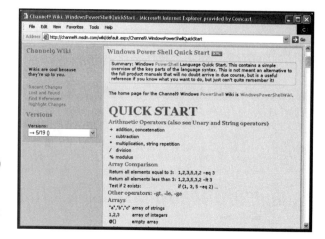

FIGURE B.6

The Channel9 Wiki Windows PowerShell Quick Start page.

Windows PowerShell News Group

Sometimes there is no better way to learn than to spend time sharing information with peers. One way to do this is via newsgroups. Microsoft sponsors a newsgroup dedicated exclusively to the PowerShell. You will find this newsgroup at www.microsoft.com/communities/ newsgroups/list/en-us/default.aspx?dg=microsoft.public.windows.powershell. Figure B.7 provides a glimpse of this web page and the kinds of discussions that occur.

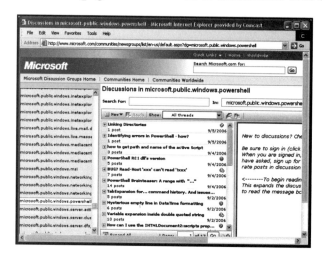

FIGURE B.7

Microsoft's Windows PowerShell Newsgroup.

PowerShell Blogs

Another extremely useful place for meeting fellow programmers and exchanging questions and answers is PowerShell blog websites. One such blog is the one belonging to the Windows PowerShell development team, located at blogs.msdn.com/PowerShell/, as shown in Figure B.8.

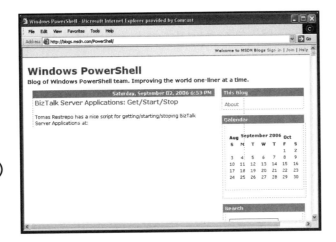

FIGURE B.8

The Windows PowerShell development team's blog.

As you might imagine, this site is very popular within the PowerShell community and you will find no shortage of technical discussion going on every day.

Another good blog website is the Monad Technology Blog, which you will find at blogs.msdn. com/monad/archive/2005/09/02/460075.aspx, as shown in Figure B.9. As the name implies, this blog was set up back in the early days, before Microsoft gave the PowerShell its new name. This blog's primary benefit is that it provides you with access to discussions dating as far back as 2005.

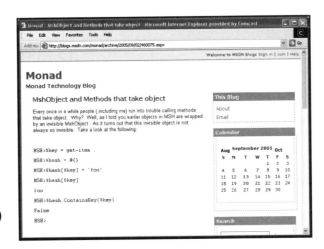

FIGURE B.9

The Monad Blog.

One more blog worth mentioning is the PowerShelled blog at mow001.blogspot.com, as shown in Figure B.10.

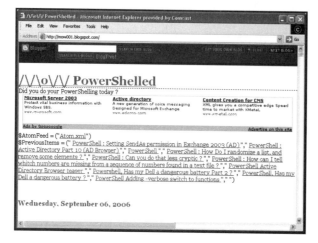

FIGURE B.10

The PowerShelled blog.

The PowerShelled blog provides a Microsoft-independent discussion area where PowerShell programmer's regularly interact and share experiences and help each other solve problems.

The Author's Website

Last but not least, you may also want to check out my website, which is located at www. tech-publishing.com, as shown in Figure B.11. In addition to learning about my other books, you will find information about both this book and Windows PowerShell. You might also want to stop by just to provide feedback on this book or to provide any input you may have on how to make it better.

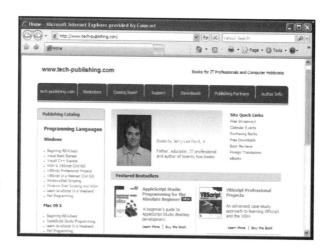

FIGURE B.11

My website at www.tech-publishing.com.

GLOSSARY

.NET Framework. A Microsoft developed framework designed to support the development of desktop, network, and Internet-based applications and scripts.

.NET Framework Class Library. A hierarchical collection of classes that can be used to instantiate objects based on those classes.

.ps1. The file extension used by Windows PowerShell scripts.

$_. A special variable created and maintained by Windows PowerShell that is automatically assigned the name of the current object in the PowerShell pipeline and, in the case of the `Where-Object` cmdlet, is used to reference each object in a collection.

Add-Content. A Windows PowerShell cmdlet that adds to the content of the specified item.

Add-History. A Windows PowerShell cmdlet that adds entries to the session history.

Add-Member. A Windows PowerShell cmdlet that adds a user-defined custom member to an object.

Add-PSSnapIn. A Windows PowerShell cmdlet that adds one or more PSSnapIn(s) to the current PowerShell console.

Alias. A shortcut to another cmdlet.

Argument. Data passed to a script or function for processing.

Array. An indexed list of values.

Associative Array. Sometimes referred to as hash or dictionary, which provides efficient and fast access to data stored in key-value pairs.

Classes. Templates for creating objects that Windows PowerShell can access and manipulate.

Clear-Content. A Windows PowerShell cmdlet that removes the content from an item or file while leaving the file intact.

Clear-Item. A Windows PowerShell cmdlet that sets the item at the specified location to the "clear" value specified by the provider.

Clear-ItemProperty. A Windows PowerShell cmdlet that removes the property value from a property.

Clear-Variable. A Windows PowerShell cmdlet that removes a value from a variable.

Cmd.exe. The predecessor to the Windows PowerShell command shell.

Cmdlets. Predefined commands, representing .NET classes, which are designed to perform a specific task.

Command Shell. A text-based interface that sits between the user and the operating system.

Command.com. The original Windows command line shell.

Compare-Object. A Windows PowerShell cmdlet that compares the properties of objects.

COM (Component Object Mode). A Microsoft technology that allows Windows PowerShell to programmatically interact with and control COM objects, including ActiveX controls and various Windows applications.

ConvertFrom-SecureString. A Windows PowerShell cmdlet that exports a SecureString to a safe, persistent format.

Convert-Path. A Windows PowerShell cmdlet that converts the path of the item given from a PowerShell path to a provider path.

ConvertTo-Html. A Windows PowerShell cmdlet that converts the input to an HTML table.

ConvertTo-SecureString. A Windows PowerShell cmdlet that creates a SecureString from a normal string created by Export-SecureString.

Copy-Item. A Windows PowerShell cmdlet that calls a provider to copy an item from one location to another within a namespace.

Copy-ItemProperty. A Windows PowerShell cmdlet that copies a property between locations.

CSV (Comma-Separated Value). A file format that is used to store comma-separated data as records separated by newlines. This format is commonly used by applications such as Microsoft Excel.

Do Until. A PowerShell statement that iterates until a specified condition is `True`.

Do While. A PowerShell statement that iterates as long as a specified condition is `True`.

ErrorRecord. An object that is created anytime an error occurs and which provides access to information about the error.

Exception. An event that occurs whenever an error is discovered in a Windows PowerShell script.

Export-Alias. A Windows PowerShell cmdlet that exports an alias list to a file.

Export-Clixml. A Windows PowerShell cmdlet that produces a Clixml representation of a PowerShell object.

Export-Console. A Windows PowerShell cmdlet that exports the changes made to the current console.

Export-Csv. A Windows PowerShell cmdlet that creates CSV strings from input.

Expression. A statement that is evaluated and produces a result.

Filter. A programming construct similar to a function but which is designed to more efficiently process large amounts of object pipeline data.

Flowchart. A tool used by programmers to graphically depict the logical flow of all or part of a script.

For. A PowerShell statement that iterates a set number of times.

ForEach. A PowerShell statement that iterates through all of the elements stored in a collection or array.

ForEach-Object. A Windows PowerShell cmdlet that applies a script block to each object in the pipeline.

Format-Custom. A Windows PowerShell cmdlet that formats output display as defined in additions to the formatter file.

Format-List. A Windows PowerShell cmdlet that formats objects as a list of their properties displayed vertically.

Format-Table. A Windows PowerShell cmdlet that formats output as a table.

Format-Wide. A Windows PowerShell cmdlet that formats objects as a table of properties.

Function. A collection of statements that is called and executed as a unit.

Get-Acl. A Windows PowerShell cmdlet that gets the access control list associated with a file or an object.

Get-Alias. A Windows PowerShell cmdlet that returns alias names for cmdlets.

Get-AuthenticodeSignature. A Windows PowerShell cmdlet that gets the signature object belonging to a file.

Get-ChildItem. A Windows PowerShell cmdlet that retrieves the child items for the specified location on a drive.

Get-Command. A Windows PowerShell cmdlet that retrieves information about a command.

Get-Content. A Windows PowerShell cmdlet that returns the content from the item at the specified location.

Get-Credential. A Windows PowerShell cmdlet that gets a credential object based on a password.

Get-Culture. A Windows PowerShell cmdlet that gets culture information.

Get-Date. A Windows PowerShell cmdlet that gets current date and time.

Get-EventLog. A Windows PowerShell cmdlet that gets EventLog data for the machine.

Get-ExecutionPolicy. A Windows PowerShell cmdlet that gets the effective execution policy.

Get-Help. A Windows PowerShell cmdlet that opens a help file.

Get-History. A Windows PowerShell cmdlet that gets a listing for the current session history.

Get-Host. A Windows PowerShell cmdlet that retrieves host information.

Get-Item. A Windows PowerShell cmdlet that gets an object that represents a namespace item.

Get-ItemProperty. A Windows PowerShell cmdlet that retrieves properties belonging to an object.

Get-Location. A Windows PowerShell cmdlet that displays the current location.

Get-Member. A Windows PowerShell cmdlet that enumerates the properties, methods, and property sets for the specified object.

Get-PfxCertificate. A Windows PowerShell cmdlet that gets the pfx certificate information.

Get-Process. A Windows PowerShell cmdlet that returns a list of active processes.

Get-PSDrive. A Windows PowerShell cmdlet that gets drive information.

Get-PSProvider. A Windows PowerShell cmdlet that returns provider information.

Get-PSSnapIn. A Windows PowerShell cmdlet that gets a list of registered PSSnapIns.

Get-Service. A Windows PowerShell cmdlet that gets a list of services.

Get-TraceSource. A Windows PowerShell cmdlet that lists trace source properties.

Get-UICulture. A Windows PowerShell cmdlet that gets the uiculture information.

Get-Unique. A Windows PowerShell cmdlet that gets the unique items in a sorted list.

Get-Variable. A Windows PowerShell cmdlet that retrieves a PowerShell variable.

Get-WmiObject. A Windows PowerShell cmdlet that creates a WMI Object or the list of WMI classes available on the system.

Global Scope. The scope that is established whenever a new PowerShell session is started.

Group-Object. A Windows PowerShell cmdlet that groups the objects containing the same property value.

If. A PowerShell statement that evaluates a comparison and then executes or skips the execution of a set of statements located in an associated code block.

Import-Alias. A Windows PowerShell cmdlet that imports an alias list.

Import-Clixml. A Windows PowerShell cmdlet that imports a Clixml file.

Import-Csv. A Windows PowerShell cmdlet that extracts data from a CSV list and passes objects down the object pipeline.

Invoke-Expression. A Windows PowerShell cmdlet that executes a string as an expression.

Invoke-History. A Windows PowerShell cmdlet that executes a previously run command.

Invoke-Item. A Windows PowerShell cmdlet that invokes an executable or opens a file.

Join-Path. A Windows PowerShell cmdlet that combines path elements into a single path.

Local Scope. Refers to the current scope, which can be global, private, or script.

Logical Error. An error that occurs when a script produces unexpected results as the result of faulty programming logic.

Loop. A set of programming statements that is repeatedly executed as a unit.

Measure-Command. A Windows PowerShell cmdlet that tracks the runtime for script blocks or cmdlets.

Measure-Object. A Windows PowerShell cmdlet that measures different aspects of objects.

Method. A predefined collection of code that can be executed in order to interact with and control its associated object.

Move-Item. A Windows PowerShell cmdlet that moves an item from one location to another.

Move-ItemProperty. A Windows PowerShell cmdlet that moves a property from one location to another.

New-Alias. A Windows PowerShell cmdlet that creates a new cmdlet-alias pairing.

New-Item. A Windows PowerShell cmdlet that creates a new item in a namespace.

New-ItemProperty. A Windows PowerShell cmdlet that sets a new property for an item at a specified location.

New-Object. A Windows PowerShell cmdlet that creates a new .NET object.

New-PSDrive. A Windows PowerShell cmdlet that sets up a new drive.

New-Service. A Windows PowerShell cmdlet that creates a new service.

New-TimeSpan. A Windows PowerShell cmdlet that creates a TimeSpan object.

New-Variable. A Windows PowerShell cmdlet that defines a new variable.

Non-terminating Error. An error that does not prevent the script from continuing its execution.

Object. A self-contained resource that contains information about itself as well as the code required to access and manipulate it.

Out-Default. A Windows PowerShell cmdlet that sets the default controller of output.

Out-File. A Windows PowerShell cmdlet that sends command output to a file.

Out-Host. A Windows PowerShell cmdlet that sends object pipeline data to the host.

Out-Null. A Windows PowerShell cmdlet that sends output to a null.

Out-Printer. A Windows PowerShell cmdlet that sends the output to the printer.

Out-String. A Windows PowerShell cmdlet that sends string output to the object pipeline.

Pipeline. A logical connection between two commands that supports the passage of one command's output to another command where it is received as input.

Pop-Location. A Windows PowerShell cmdlet that changes the current working location to the location specified by the last entry added onto the stack.

Precedence. The order in which mathematic operations are executed.

Private Scope. A scope that is not visible or accessible to other scopes.

Properties. Object attributes that describe particular features of the object.

Provider. A model that provides Windows PowerShell with access to hierarchical repositories including the Windows file system and the Windows registry.

Pseudocode. A term used to describe an English-like outline of all or part of a script or application.

Push-Location. A Windows PowerShell cmdlet that pushes a location onto the stack.

Read-Host. A Windows PowerShell cmdlet that collects a line of input from the host console.

Registry. A Windows repository that stores configuration data for the operating system as well as for hardware, software, network, and user settings.

Registry Key. Logical containers used to store registry keys and values.

Regular Expression. A pattern used to describe matching data.

Remove-Item. A Windows PowerShell cmdlet that calls a provider to remove an item.

Remove-ItemProperty. A Windows PowerShell cmdlet that removes a property and its value from the specified location.

Remove-PSDrive. A Windows PowerShell cmdlet that removes a drive.

Remove-PSSnapIn. A Windows PowerShell cmdlet that removes PSSnapIns from the current console.

Remove-Variable. A Windows PowerShell cmdlet that deletes a variable and its value.

Rename-Item. A Windows PowerShell cmdlet that changes an item's name.

Rename-ItemProperty. A Windows PowerShell cmdlet that renames a property.

Reserved Word. A keyword that Windows PowerShell has predefined as having a special purpose.

Resolve-Path. A Windows PowerShell cmdlet that resolves the wildcard characters in a path.

Restart-Service. A Windows PowerShell cmdlet that restarts a service that has been stopped.

Resume-Service. A Windows PowerShell cmdlet that resumes a service that has been suspended.

Runtime Error. An error that occurs when a script attempts to perform an illegal action such as the division of a number by zero.

Script Scope. The scope that is established whenever a script is executed and which ends when the script stops executing.

Select-Object. A Windows PowerShell cmdlet that selects objects based on parameters specified in the command string.

Select-String. A Windows PowerShell cmdlet that searches through strings or files for matching patterns.

Set-Acl. A Windows PowerShell cmdlet that sets Access Control List properties.

Set-Alias. A Windows PowerShell cmdlet that maps an alias to a cmdlet.

Set-AuthenticodeSignature. A Windows PowerShell cmdlet that places an authenticode signature in a PowerShell script.

Set-Content. A Windows PowerShell cmdlet that sets the content in the item.

Set-Date. A Windows PowerShell cmdlet that sets the system time.

Set-ExecutionPolicy. A Windows PowerShell cmdlet that establishes execution policy.

Set-Item. A Windows PowerShell cmdlet that sets the value of a pathname within a provider to a specified value.

Set-ItemProperty. A Windows PowerShell cmdlet that sets a property to a specified value.

Set-Location. A Windows PowerShell cmdlet that sets the current working location.

Set-PSDebug. A Windows PowerShell cmdlet that turns on PowerShell's script debugging features.

Set-Service. A Windows PowerShell cmdlet that makes changes to service properties.

Set-TraceSource. A Windows PowerShell cmdlet that modifies options and trace listeners from the specified trace source instance.

Set-Variable. A Windows PowerShell cmdlet that assigns a value to a variable or creates a variable if it does not exist.

Sort-Object. A Windows PowerShell cmdlet that sorts the input objects based on property values.

Special Variables. A collection of variables created and managed by Windows PowerShell that provide access to commonly used information.

Split-Path. A Windows PowerShell cmdlet that streams a string with the qualifier, parent path, or leaf item.

Start-Service. A Windows PowerShell cmdlet that starts a service that has been stopped.

Start-Sleep. A Windows PowerShell cmdlet that suspends shell, script, or runspace activity for the specified amount of time.

Start-Transcript. A Windows PowerShell cmdlet that starts a transcript for a command shell session.

Stop-Process. A Windows PowerShell cmdlet that stops an active process.

Stop-Service. A Windows PowerShell cmdlet that stops an active service.

Stop-Transcript. A Windows PowerShell cmdlet that stops the transcription process.

Subclass. A class that inherits base object definitions from its parent class and includes its own modifications.

Suspend-Service. A Windows PowerShell cmdlet that suspends an active service.

Switch. A statement used to define a collection of different test and code blocks, each of which evaluates against the same expression.

Syntactical Error. An error that occurs as a result of not following the syntax requirements of the PowerShell scripting language.

Tab Completion. An editing feature that enables you to type a part of a command and then to press the Tab key to obtain assistance in filling out the rest of the command.

Tee-Object. A Windows PowerShell cmdlet that sends input objects to two different places.

Terminating Error. An error that halts the execution of a PowerShell script.

Test-Path. A Windows PowerShell cmdlet that returns `True` if a path exists and `False` if it does not.

Trace-Command. A Windows PowerShell cmdlet that enables the tracing of a trace source instance.

Trace. The process of tracing the execution of script statements when executing a script.

Trap Handler. A collection of statements that are executed when an exception occurs.

Update-FormatData. A Windows PowerShell cmdlet that modifies format data files.

Update-TypeData. A Windows PowerShell cmdlet that updates the types.ps1xml file.

Values. Containers in which actual data is stored in the Windows registry.

Variable. A reference to data that is stored in memory.

Where-Object. A Windows PowerShell cmdlet that filters the input from the object pipeline.

While. A PowerShell statement that iterates as long as a specified condition is `True`.

WMI (Microsoft's Windows Management Instrumentation). A system management interface designed to facilitate access to system information.

Write-Debug. A Windows PowerShell cmdlet that writes debug messages.

Write-Error. A Windows PowerShell cmdlet that creates an error object and passes it through the object pipeline.

Write-Host. A Windows PowerShell cmdlet that displays object data.

Write-Output. A Windows PowerShell cmdlet that adds an object to the object pipeline.

Write-Progress. A Windows PowerShell cmdlet that sends progress records to the host.

Write-Verbose. A Windows PowerShell cmdlet that writes a string to the host's verbose display.

Write-Warning. A Windows PowerShell cmdlet that writes warning messages.

XML. A markup language that facilitates the definition, storage, and transmission of data between applications.

INDEX